TRADITION AND CHANGE IN A TURKISH TOWN

Paul J. Magnarella

A Halsted Press Book

Schenkman Publishing Company

JOHN WILEY AND SONS

New York — London — Sydney — Toronto

Copyright © 1974
Schenkman Publishing Co., Inc.
Cambridge, Massachusetts 02138

Distributed solely by Halsted Press, a Division
of John Wiley & Sons, Inc., New York.

Library of Congress Cataloging in Publication Data

Magnarella, Paul J
   Tradition and change in a Turkish Town.

   (Schenkman series on serio-economic change, 5)
   Bibliography: p.
   1. Susurluk, Turkey.   I. Title.
DS51.S94M3   309.1'562   74-14927
ISBN 0-470-56338-9
ISBN 0-470-56339-7 (pbk.)

To
Sharlene, Chrisy, Mark, and Brad

Table of Contents

Tables

Maps

Chart

Note on Exchange Rate

At the time of this study (1969-70) two official exchange rates were operative in Turkey: nine Turkish lira (TL 9) to $1.00 for Turkish citizens, and TL 12 to $1.00 for foreign visitors. For convenience, the reader might equate TL 10 to $1.00.

Foreword

Dr. Magnarella's study provides an exciting new insight into the social-political-economic dynamics of modern Turkey, a society in continuing transition. The author's thorough competence as an anthropologist and his intimate knowledge of both Susurluk — the town of his research — and its national environment provide a certain solid validity to his analysis that is lacking in similar studies made by those only superficially knowledgeable of the country's social order and history.

I have long been aware that the anthropological approach to social change — "modernization," if you will — comes closer to describing and explaining both economical and political development than the works of many economists and political scientists. (I hesitate to say most, but that is what I really mean.) From the vantage point of my much less sophisticated observation of the dynamics of Turkish society made in the late 1940s and early 1950s, every page of Dr. Magnarella's study rings true. What is particularly appealing is his ability to intermingle anthropological models with meaningful statistics and anecdotal snapshots of life. His final anecdote, the story of Mustafa the tailor, in a way incapsulates the whole process of social change in the Turkish context, with its joy and sorrow, its opportunity and dilemma. One suspects that the story of Mustafa the tailor will be referred to by other analysts with the same frequency as Daniel Lerner's "Grocer and Chief" of Balgat.

My first view of the Balikesir region, in which the town of Susurluk lies, came in early September 1948. I find the following paragraph in my journal for September 2 of that year.

> Our way led across fertile valleys and rolling green hills. The villages looked good, many of the houses being of wood construction. The countryside is full of animals, particularly horses. We saw very few oxen and no solid-wheeled carts typical of Central Anatolia. We stopped at one place where a thrashing machine was in operation. It was an old model, but the power came from a modern tractor. We learned that it was owned by the Mayor of Susurluk. His rental charge is 10 percent of the wheat thrashed. The farmers using it seemed satisfied with the machine, said it saved considerable wheat as compared with the use of oxen (and wooden sleds). The men said that thrashing machines had been used in the region for 30 years and that there were several others.

I introduce this paragraph only to alert the reader that Susurluk had already been touched by change back in 1948, indeed prior to that. Apparently horses had replaced oxen as the primary draft animal some years before, so likewise the relatively light four-wheel wagon for the heavy two-wheel ox cart. Some rural people had even been exposed to the use of mechanical power. Of even greater significance was the apparent shift in attitudes revealed by these changes in traditional technology. Economic incentive was obviously operating here in 1948. A willingness to innovate had appeared, a necessary (if not sufficient) prerequisite of which was possibly the elevation of living standards above subsistence. Innovation was no longer seen as an intolerably high risk proposition. One of the technological change agents here, the Mayor of Susurluk, demonstrates the conduit function of the provincial town in linking metropolis and village.

When Dr. Magnarella appeared on the scene in 1969 the process of "modernization" had developed sufficiently to make it possible for him to plot in a meaningful way directions of social change, whether in respect to values, kinship, sex roles, social and geographical mobility or to such institutions as represented in the social, religious, economic and political sectors. Even in this less developed country environment where the initial change process has moved relatively slowly (relative, that is, to many LDC's or even to other parts of Turkey), many of the stresses and strains being generated in Susurluk seemed almost intolerable at the personal level. That is the story of Mustafa the tailor. In other communities in which the modernization process has started more recently and proceeded at an even more rapid pace, breaking points have been reached, such as the almost complete breakdown of the extended family ideal. In such cases, intergenerational conflict tends to be too great to tolerate any continued sense of obligation to large kin groups, and personal mobility in a geographical sense so heightened as to erode any sense of community loyalty.

The million Turks who have either worked in Western Europe within the past decade, or are there now, plus the additional million who have registered their desire to go, are tangible evidence of the degree to which the hold of traditional Anatolian society has broken. Impatient with one's ability to change his home environment immediately to the extent deemed desirable, the individual may well opt to escape — first to the metropolitan area, then abroad. But he is never fulfilled in a fundamental sense for he is not really part of his new environment. Yet he cannot return to the old. That is the tragic story of Mustafa the tailor. The tragedy lies in the casting aside of the more desirable elements of traditional society along with those really incompatible with the new philosophy that gives Man the belief in his capacity to influence his fate and in his obligation to do so. But Mustafa the tailor has neither the faith in rewards in other worlds nor the capacity to influence his environment in any meaningful manner, though he feels compelled to try. Indeed, as Dr. Magnarella points out so eloquently in his final chapter, we may all face the same danger, the realization of which can only lead to human defeat and complete resignation to the material joys of the moment regardless of their cost.

Richard D. Robinson
Professor of International Management
Massachusetts Institute of Technology
September 1973

PREFACE

by DAVID BROKENSHA

This book (the fifth in the Schenkman Series on Socio-Economic Change) should be a welcome addition to the ethnographic literature of the Middle East. First, relatively few studies of rural and urban Turkey have been published in English; and second, even fewer emphasize recent changes in society. The lively description and thoughtful analysis of the community of Susurluk provides an excellent introduction to contemporary Turkey.

Dr. Magnarella examines all the major aspects of society in a way that combines perceptive observation and keen insights. In addition, his warm attachment to the people he studied is readily apparent.

Acknowledgements

Many people kindly contributed to the research, writing, and publication of this book. Unfortunately, I can acknowledge only some of them here. Dr. Abbas Alnasrawi, Dr. Gardiner Barnum, Dr. William Haviland, Dr. David Huddle, and Dr. Frederick Schmidt of the University of Vermont; Dr. Zekiye Eglar and Mr. Derwood Lockard of Harvard University; Dr. Walter Weiker of Rutgers University; and Mrs. Füsun Tiregol Floyd and Mr. James Meeder offered helpful suggestions and encouragement at critical points in the project. Dr. Richard D. Robinson of M.I.T. not only contributed an important "Foreword," but stimulated my interest in Turkey with his scholarship and exciting course on modern Turkish history. The editor, Dr. David Brokensha, and the publisher, Mr. Alfred Schenkman, assisted me unstintingly during the writing and publication phases. Miss Mary Gilbertson shared the burden of typing the manuscript with Mrs. Kathryn Greer and offered invaluable editorial assistance. To all of them, thank you.

The research upon which this book is based could not have been accomplished without the kind permission of the Turkish government and the hospitality of the people of Susurluk. My gratitude to the latter, especially to the Andiç family and my Turkish "parents," and to my wife, Sharlene, who contributed to practically every phase of the study, defies verbal expression.

Financial support for this study was provided by a Fulbright-Hays Graduate Fellowship, a Harvard University Sinclair Kennedy Travelling Fellowship, a University of Vermont Institutional Grant, and two University of Vermont Summer Faculty Fellowships. I am grateful to the members of the institutions which granted this support for their interest and confidence in my work.

Paul J. Magnarella

Burlington, Vermont
October, 1973

CHAPTER I

Introduction

Modernization: Model, Concepts, and Assumptions

Modernization is an all-encompassing and global process of cultural and socio-economic change whereby developing countries seek to acquire some of the characteristics common to industrially advanced countries. This process is stimulated by international contact and inevitable comparisons between rich and poor nations with respect to technological achievement, military power, and standards of living. The quest for modernity is evident in practically every underdeveloped country, and the consequences of this process represent one of the world's most vital concerns.

A competent study of modernization requires the expertise of the economist, political scientist, sociologist, anthropologist, and historian, as each is qualified to analyze different, but complementary, features of this complex phenomenon. The anthropologist distinguishes himself from his colleagues in these other disciplines in at least three respects. First, he is interested in all the topics covered by the social sciences. Because of his holistic perspective, the anthropologist is concerned with the interrelationship of economic, cultural, social, and psychological variables. Second, Anthropologists generally investigate the empirical realities of modernization in diverse societies by working on the microscopic level. Equipped with the methods and concepts that facilitate the intimate analysis of small communities, anthropologists can provide rich descriptions of the various social institutions in the process of change and apply the major models and hypotheses of modernization to the empirical realities of the communities studied. This system of hypothesis testing, and the verification, reformulation, or rejection which it entails, constitutes the basis upon which a social scientific study of modernization can develop.

The anthropological view of microscopic investigation has changed greatly in recent decades. Formerly most anthropologists specialized in the study of esoteric peoples, without recorded histories, who lived isolated and insulated from national and international influences. Under such conditions it was often valid to analyze their cultures and societies as though they existed in a vacuum. This can no longer be the case. Politics and war, international trade, advances in communication and travel, and the diffusion of modern industry and technology have brought almost all societies under the powerful influences of outside forces. Today, the anthropologist studying a village or small town must treat the modernization of that community as an historic process within a larger setting of regional and national development.

Third, the anthropologist combines a social scientific approach with an effort to empathize with the subject people and fully appreciate their own perceptions of change and what change means to their lives. The anthropologist benefits from the concepts, methods, and theories of all the disciplines concerned with modernization, but he uses them to gain a deeper understanding of the human drama, with its happiness and grief, its successes and failures.

An appreciation for any people's experiences with change requires an understanding of their country's history. Although each history is unique, many countries have been stimulated to initiate development programs in the same general way. Like Turkey, these countries had contact with the technologically advanced West. Their leaders found them lacking by comparison, and became especially dissatisfied with the low standard of living that their economies could afford the general population. These leaders aspired to "advance" their countries so that they, too, might take places among the modern nation-states of the world. In most, if not all cases, economic modernization was perceived as the means to this goal.

Unfortunately, a generally accepted and empirically valid socio-cultural theory of modernization, with systematically organized propositions explaining culture and social behavior in the process of change, does not exist. In this book I employ a general orientation to the study of modernization which has been borrowed from Smelser (1968). Although Smelser presented his model or partial theory as an ideal construct in the tradition of Max Weber, the model has general cross-societal validity; the processes comprising the model are being experienced currently by many countries in the Third World.

Smelser's modernization model involves four interrelated sub-processes:

1. *Technological Development.* The developing society moves from the near exclusive application of simple and traditionalized knowledge and techniques toward the greater application of scientific knowledge and techniques borrowed primarily from the West.

2. *Agricultural Development.* The developing society moves from subsistence farming toward commercial farming, emphasizing the production of cash crops, agricultural wage-labor, and a greater reliance on a cash economy and markets for the sale of farm products and the purchase of manufactured goods.

3. *Industrialization.* The developing society progressively industrializes, placing greater emphasis on the use of inanimate forms of energy, such as oil

and coal, to power machinery, and less emphasis on human and animal power and handicrafts.

4. *Urbanization*. The developing society experiences population movements from rural communities to growing urban centers.

Once these processes are underway, they act as causes and catalysts for other changes throughout the culture and society. For example, the governmental system may become westernized with the addition of political parties, elections, and civil-service bureaucracies. In education there is a greater emphasis on expanding learning opportunities, increasing general literacy, and training an indigenous educated elite. In the religious sphere, secularization (the process whereby religion becomes progressively less important in more and more areas of thought and behavior) undermines the scope of traditional beliefs and practices. In the kinship sphere, the traditional and reciprocal rights, duties, and obligations of kin become altered or, in the case of more distant kin ties, reduced or eliminated. In the stratificational sphere, better educational opportunities, geographical, and socio-economic mobility work to alter traditional class structures which rank people primarily on the basis of ascriptive criteria, factors over which they have little or no control, such as family connection, race, sex, religion, ethnicity, and age. The emerging system of social stratification places greater emphasis on achievement criteria, such as individual ability, skill, and accomplishment.

Permeating these processes and spheres of change are two further dimensions of modernization: structural differentiation and integration. The former is the process whereby existing roles and organizations become individually divided into two or more distinct and more specialized roles and organizations, which perform the functions of their former unit more efficiently in the new historical setting.

> [Structural] differentiation is the evolution from a multi-functional role structure to several more specialized structures. In illustration, we may cite . . . typical examples. During a society's transition from domestic to factory industry, the division of labor increases, and the economic activities previously lodged in the family move to the firm. As a formal educational system emerges, the training functions previously performed by the family and church are established in a more specialized unit, the school [Smelser 1971:356].

Structural differentiation creates an increasingly complex socio-economic system in which many people occupy new roles and pursue special interests. To prevent fragmentation new mechanisms of integration are needed to organize and coordinate specializing and diversifying roles and organizations and provide people with norms which establish new forms of social interaction. These new integrative mechanisms commonly appear in the form of nationalistic ideologies, governmental structures, political parties, legal codes, labor and trade unions, and associations. Smooth, stable development requires a balance between differentiation, which creates diversity, and effective integration, which organizes the newly differentiated structures on new bases. Lacking such a balance, a developing society is likely to experience social and political disruption. Modernization has been described as "a three-way tug-of-war among the forces of tradition, the forces of differentiation, and the new forces of integration" (Smelser 1971:369). The total process may be considered a dynamic system of tension-management.

Smelser's model of modernization consists of a generalized series of assumptions and hypotheses about the nature of socio-cultural change associated with the economic development of traditional societies. On the more specific level of empirical reality, developing societies experience unique differences, deriving from such factors as their peculiar cultures, population compositions, economic structures, and social organizations prior to the initiation of modernization; their unique histories; the reasons for their commitment to modernize; and, the differing paths to modernization chosen by each (Smelser 1967:31-32).

Although modernization brings new and different ways of life to traditional peoples, we must be careful not to regard modernity and tradition as antithetical polar opposites. Traditional values and social structures are not always in conflict with modernity. In some cases the two may be congruent, even mutually reenforcing. For example, in Susurluk the traditional extended family with its diffuse kinship bonds has proven an effective social group for the successful financing and operation of modern retail business. In turn, the modern family-run business functions to maintain kinship solidarity by providing jobs and financial security for the extended family's members.

Modernization does not necessarily sweep all aspects of tradition from its path. Certain traditional practices may and often do survive the appearance and acceptance of modern, scientific techniques. Essentially, modernization provides a people with an increased range of alternative choices of action. For instance, modern medicine and magical folk cures can co-exist and be resorted to alternatively or simultaneously by the same person. In some instances, modernization may actually enhance tradition. In Turkey, economic development has contributed to increased income and improved transportation. These advances have enabled more Turkish Muslims, than ever, to make the traditionally prestigious pilgrimage to Mecca, and thereby fulfill one of the obligations of Islam.

Finally, we must be careful not to equate industrial might with cultural superiority. The technologically advanced West has much to learn from the Third World about human values and personal relations.

In this book, the model, concepts, and assumptions outlined above are employed in an historical, regional-national, and comparative perspective to the study of tradition and modernity in Susurluk, a Turkish town. I will preface the introduction of this particular town with a brief discussion of Turkey and the role of towns in her history.

Turkey and the Turks

The origin of the Turks is not the Middle East, but inner-Asia. The first written evidence of their language dates to the eighth century A.D. runic inscriptions on steles found along the Orkhon River near present-day Ulan Bator, Mongolia. The Turkish language is not a member of the Semitic family as are Arabic and Hebrew, nor of the Indo-European family as is Persian; it belongs to the Altaic language family along with Mongolian, Manchu-Tungus, and Chuvash.

During the ensuing centuries, the famed Turkish horsemen of the Asiatic steppe galloped west into Muslim lands, where they found employment as soldiers and body guards under Persian and Arab rulers and converted to Islam. They eventually surpassed their employers, and Turkish dynasties, such as the Seljuks and Ottomans, gained military and political prominence. The Ottomans organized the vitality and aggressiveness of the formerly loose-knit Turkish tribes into a supreme military force that conquered Constantinople (Istanbul) in 1453 and then the Balkans, much of the Middle East, and large stretches of North Africa. By virtue of its strength and geographical position, the multi-ethnic Ottoman Empire enjoyed a dominant status in the cultural, political and economic affairs of East and West until the end of the eighteenth century, after which it declined steadily due to internal decay and external pressure from expansionist Russia and Western Europe.

After her defeat in the First World War, the Ottoman Empire was dissolved and the state of Turkey emerged through the efforts of nationalist Turks who hoped to create a new country without ambitions of Empire. Her new leadership, headed by Mustafa Kemal Ataturk, embarked on a social, cultural, political, and economic revolution with the ultimate goal being the creation of a modern, democratic nation-state with an advanced economy and a secular-minded, progressive people. The story of Susurluk, in large part, reflects the principles and policies of these national leaders.

Today Turkey's size is 300,600 square miles — only slightly smaller than Texas and Louisiana combined. Her 1970 population of 35,666,549 results from a hefty average annual growth rate of 2.5 since World War II. About 98% of her population is Muslim and close to the same proportion speaks Turkish. Her literacy rate is approximately 50%.

Turkey's economy is predominantly agrarian, with about 72% of her labor force engaged in agricultural or related pursuits and only 9% in manufacturing. In this latter area, small firms are especially important, as 60% of those working in manufacturing were employed in establishments with less than ten people.

Turkey's per capita national income rose from $197 in 1960 to $362 in 1968 as compared with increases in the same period for the entire Middle East of from $220 to $360, for all of Africa of from $120 to $160, and for Europe of from $970 to $1,690. The 1968 per capita income for the United States was $3,898. In comparison to some other Third World countries, Turkey's achievements are notable. Her roads, power plants, and port facilities are substantial; her agricultural production is improving, and with greater use of irrigation and fertilizers her land has the potential to support her growing population; her climate allows for cultivation of a large variety of quality crops; and, she possesses a good supply of certain mineral resources, especially coal, iron, and chromium.

One of Turkey's major developmental problems is her growing population which keeps her per capita income around the subsistence level, thereby prohibiting the degree of savings and investment that economists believe necessary for vigorous economic growth. The process of modernization has infected the Turkish people with rising aspirations for better living standards. While these aspirations are often considered beneficial to development, because they impel people to seek ways of improving their income, they may also generate high levels of frustration, if people cannot find the means to satisfy their newly created consumption needs.

The Town in Turkish History

The position of the town within Turkey's historical process is somewhat ambiguous. It is both transitional and traditional — a catalyst for change and a stronghold of conservatism. Historically, the town has performed important traditional functions for its own residents and those of the surrounding rural area. For instance, it provided regional markets, educational facilities (i.e., religious schools), places of worship, religious judges, public baths, and Ottoman administrators. In Redfield and Singer's terms (1954), the town was an orthogenetic community existing primarily for the purpose of carrying forward, developing and elaborating a long-established local culture and civilization.

However, since the establishment of the Turkish Republic in 1923 and subsequent attempts at modernization and secularization, the town no longer provides some of these traditional functions in the same form (e.g., adjudication, government administration), and it has added new functions based on Western models (e.g., secular education). It is now the seat of a secular bureaucratic governmental administration which regulates many of the area's social, educational, commercial and religious activities. Its schools are largely staffed by teachers who were educated in the Western oriented secular institutions of the larger, modern cities. The values inculcated in these schools are no longer primarily Islamic and Oriental, but increasingly secular and Western. The town's judges and lawyers have studied modified European codes and are now devoted to their administration. The banking institutions are also operated on Western models and are often directed by people born and educated in Istanbul, Ankara, or Izmir. In fact, a large proportion of the town's professional elite is not indigenous.

In effect, the town may be viewed as a socio-cultural, economic and political mechanism of integration operating on two levels. On one level it provides a traditional context for the multi-purpose relationships of villagers and townsmen. It is a traditional scene for interaction within a rather limited geographical range. On another level it is a mechanism for integrating townsmen and surrounding villagers into the various institutions of the modernizing national society.

Because many of Turkey's 35,000 or more villages are town satellites, the town occupies a critical mediating position between Turkey's folk cultures and the culture of her urbanizing national elite. Towns are also important because in some cases they serve as step one in the two-step pattern of peasant migration to the large metropolises.

The Setting

The town of Susurluk with its population of 12,357 in 1970 is located in the northwestern corner of Asia Minor. It has experienced a dramatic series of changes in recent years. During the 1930s and 1940s it was a quiet peasant community of about 4,000 citizens that served as a market center and sub-provincial seat for its surrounding villages. Its economy was one of near subsistence, characterized by a lack of industrialization and a low degree of differentiation in production and marketing. The town's secular educational facilities were limited to one complete primary school (grades 1-5) attended mainly by boys. Poor transportation, widespread illiteracy, and a paucity of radios greatly restricted exposure to national and international affairs.

Because of a number of political and agricultural considerations, Susurluk became the site of a modern, government sugar beet refinery which began operation in 1955. This large plant created full and part-time employment for approximately one thousand males from the town and its surrounding villages and also provided the region's peasants with a market for their first cash crop and technical assistance to cultivate it.

The construction and subsequent operation of the refinery stimulated the expansion of the town's crafts, services, banking, and other support activities. As a result, the town changed from a condition where the overwhelming majority of its adult population was primarily engaged in subsistence farming to one in which only a small proportion derived their livelihoods chiefly from such pursuits.

The availability of numerous wage jobs attracted many villagers to town, and by 1960 Susurluk's population reached 11,450. Included in this figure were over one hundred administrative and technical personnel and their families who had recently moved to Susurluk to occupy high and intermediate level positions in the sugar refinery, banks, government, and schools. Most of these people had lived and studied in Turkey's larger and more modern cities, and they brought to Susurluk an urban style of life and a cosmopolitan air. Concomitant with these changes were a number of advances in the fields of education, news media participation, and travel.

Because of its traditional background and recent history, Susurluk represents an ideal case for the analysis of modernization.

Levels of Comparison and Baseline

Any research strategy of social change must make explicit its method of handling two methodological problems. The first concerns levels of comparison. One must distinguish ideal rules for social behavior from actual social behavior — or, put differently, one must discriminate between ideal norms of conduct and statistical norms, what people do most frequently. The two are not always congruent. Statistical data may not uncover the ideal decision models which members of a society share. For instance, Goodenough (1956) has demonstrated that statistical patterns of social behavior, specifically post-marital residence, can vary widely under different demographic and ecological conditions, even when the ideal norms upon which decisions are based remain constant.

In addition to the ideal-real dimension of this problem, there is the interclass dimension: ideal and statistical norms often vary among the various social classes of any one society. Therefore, researchers should not assume that the documented social behavior of a country's past nobility, for whom data are usually available, was representative of the country as a whole. Also, the comparison of their behavior with that of the present-day middle class may be invalid for the same reason. To avoid these possible pitfalls, comparisions should be made on either the ideal or the behavioral level within the same social class.

The second methodological problem in the analysis of social change is the establishment of a baseline for comparison, with sufficient data on both the ideal and the behavioral levels for the community under investigation. In the face of inadequate historical information, some social scientists have resorted to comparing social structures in urban settings to those in rural ones, under the assumption that the urban situation represents the new and the rural the old. At best, this is a hypothesis to be tested, not assumed. The same urban-rural differences may have existed over a long period of time, or both urban and rural social structures may be changing independently of one another. Their differences may not be explainable in terms of modernization, but in terms of demographic factors.

In summary, to study social change it is most desirable to have sufficient past and present information on both the ideal norms and actual behavior of comparable social classes in the same society. The present study approaches, but unfortunately does not attain this ideal. For a baseline I have chosen pre-1950, a period which predates most of the prominent changes in Susurluk's socio-economic structure.[1] I do not assume that the town was static prior to 1950; the history section will show that it has experienced substantial socio-cultural change, primarily as the result of war and migration. More recently, however, a new kind of change — modernization —, which differs in kind and degree, has made its impact on the town.

The sources of information for the past are several, the most important being local informants. Because the baseline is within the living memory of the present adult population, informants have been able to supply a great deal of information about both ideal norms and actual behavior. From the statements of a large number of informants a consensus picture was drawn and then compared with several written accounts of pre-1950 Susurluk and other nearby communities. In several cases not only statistical data for both the past and the present are available for comparison, but observable behavior as well. In many respects this study deals with the living past; some pre-1950 social practices have been maintained by certain members of the community, while other members have opted for change. Studies conducted in other small Turkish communities and ethnographies of Caucasian peoples were also consulted. These other communities are not assumed to be identical to Susurluk; taken together with Susurluk data, however, they will help reveal general trends. Where baseline evidence is insufficient, I offer present-day data as a description of current patterns and a basis for future comparison.

The conclusions reached in this study should not be interpreted as final; they are hypotheses about change based on available data and personal assumptions. Like all hypotheses, they are open to further testing and reformulation.

Fieldwork

Before embarking on this study, I had already gained a good background knowledge of Turkey and a proficiency in Turkish as a result of two years

Author's Turkish "parents"

residence in the provincial capitals of Burdur (1963-64) and Antalya (1964-65), where I taught English as a foreign language in public schools; extensive travel throughout Turkey; and graduate study of Turkey's history, government, culture, and language. Agreeing with many scholars and development experts who believe that towns are critical to the understanding of social change in Turkey and the Middle East, I decided to study the changing culture and society of a Turkish town through the use of anthropological and sociological techniques. I hoped to find a town small enough for one anthropologist to study, that had recently experienced economic development, but which remained a distinct entity, rather than a large city's suburb. I chose Susurluk from a number of towns recommended by Turkish friends because it met these criteria best, but more importantly because local officials appeared genuinely interested in my project and sincere in their willingness to allow me to proceed.

I arrived in Susurluk during the last week of August 1969 and took up residence at the sugar refinery where I remained for three weeks. Because this period marked the beginning of the sugar beet harvest and processing season, I was able to observe the operations of the refinery during its busiest time. While I was studying the factory and becoming acquainted with the town, friends were helping me find an indigenous family with whom I might reside. I was warned that this would be no easy task, as local families are conservative and do not adopt strange men into their households. As no consenting family had been discovered by the end of the third week, I decided to move from the factory to town and rent an apartment in a two-family house located on a busy street near the edge of the town's center. It was a good location, as a great deal of town activity could be observed from my window and doorstep.

Once there, I systematically set about meeting people — neighbors, local merchants, craftsmen, teachers, bank officials, and town and district officials with whom I was not already acquainted. Many of these early acquaintances became good friends and helped me throughout my stay. My daily activities usually involved a stop at the local newspaper office to chat with friends and learn of recent events, a tour of the market place and business district, and visits with merchants, craftsmen, and friends. I also made frequent visits to the mayor and chief of police.

About three weeks later several friends told me they had found an elderly Manav couple who might rent me a room in their home. As I later learned, this family had known I wanted to live in a local household for some time, but only after a number of people had gone to them repeatedly imploring on my behalf did they even consent to consider me. Meanwhile, they and their relatives had been observing my activity in town for the past three weeks. At a very pleasant meeting in the backyard garden of their humble three-room home, the couple and I discussed the matter over coffee. After asking me numerous questions about my family, background, and plans, they promised to decide in a few days. Fortunately their decision was positive, and I shared their home for the next ten months.

At first our relationship was correct and formal. Eventually, however, we became more than good friends; not only did they open their home to me, but their hearts as well. In time they were inviting me to participate in practically all of their home activities: we shared meals, entertained guests together, and passed many hours of enjoyable conversation either seated in the sun of their garden during the warm seasons or huddled about their wood-burning stove in winter. As they were basically illiterate I was entrusted with reading and writing their correspondence. I even shared some of the household duties, such as shopping and caring for the garden. I became their *ahret oğlu* (adopted son) and they my parents, and we addressed each other exclusively in kinship terms.

It was through my Turkish mother and her friends that I learned something of the life of Turkish women in the home. She was extremely helpful in other phases of the study as well. She was in her seventies and knew practically every local family and their immediate ancestors. In addition to helping with genealogies and local history she explained local beliefs and folklore associated with life-cycle rites and curing. She herself was a popular curer and fortune teller *(falcı)* as well as a famous matchmaker. Many local families in need of cures or searching for spouses came to her for help, and much of her correspondence dealt with these marital matters.

In addition to participant observation and formal and informal interviews, I utilized a questionnaire and an interview schedule. The questionnaire was administered to 307 twelve and thirteen year old students, who comprised seven of the town's first year middle school *(orta okul)* classes and the only middle school class in the nearby village of Sultançayır. It consisted of ten questions concerning occupation, education, residence, and ethnicity of parents; and occupational goal and favorite subject of student.

The interview schedule dealt with family, kinship, occupation, residence, education, recreation, and general attitudes. It was administered in the last months of my field work, after I had gained familiarity with the town and knew the kinds of questions that were appropriate to the problems under investigation. Many of the questions were adapted from schedules previously administered in Turkey, e.g., Kiray (1964) and the Rural Development Research Project conducted in 1962 by the Research and Measurement Bureau of the Turkish Ministry of Education under the joint sponsorship of the Turkish State Planning Office and U.S. AID. Other questions were of my own creation. All questions were read and checked for clarity and meaning by local Turks, and on the basis of their recommendations many changes were made, even in questions which reportedly were administered successfully in other parts of the country.

This done, a pilot survey of fifteen informants was conducted with the help of a local high school graduate whom I trained. The schedule proved too long for convenient administration and several of the questions were still unclear. Therefore, it was shortened to a half-hour or less, and with the help of local Turks the confusing questions were reworded. The revised schedule was then administered by two local young men, whom I trained, to a quota sample of 182 men.

A more ideal random sample was impractical for several reasons. For one, it would have required interviewers to seek selected respondents in their homes, and if they were not in, the interviewers would be forced to deal directly with women. This action would have offended some townspeople. A second reason was the political atmosphere. Some people in town were xenophobic and especially anti-American. They not only would have refused to be interviewed, but probably would have complained vociferously to the government, townspeople, and press about my alleged "espionage" activities. This may have terminated the survey and placed the rest of the research in jeopardy as well.

With these and other considerations in mind, the interviewers were instructed to select a quota sample of married males from the various occupational, ethnic, age, and educational groups and residence quarters of town. One non-Turkish ethnic group — Circassians — was somewhat over-represented so that inter-ethnic comparisons might be facilitated. Interviews were conducted in private with the anonymity of the respondent guaranteed; no more than one male from any one household was interviewed; and people who might be antagonistic to the study were avoided. As the interviews progressed, respondents were tallied according to the above variables to determine what kinds of people were being under- or over-represented. After 127 married males were interviewed in this manner, a similar procedure was used to interview 55 young adult bachelors. To my knowledge no complaints resulted. Appendix A lists the ethnicity, occupation, age, education, and residence quarter of the respondents.

An abundance of useful information was obtained from the study of official statistics and local documents and the content analysis of two local newspapers: one covering ten years (1961-1970) and the other about one and one-half years (1968-69, revived in 1970). Several regional papers were also examined daily during the time of the field work.

During the summer of 1972, I returned to Susurluk to collect additional information and discuss my earlier findings with local townspeople so as to profit from their comments, criticisms, and additions. Their own evaluations of my data and preliminary conclusions added a further element of indigenous insight to the study.

Notes to Chapter I
Introduction

[1]It appears that the time chosen as a baseline here has also proven critical for many other countries in the Middle East. After a thorough examination of the family literature on the Arab World, Goode (1963:162) writes: "It is clear that, in the main, Arab family institutions had not changed very much until the decade of the 1950s. In this decade, however, a substantial number of legal and social innovations were inaugurated whose consequences in marital and kinship life will not be fully evident until the succeeding decade, when an increasing number of empirical studies may be expected to report them."

CHAPTER II

History and Geography

Historical Background

The history of Susurluk and of the Balıkesir region in general is characterized
by two enduring dimensions: the presence of diverse ethnic groups and the
interaction of Eastern and Western cultural forces. The integration and disintegration of these socially and culturally differentiated dimensions form a major
theme in this region's story. In setting the background to this study, it may not
be necessary to reach far back into history, but the region's past contains such
riches that it justifies at least brief mention.

Blessed with a fertile soil, an adequate water supply, numerous edible plants
and animals, and mineral resources, Balıkesir must have appeared attractive to
the Mysians who migrated there from Thrace in the second millenium B.C. and
gave the region its name. Herodotus described them as a primitive people
dressed in fox skin hats and deer skin garments. In time, however, these
nomads came under the influence of Greek civilization. They appear on the list
of Trojan allies in Homer's *Iliad* and were widely employed as mercenaries
during the Hellenistic period. The geographer Strabo recorded that the Mysians
spoke a mixture of Lydian and Phrygian and shared access to the Temple of
Carian Zeus at Labraunda on the basis of kinship with the Carians and Lydians.

During 1660-1490 B.C. Mysia was under the control of the Hittites who
extended their rule across Anatolia to the Aegean Coast. After the Hittites, the
Phrygians, Lydians, Persians, Hellenes, Romans, and Byzantines all enjoyed
successive periods of rule. In the 12th century the armies of the Second Crusade
(1147-49) under Louis VII and the Third Crusade (1189-91) under Friedrich I
crossed Mysia. The Latin state, established after the Fourth Crusade (1202-04),
included the northwestern portion of Mysia in its domain.

Historically this region has provided an important link between East and
West. For example, during the 7th and 6th centuries B.C. the Lydians carried
on a brisk trade with the Greeks which they facilitated by the invention of
coinage, and the Etruscans who provided Italy with a strong cultural foundation
most likely emigrated there from Lydia. This period of Western orientation
temporarily terminated with the Persian conquest and the ensuing era of

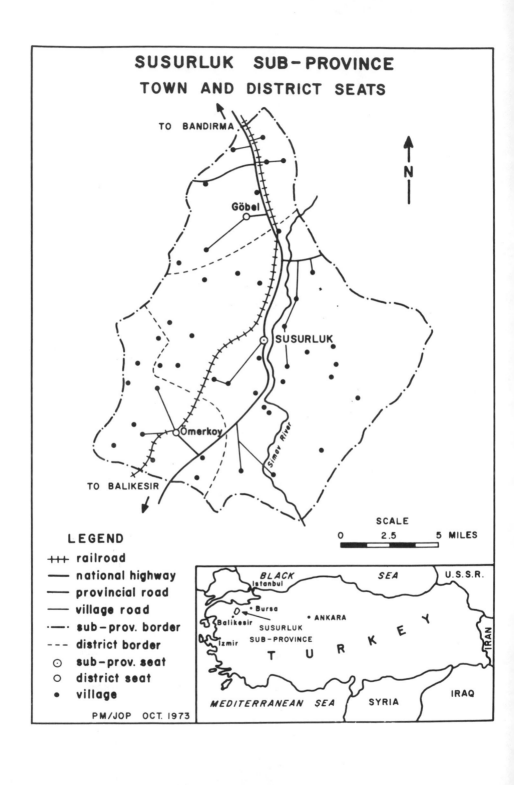

SUSURLUK SUB-PROVINCE
TOWN AND DISTRICT SEATS

TO BANDIRMA

N

Göbel

SUSURLUK

Ömerköy

Simav River

TO BALIKESIR

SCALE
0   2.5   5 MILES

LEGEND

+++ railroad
— national highway
— provincial road
— village road
—·— sub-prov. border
--- district border
⊙ sub-prov. seat
○ district seat
• village

PM/JOP OCT. 1973

BLACK   SEA   U.S.S.R.
Istanbul
• Bursa
Balikesir   • ANKARA
SUSURLUK
Izmir   SUB-PROVINCE
T U R K E Y   IRAN

MEDITERRANEAN SEA   SYRIA   IRAQ

Oriental rule, but later revived under the Western influences of the Hellenes and Romans. East-West cultural forces found a synthesis of sorts during the Byzantine period, when the inhabitants of ancient Mysia were exposed to a combination of Greco-Roman civilization and Eastern despotism. With the arrival of Turkish tribes in the 13th century, the hegemony over the region shifted decisively back to an Eastern people.

The defeat of the Byzantine army in 1071 at Manzikert in Eastern Anatolia opened Asia Minor to the invasion of various Turkic tribes. By the middle of the 12th century numerous *ghazi beyliks* had been established across Asia Minor. These could be described as relatively autonomous emirates each ruled by a Turkish dynasty and containing a party of "warriors of the faith" or *ghazis* who existed in large part to battle the Christian infidel. As long as they could plunder beyond the frontiers of Islam, they remained economically viable. When they could not raid the infidel, they turned on one another.

From about 1155 to 1243, a Turkish dynasty known as the Seljuks of Rum was able to hold these *ghazi* warriors in check and thereby attain supremacy in Anatolia. However, the Seljuks suffered a devastating defeat at the hands of the invading Mongols in 1243, and in a short time the *ghazis* again set about establishing autonomous *beyliks*.

In about 1300, a *beylik* by the name of Karasi was established in Mysia by Kara Isa (Dark Isa) and his father, Kalem Bey. These founders were descendants of the great *ghazi* Melik Danishmend (Uzunçarşılı 1969. 96-103). Prior to the Seljuks of Rum the Danishmend Beylik with its capital at Sivas had been one of the most powerful in Anatolia. Its descendants were to continue the *ghazi* tradition in Mysia.

Kara Isa and his father made the present-day city of Balıkesir their capital. This city may rest on the site of Hadrianoutherai, one of the many products of the Roman Emperor Hadrian's mania for building. Later, during the Byzantine period, it was called Akhyraous. The settlement was situated on the great Roman and Byzantine land routes to Miletopolis (the Karacabey of today) and Constantinople from points south. During the 12th or 13th century, it was elevated to the rank of metropolis, thus evidencing its importance. Kara Isa Bey changed its name to Balık Hisar. (*Balık* is an antiquated Turkic word meaning town, city, palace, or tower, while *hisar* means fortress.) In time its pronunciation and spelling were changed to Balıkesir.

Mysia, now known as the Karasi Beylik, or the Emirate of Kara Isa, became a magnet for many Turkic tribes seeking either refuge from the Mongols or a frontier from which they could plunder the infidel. By their immigration the region's population increased in strength and diversity. The Karasi Beylik boasted quick-striking equestrian land forces, and a navy, made up of both Greeks and Turks, which attacked Byzantine towns along the Dardanelles. By alternately opposing Byzantium and allying with it against its Balkan enemies, the Karasi Beylik was able to expand its boundaries. After the death of Kara Isa Bey his emirate was divided between two of his three sons. Yahsi Khan took control of Bergama, and Demir Khan acquired Balıkesir and the lands to its north and west.

Shortly thereafter, in 1335, the famous Moroccan traveler Ibn Battuta journeyed through the area and left us the following account of his visit to Balıkesir and Bursa, the capital of the surging Ottomans.

We went on next to Barghama [Bergama] which is in ruins but has a strong fortress on the summit of a hill. Here we hired a guide and travelled among high and rugged mountains to the town of Balikasri [Balıkesir]. The sultan, whose name was Dumur Khan, is a worthless person. It was his father who built this town, and during the son's reign it attracted a vast population of knaves, for 'Like king, like people.' I visited him and he sent me a silk robe. In this town I bought a Greek girl named Marguerite.

We journeyed next to Bursa, a great city with fine bazaars and broad streets. . . . The sultan of Bursa is Orkhan Bek, son of Othman Chuk. He is the greatest of the Turkmen kings and the richest in wealth, lands, and military forces, and possesses nearly a hundred fortresses. . . . He fights the infidels and beseiges them (Ibn Battuta 1929:135-36).

Demir Khan, like his father Kara Isa, profited from the Byzantines' internal strife and their external threats from the Slavs and Bulgars. However, Demir Khan had his own internal problems. He was not a well-liked ruler, and his own generals intrigued against him with the Ottoman Sultan Orkhan, who annexed Karasi Beylik without opposition in about 1340.

The Ottoman Sultan had already taken Bursa in 1326, Nicaea in 1331, and Nicomedia in 1337. Fighting men from the other *ghazi* emirates as well as Greeks and the Spanish Catalans[1] had flocked to the successful Ottoman banner. Now the Karasi land and the sea forces also joined the Ottomans in their conquest of Byzantium and expansion into the Balkans, where large numbers of Turks from Karasi were later resettled as part of the Ottoman Turkification program there.

For five centuries after its annexation, the Karasi Beylik was a *sanjak* (sub-province) administratively tied to the *vilayet* (province) of Hudavendigar (Bursa). Its capital, Balıkesir, continued to develop under the Ottomans. In the 17th and 18th centuries it boasted a number of large inns, caravansaries and commercial buildings and exported woolen cloth and agricultural products to Istanbul and other large cities. In 1923 the Karasi Beylik became a *vilayet,* and in 1926 its eponym was dropped and the name "Balıkesir" was adopted for the whole province. Today its capital is a modernizing and industrializing city of 70,000 inhabitants.

While we can trace the past of Balıkesir Province back to the Mysians, the historical evidence pertaining specifically to Susurluk is much more limited. Although its present-day site appears to have been on or near the Roman and Byzantine routes which passed through Balıkesir to Karacabey, there is no evidence of a settlement there at that time. Only the remnants of a large Byzantine bridge are visible in the Simav River a few miles south of Susurluk.

A title deed dated 842 H./1439 A.D. may be the oldest known document directly related to this sub-province. With this deed one Koca Mehmet Pasha obtained title to lands in and around the present-day village of Kepekler, about thirteen miles north of Susurluk. This agricultural estate was set up as a *vakif* (trust) to be administered by his heirs. Today, associated with this title deed is a genealogy delineating Koca Mehmet Pasha's heirs down to the present. Both documents are owned by the Susurluk family, his living descendants, and have been submitted as evidence in a current legal case to establish ownership of certain lands more recently settled by immigrants. Ozer (1963:29, 33), a local historian, claims that Koca Mehmet Pasha was a descendant of the Karamanids, a *ghazi* dynasty that resided near Konya. A Kepekler villager and descendant of the Pasha holds that his ancestor was also the vizier and son-in-law of Murad II (Sultan from 1422-51). He reportedly died at his estate and was buried in Kepekler, although the exact location of his grave is not known.[2]

During the 16th century the site of Susurluk along with its surrounding forests, marshes, and pastures constituted the agricultural estate of the heirs of another Turkish noble named Inebey. It was known as "Susığırlık" (*su* = water; *sığır* = cattle), because of an important function carried on there — that of watering cattle in a large marsh fed by waters from the passing Simav river and located in what is now the center of town. (Much later its pronunciation was altered to Susurluk, and it began to be spelled officially as such in the 1940s.) The old Byzantine trade route was still in use and many caravans stopped at Susurluk to water animals and rest. In 974 H./1566-67 A.D. a police chief named Mustafa Celebi had a *han* or caravansary and a mosque built there to accommodate these travelers.[3]

These structures increased the importance of Susurluk and provided the nucleus for expansion. In 1050 H./1640-41 A.D. a group of Koca Mehmet Pasha's descendants moved to Susurluk where they were soon joined by migrants from other nearby settlements. With these influxes of people Susurluk developed into a village with a formal local governmental administration.

The next major events affecting Susurluk and the character of this region occurred in the second half of the 19th century. The first of these concerned the Yürük and Turkmen — the independent minded, nomadic pastoralists who grazed their flocks of sheep and goats on the plains and in the river valleys during the winter and in the mountains during the summer. They probably lived much as their ancestors had centuries before. Based on an examination of local documents of the 1858-65 period, the local historian Kamil Su (1938) concluded that there were more than thirty-six Yürük and Turkmen tribes in the Karasi Sanjak at that time. They had descriptive tribal names such as: White Sheep, White Goat, Black Goat, Red Goat, Woolgrower, Horsemen, Dark Moses, Arab, Martyrs of Islam, and The Furious.

In order to facilitate government control and tax collection, the Governor-General of Hudavendigar (Bursa), Ahmed Vefik Pasha[4], ordered these tribes to cease their nomadic way of life and settle down. Many nomads chose to ignore this order, but they were systematically hunted down by the military who punished them by destroying their tents. Within a short time most of the tribes broke up into small groups and established permanent settlements in the hills. As years passed, their tribal organization, which had functioned to coordinate migrations and maintain unity in the face of opposition, lost its reason for being and was not retained. Yet today the elderly Yürük and Turkmen still know their tribal affiliations and refer to Ahmed Vefik as the ''Tent Tearing Pasha.''

With the nomads under control the Governor-General focused his attention on the problems of travel, and in 1871 had a new road built from Balıkesir to the North which passed through Susurluk. This structural change facilitated Susurluk's development. Because of its central position and improved access, it began to function as an important market center for the surrounding villages.

At this point in time Susurluk's population was composed of both Muslim and Christian peoples. Among the Muslims were sedentary Turks, the vast majority of whom were engaged in near subsistence agriculture. Their agricultural techniques and level of living were rather primitive. They farmed the fertile plains and river valleys, living in homes of reeds and thatch. They had long since acquired the appellation ''Manav'' (fruit and vegetable people) probably to distinguish them from the pastoral nomads, who had only recently taken on a sedentary life in newly established hill settlements. Interspersed among these Turks was a small number of Arabs whose forefathers may have been either *ghazi* warriors or caravan travelers who decided to stop their wanderings.

Susurluk also had an important minority of skilled Greeks and Armenians employed as builders, shoemakers, metal workers, tool makers, bakers, wine-makers, and retail tradesmen. About 25 to 30 such families resided in the center of the village. In addition, over 100 Armenian workmen lived at a boracite quarry four miles to Susurluk's south. Operations began there in 1865 when the mineral rights were purchased by a Frenchman. Later they were acquired by an Italian, then finally by an English firm which worked the quarry up to 1956.[5]

Susurluk's weekly market provided an important mechanism for the integration of these spatially distributed and economically as well as ethnically differentiated groups. People from Susurluk and the surrounding villages could exchange their products for the provisions, clothing, or tools which they lacked. The Manavs provided poultry, eggs, grains, and vegetables; the Yürüks and Turkmen brought yogurt, milk and cheese, hides, meat on the hoof, and woven bags, rugs, and carpets; the Christians supplied crafted leather and metal products such as shoes, boots, axes, agricultural implements, containers, and cooking utensils. The Greek grocers carried a few non-local items like salt, sugar, and tea. Both barter and monetary systems of exchange were in operation. For these rural people, market day constituted a great economic and social event; it provided an opportunity to see relatives and friends, to exchange gossip, and to learn the news of recent events.

Economic interdependence was not confined to market day. Prohibited from making alcoholic beverages themselves, many Muslims appreciated the proximity of their Christian neighbors whose products added warmth and glow to festive occasions. Large landowners hired the services of Greek and Armenian craftsmen to built them homes of stone and mudbrick, while Christian craftsmen took on Turkish boys as apprentices and taught them their trades.

This ethno-economic mosaic attained a further degree of complexity as a result of international events in the 1870s, the penultimate phase in the deterioration of the Ottoman Empire. The Balkan countries were gaining their independence and Russia was annexing Ottoman lands on the Black Sea and in the Caucasus. As a consequence many Muslims were fleeing these areas seeking refuge in Anatolia. From the Balkans came descendants of Turks settled there during the early days of Ottoman expansion; Albanians, Bulgarians, and Bosnians whose ancestors had converted to Islam; and Muslim Gypsies. From the Crimea came Turkish Tatars, and from the Caucasus came Circassians, Georgians, Dagistanis and Turkish Nogays. These immigrants were assigned to areas throughout the remaining Ottoman Empire. However, many of them disliking their assigned places chose to make their way to the rich Aegean-Marmara region and to Susurluk.

These immigrants added to the skilled and semi-skilled manpower of the district. The Balkan refugees included builders, craftsmen and farmers whose agricultural techniques were superior to those of local Manavs. Georgian builders brought their own peculiar techniques and architecture, while Gypsies brought their music, basketmaking, tinning, and tinkering skills.

Except for the Gypsies, who settled on the edge of Susurluk, most of these immigrants either established new villages or settled in existing ones. About twenty-five villages were created at that time, and approximately one-fourth of them were ethnically mixed. Of the existing villages in which immigrants settled, five were Manav and eight were either Yürük or Turkmen.

Due to this increase in population, Susurluk was elevated to a township in 1901. The proliferation of villages in the immediate area had added to her economic and administrative importance, and on several occasions during the ensuing twenty years the *nahiye* (seat of the district) was shifted back and forth between Susurluk and Omerköy, a rival township thirteen miles to the southeast.[6]

In October of 1914, the leaders of the Ottoman Empire made the fatal mistake of entering World War I on the side of Germany and Austria-Hungary. Defeat and dissolution were the result. The war had a very depressive effect on Susurluk; a large part of her male population was conscripted into the army and never returned. Some lost their lives in far off places like the Yemen, others found death as nearby as the Dardanelles. Few households did not sacrifice a son to the cause. After the war, Greek forces occupied Western Turkey, a small contingent of 150 to 200 soldiers being stationed in Susurluk. A few local Greeks joined the occupation army. Informants say that these troops kept strict order in the area, but they remember no unusual cruelty in Susurluk. In other parts of Anatolia Turkish liberation forces took up arms against their conquerors. By 1922, the tide shifted in their favor and the Greeks began retreating to the west. With the Turkish breakthrough at Afyon, the Greek retreat became disorderly; fleeing soldiers, murdering and destroying on their way, attacked and burned many small settlements.

At this time the Greek contingent in Susurluk evacuated, and the Greek citizens, fearing reprisals by the Turkish Liberation Army, wanted to leave also. However, the Turkish mayor, Daniş Bey, pleaded with some of them to stay behind to protect the town against the retreating troops. As a final tribute of loyalty to their neighbors and friends of many generations, a few Greek families did remain to persuade or oppose, if necessary, any malicious Greek troops who might want to attack Susurluk. The strategy worked. As the locals now say: Not a person was injured, not a brick was disturbed. Shortly before the arrival of the Turkish liberation forces, the Muslims of Susurluk bade a last farewell to their Christian neighbors, who now had to flee to the coast to save their own lives. By this time almost all of the Armenians had already gone.

Susurluk's official liberation came on September 4, 1922,[7] and after an initial period of celebration townspeople set about reestablishing normalcy. The recent Balkan immigrants who possessed skills in the various crafts and trades began moving from their villages into Susurluk to fill the occupational vacuum created by the Christians' departure. In 1926, Susurluk was elevated to the rank of *kaza* (sub-provincial seat, now called *ilçe*), a position it has maintained ever since.[8]

During the thirties and forties Susurluk served as a market town, a sub-provincial seat, and a brief halting place for travelers. As a whole, the area's economy remained one of near subsistence; people consumed what they produced and shared surplus crops with neighbors, friends, and kin. Except for the steadily decreasing quarry activity and the limited craft work in town, there was little non-agricultural employment. Even in agriculture the market for labor was restricted as people preferred to observe the tradition of mutual aid during planting and harvest rather than work or hire for wages. The local economy was characterized by limited participation in the national economy, little industrialization, and a low degree of differentiation in production and marketing.

In the related areas of government and politics the same lack of differentiation prevailed. Most of the authority and responsibility for the town and sub-province rested with the sub-provincial governor, an official appointed by the central government. Before the advent of a true multi-party system in 1950, all locally elected officials were members of the Republican People's Party. An absence of political organization outside this single party, greatly restricted local self-government and political expression.

In the cultural realm, differentiation did exist. Thanks to its multiplicity of ethnic groups, the district boasted a rich array of folk cultures. In 1950-51 international events again contributed to this array, for in these years over 150,000 Muslims, mostly Turks, were forced to leave Bulgaria and were granted refuge in Turkey. Of these immigrants, 225 families (957 persons) were assigned to Susurluk. About forty families were settled in the town itself, while the rest were dispersed among its villages. The government tried its best to supply the refugees with land, agricultural equipment, homes, and long term credit.

While these and previous immigrant groups had to make adjustments during their process of adaptation, they tried to maintain the most valued elements of their cultures. As a result, life among them could be described as traditional. For example, kinship loyalties and ethnic identity remained strong. Despite the discouragement of the pre-1950 secular government, almost all these peoples maintained a firm adherence to religion and religious values. A marked segregation of the sexes prevailed, with women customarily entertaining themselves in their homes, while men gathered in groups in *odas* (meeting rooms in the homes of well-off males who were usually kin group and/or community leaders).

Notwithstanding its traditional community life, the town of Susurluk did not represent the pure and isolated "folk culture" of the ideal "folk-urban" dichotomies. Owing to its location, the community was constantly exposed to travelers from other parts of the country, and many of the residents' parents or grandparents had come to Susurluk from relatively distant and different lands like the Caucasus and the Balkans. The town and its surrounding villages portrayed an ethnic mosaic, and a strong preference for marriage within ethnic groups operated to maintain certain basic cultural and social boundaries through time. However, adherence to a common religion, Sunni Islam, and common Turkish citizenship functioned to promote interethnic relationships and solidarities.

Geographical Setting

The sparkling Marmara and Aegean Seas, situated to Susurluk's north and west, have a moderating effect on the area's weather. The town's temperature annually ranges from a high of 40 C. (104 F.) to a low of − 19 C. (−2.2 F.) with an average of 18 C. (64.4 F.), and its hottest months are July and August, while its coldest is January. Most of the 167 mm. average annual rainfall precipitates during the winter between December and March. The predominant breezes blow from the southeast (*poyraz*), but occasionally give way to southwesterlies (*lodos*). The summers are hot and dry, while the winters vary from pleasantly mild to a ruthless cold that has inflicted frozen death on poor peasants sleeping in their unheated huts or in pastures by their flocks.

Villagers are also plagued by frequent earthquakes, as the entire 601 square kilometers of the sub-province lie in one of Turkey's most dangerous seismic zones. Potential loss of life and home to the tormenting tremors is one more worry peasants must shoulder. Townspeople are more fortunate because Susurluk's geological base has consistently absorbed even the most violent shocks.

The sub-province's chief water feature is the Simav River, which connects with six tributaries as it flows the length of the sub-province from south to north. Their waters offer the people a mixed blessing: flood dangers in winter and potential sources of irrigation in summer. The sub-province also boasts a number of hot springs and mud baths, which are central to the practice of folk medicine. Dere Village water reportedly cures stomach and intestinal ailments, while the bathing waters of Ilicaboğaz Village are resorted to for rheumatic and skin disorders. Because peasants living near these springs and mud baths praise their medicinal powers and relate numerous stories of miraculous cures, their reputations have spread and have allured visitors from Istanbul and other major cities. Consequently, these attractions are responsible for periodic social interaction between Turkey's urbanites and Susurluk's peasantry.

Most of the southeastern and western sections of the sub-province are hilly to mountainous and are covered by an infertile podzolic soil consisting of a thin, ash colored layer above a brown acidic humus. The most fertile areas consist of an alluvial valley along the Simav River, which begins a little south of Susurluk town and extends north to a point above Göbel, and a rich alluvial plain that constitutes most of the sub-province's northern section. The rest of the sub-province — the central, south, and southwestern sections — varies from low to medium fertility and is characterized by hilly topography and brown soil with low lime content. In general, villagers living on the plain and in the valley work more fertile lands and enjoy a higher standard of living than villagers in the hills.

In 1968, the sub-province's 68,600 hectares [9] were divided into the five use categories represented in Table 1.

TABLE 1
1968 Land Use in Susurluk Sub-Province
in Hectares (Altunbaş 1969:4)

Grains, vegetables	23,044
Orchard and vineyard	1,190
Pasturage	6,174
Forest	12,014
Land useless for agriculture	26,178
Total	68,600

The area's most common crops are wheat, barley, rye, corn, beans, oats, sunflowers, sugar beets, and garden vegetables. Animal husbandry is also important as evidenced by the 1969 veterinarian's report, which listed 16,152 head of cattle, 93,564 sheep and goats, and 40,169 poultry in the sub-province. Animal production that year contributed an estimated TL 4,200,000 to Turkey's gross national product.

The poor agricultural conditions and the growing rural population which typify a large proportion of the sub-province have had at least three major social consequences. The first is intensified conflict between neighboring villages over land use and boundaries. For instance, in 1965 peasants from the south-western villages of Kulat and Paşaköy resorted to their rifles in an attempt to settle a border dispute, and fights between shepherds over grazing areas are reported weekly in local newspapers. The second major consequence is migrant labor. During spring, summer, and fall men and sometimes whole households from the villages of Reşadiye, Asmalidere, Kayalıdere, Gökçedere, Alibey, Kulat, Kiraz, Paşaköy, Danaveli, Babaköy, and Eminpinar earn their meager livings by migrating to the nearby provinces of Manisa, Edremit, Akhisar, and Ayvalik to work in cotton and tobacco fields and olive groves. Their homes are places where they spend the idle winter. The third effect is permanent population movement from village to town or city. Heavy rural migration to the town of Susurluk began in the 1950s and has continued to the point where housing and unemployment are becoming major problems. However, these problems are much more serious in Turkey's larger cities.

Appendix B contains a list of villages in the sub-province with their distances from town, terrain descriptions, 1965 populations, and major ethnic groups.

Notes to Chapter II

History and Geography

[1] The Catalan Grand Company, an army of about 6,500 Spanish mercenaries accompanied by their wives, mistresses and children, had originally been hired by the Byzantines in 1302 to combat the aggressive Turkish *ghazi*s (Ostrogorsky 1957:439). It is probable that in time some of them melded into the Anatolian population.

[2] As this writer is not an Ottoman historian and the documents under discussion were not available for inspection, he cannot comment on the authenticity of the above claims. Suffice it to say that an important historical figure by the name of Karamanı Mehmet Pasha can be the personage to which Ozer and the villager refer. Karamanı Mehmet Pasha, as his name implies, was a Karamanid probably born near Konya at Karaman. He was a descendant of the great mystic Jelal al Din al Rumi. Educated in Istanbul, he attained a rank of vizier, Secretary of State to the Signet (*nishandji*), at an early age in 1464. He was an advisor to Murad II's son, Mehmet the Conqueror, and became Grand Vizier in 1478. On 4 May 1481 he was murdered by mutinous janissaries and most likely was buried in Istanbul (Babinger 1927).

[3] Unfortunately, the remains of this historic *han* have been removed and new buildings have taken its place. The original mosque has been reconstructed into the present Çarşi Mosque which stands in the center of town.

[4] Ahmet Vefik Pasha (1823-91) is one of the most interesting figures in the late Ottoman period. He was born into a family of interpreters. His grandfather, a convert to Islam, had been a dragoman to the Porte. Ahmet served as Ambassador to Paris, inspector of the Western Anatolian Provinces, President of the First Ottoman Parliament of 1876, and Governor-General of Hudavendigar. He translated and produced Moliere's plays on stage in Bursa and also sold land to Robert College, an American institution in Istanbul (Deny 1960:298).

[5] At first the minerals were transported overland by oxcart to the Marmara port of Bandırma and shipped from there to Europe. In 1912 a railroad track was laid between Balıkesir and Bandırma which passed through Omerköy and Susurluk. Thereafter shipments were made by train from Omerköy. Throughout most of the 1865-1956 period European supervisors lived at the quarry, thereby exposing local Muslim and Christian workmen to European patterns of authority and work organization. For the Ottoman documents pertaining to this quarry see Mutluçağ (1967).

[6] For a while during this period Susurluk was officially known as Fırt, a Turkish word somewhat similar to the word "zip" in English. The locally accepted reason for this change is as follows: After the district seat had already been transferred between Susurluk and Omerköy twice, it was about to be switched back to Susurluk again, when in Istanbul a high official in the Ministry of Interior became perplexed and exclaimed, "What is this! Zip (i.e. *fırt*) the *nahiye* is here, zip it is there!" And supposedly, in a fit of irritation, he changed Susurluk's name to Fırt (Ozer 1963:30).

[7] This is now a local holiday celebrated with parades and speeches each year. Susurluk's first school was named "September Fifth" (*Beş Eylul*).

[8] Susurluk's 1927 population is given as 5,510 (*Iller Bankasi Belediye Yilliği* 1950:400). However, it should be pointed out that this, like all other population figures to be given for the town, includes the military contingent stationed there. The military figures are not available, but it is known that the size of the military presence in Susurluk has varied greatly over the years. In 1927 it may well have comprised 25% to 30% of the above figure.

[9] A hectare equals 10,000 square meters or 2.471 acres.

CHAPTER III

The Town Today

If one had compared Susurluk to some other towns and cities in this area before 1950, it would have seemed a lonely, poor, and quiet place. It was undeveloped and poor; its economy operated within a limited agricultural framework. The 1950s, however, saw a great change, due in large part to the establishment of the sugar refinery, which has contributed to Susurluk's social, agricultural, and economic development. It has enabled the peasant to emerge from the age of the *çarık* [raw-hide sandal, a symbol of destitution].

This factory, the town's biggest step toward progress, has helped Susurluk face its other problems. Formerly only one primary school existed; now there are three, along with a middle school and plans to complete a high school. A large bus station and public garage have been created, and they will be expanded. These improvements give us all pride.

The Democratic Party, which came to power in 1950,[1] has recognized the middle class and helped it develop. As a result our crafts are flourishing. Susurluk has become famous for the quality of its carpentry tools (especially the plane), its iron products (axes, hatchets), and its wooden chairs. As part of this economic development the number of banks here has increased from one to four.

These are only some of our accomplishments. In a short time period, our people have shown themselves to be industrious, honest and determined. They combined government help with their own energies. Water flows from our fountains; smoke rises from our chimneys. Our sick are cared for in our own hospital; our children are educated in our own schools. Natives of Susurluk have become doctors, engineers, teachers, and tradesmen. Many of them have gone to other parts of Turkey to represent us. Susurluk has been saved from ignorance. This gives us pride.

However, we do not stop here. Our newest goals include a larger high school, a primary school in Orta Quarter, and the pipage of water from Çaylak. These will improve our town even more.

Above is the translation of an editorial which appeared in a local newspaper, the *Susurluk Beş Eylul Ekspres* in 1968.[2] The ideas expressed concerning the impact of the sugar refinery represent local opinion. Its author, Mehmet, a young man in his mid-twenties, was born and raised in Susurluk. After finishing the Boys Trade School in Balıkesir he served in the military and then went to Germany where he worked in a factory for two years. While there he improved his technical skills and learned German. Mehmet returned to Susurluk and found a position with a modern cannery in a nearby town as foreman of the container production section, a position requiring both technical knowledge and supervisory skills.

The education, experience, and skills which Mehmet has acquired would classify him as a modern man. He is an active part of the technical world which symbolizes westernization, and he takes great pride in his town's educational and economic achievements. Yet he is the product of a traditional family and considers himself a devout Muslim. Recently married, he and his young wife reside, by his choice, with his parents and two younger unmarried brothers. His father is a local *müezzin* (one who calls Muslims to prayer). They admire one another a great deal and are often seen together. In effect, Mehmet has harmoniously combined two life-styles often reputed to be antithetical. He is an important part of a modern factory tooled with Western equipment and organized on a Western model. Yet he chooses to live in a traditional extended household with devout Muslim parents.

Unfortunately, many of Turkey's self-proclaimed leftists and progressives label people of Mehmet's genre reactionary. The poor communication and lack of empathy between these differently oriented peoples not only hinders Turkey's economic development, but prevents the country from enjoying the degree of internal harmony that most Turks desire.

Many of the points which Mehmet raises will be taken up in later chapters. Before that, the actors in this story, Susurluk's people, should be introduced.

The People

The construction of the sugar refinery in 1954 caused a substantial increase in Susurluk's population. During ensuing years the refinery, along with newly developed support activities in transportation, industrial crafts, commerce, and housing construction created additional jobs which attracted villagers to town. Table 2 illustrates population levels from 1940 to 1970.

TABLE 2
Population for Susurluk Town and Villages

	1940	1945	1950	1955	1960	1965	1970
Town	4,833	6,147	6,701	10,022	11,450	11,268	12,357
Villages	25,824	27,163	27,504	28,024	28,304	28,495	27,782

The decrease in town population from 1960 to 1965 is partly attributable to the emigration of an estimated 100 workers to Western Europe and a decrease in the size of the local military unit, that numbered about 150 in 1970. The increase in town population from 1965 to 1970 and the corresponding decrease in village population is due to sectoral relocation, or the movement of labor from rural agricultural pursuits to urban jobs. This population mobility has affected the area's inter-ethnic relations.

Through time the boundaries of the various pieces comprising Susurluk's cultural mosaic have been diminished to the point where today all ethnic groups share a relatively common Turkish culture. However, each group still considers itself unique and somewhat superior. Even Gypsies, who are universally regarded as the most inferior people, boasted to me that they were the only ones who really knew how to enjoy life. One reason for the assimilation of the non-Turkic peoples has been the official position of the government, especially during the early years of the Republic when the establishment of a Turkish national homeland and identity was of prime importance. According to official Turkish histories all Muslim peoples living in Turkey are racially and ethnically Turks, and Kurdish, Circassian, and Georgian are mere dialects of Turkish. However, speakers of such languages have been pressured to learn and use "true Turkish," and publication in these non-Turkic languages is prohibited.

At present all residents of Susurluk speak Turkish in public and the vast majority do so in their homes also. Other languages, like Circassian and Georgian, are spoken in the villages by the elderly who know little Turkish. But most young people in these villages have not learned the languages of their grandparents and speak only Turkish. All the Turks of this area — Manavs, Balkan Turks, Chepnis, Yürüks and Turkmen—speak mutually intelligible Turkish with some accentual and vocabulary differences.

Religion has acted as another leveling force; all peoples of the sub-province, with the exception of the Chepnis, publicly indentify as Sunni Muslims of the Hanafite rite.

The absence of marked physical differences among the ethnic groups has also facilitated their assimilation. The Balkan immigrants, Circassians and Georgians tend to have light to medium complexions, blue eyes, blond to brunette hair, medium to tall stature (5'6" to 5'10" for men), and lean to stocky physiques. By comparison, Manavs are darker and somewhat shorter, but more European looking than Central Anatolian peasants. Yürüks, Turkmen, and Chepnis are very mixed, although most resemble Manavs, while Gypsies are generally darker-complected with medium stature and medium to lean physiques.

The estimated proportions of the various ethnic groups in Susurluk Town and

Sub-province for 1970 are contained in Table 3. Official statistics of this type do not exist.

TABLE 3
Susurluk's Population by Ethnicity

Village Population (1970 = 27,782)		Town Population (1970 = 12,357)	
Balkan Turk	60%	Mixed Balkan Turk-Manav	20%
Manav	15%	Balkan Turk	40%
Yürük-Turkmen	10%	Manav	15%
Circassian	10%	Circassian	10%
Other	5%	Gypsy	4%
	———	Georgian	4%
	100%	Other	7%
			———
			100%

Balkan Turks, Manavs, and Circassians are the most numerous peoples both in town and in the villages. In the past Circassians represented an even larger proportion of the town population, but many have emigrated to Istanbul and other large cities. While Yürüks and Turkmen represent about 10% of the village population, comparatively few have moved to town.

In the following pages the various ethnic groups will be discussed separately, and the historical and cultural elements contributing to their uniqueness will be treated.

Manav

Manavs regard themselves as direct descendants of the area's first Turkish settlers. However, the actual backgrounds of many Manavs are mixed and uncertain. Some claim their ultimate ancestors were nomadic Turks and others have a few Arabs in the upper reaches of their vague genealogies. The only Manav families with a ''documented'' genealogy trace their ancestry to the fifteenth century with Koca Mehmet Pasha acting as the apogee figure. Reportedly, the great pasha has 146 living descendants, most of whom reside in Susurluk or Kepekler village. This genealogy, which is by far the most extensive in this area, has functioned as a charter supporting claims of ownership to rich agricultural lands. With the development of cash cropping, the Manav families working these lands were able to accumulate small fortunes, which some of them have invested in town-based retail businesses and real estate. Their identification with the area is so great that several families chose Susurluk as their surname in the 1930s. Today these families and their close relatives are considered the town's ''blue bloods.''

Balkan Turk *(Muhacir)*

Most of the Balkan Turks in the sub-province are descendants of nineteenth century immigrants from Grecian Thrace, Bulgaria's Osman Pazar, and Romania's Dobruja. They and the more recent immigrants from these areas are referred to collectively as *"Muhacirler"* (singular = *Muhacir*), although, twentieth century immigrants differentiate among themselves by region of emigration. Balkan Turks and Manavs are similar culturally and socially, with the exception that the heterosexual relationships of the former tend to be more conservative. Balkan Turkish women observe more rigid rules of male avoidance *(kaç göç)* and subordination to male authority. Balkan Turks have traditionally been admired for their skill and industry as farmers and craftsmen, but today they are found in all occupations.

Yürük and Turkmen

Formerly these Turks were tribally organized and led nomadic or transhumant lives grazing their flocks of goats and sheep. During the last part of the nineteenth century they were forced to settle down in the hill villages which they still occupy. Today, no form of tribal organization remains, but animal husbandry is still a main source of livelihood for many. Others, who own few animals and poor farm land, have continued a nomadic existence of sorts by working as migrant laborers gathering cotton and harvesting olives in neighboring sub-provinces. Yürük and Turkmen women provide a colorful spectacle on market days when they descend on Susurluk in their traditionally bright orange and red dresses to sell eggs, cheese, yogurt, and butter.

Chepni

The Chepnis, who occupy one hill village and number about 320, represent the only outcast Turkish people in the sub-province. Their ancestors were among the Oghuz tribes that entered Anatolia before the establishment of the Ottoman Empire and subsequently played an important role in the Empire's political and religious history. They are credited with the conquest of the Ordu-Giresun region on the Black Sea in the fourteenth century, and during the sixteenth century a province near Trabzon was named Chepni. Later, a Chepni tribe known as Bashim Kızdılu (The Angry Ones) migrated to Western Anatolia and settled in the provinces of Izmir, Aydın, Manisa, and Balıkesir. These people are historically known for their adherence to Bektashi and Kizilbash doctrines — heterodox beliefs strongly opposed by Sunni Muslims. Today, they refer to themselves and are called Bektashis (members of a heterodox order) and Alevis (followers of Ali), and a number of erotic and incestuous practices are wrongly attributed to them.

Their more immediate ancestors were among the nomadic tribes forcibly settled in the nineteenth century, and today many eke out their livelihoods through a combination of animal husbandry, farming, and migrant labor. During the spring, summer, and fall a large part of the adult population leaves the village to find work in other areas.

Circassians

Circassians, who call themselves Adighe, embraced Sunni Islam during the sixteenth and seventeenth centuries while they were still living in the Caucasus Mountains. After the Russian conquest of their homeland in 1864-65, many Circassians sought refuge in the Ottoman Empire. The most noted emigres went south and became the royal guard of Jordanian Kings; many of the less famous fled to Anatolia in a destitute condition and created havoc among the Turkish peasantry from whom they extracted their daily bread. As a result of these hard times, the Circassians, who traditionally considered robbing strangers an honorable act (Luzbetak 1951:148), earned a reputation for theft that still lives on in Turkey. Many of those who finally settled in Susurluk Sub-province came via Romania and are mostly of the Abzakh and Shapsi branches of the Circassian nation.

Luzbetak (1951:205) reports that in the Caucasus the Circassians' traditional kinship system was similar to that of their Turco-Mongolian neighbors. In the Susurluk area, Circassians not only conform to Turkish social and cultural practices, but accentuate them. For example, while the ideal authority patterns of all ethnic groups are patriarchal, it is the authoritarian Circassian patriarch who is notorious for his stern and demanding demeanor. Although all groups engage in the bridewealth practice, none asks for more than the Circassians. However, it is for a basic cultural difference, involving the great relative freedom of Circassian girls, that they are really famous. From the time of the Ottoman Sultans, whose harems they filled, to the present day, Circassian girls have been renowned for their beauty. In Susurluk, this reputation partly derives from their openness and fair complexions. Unlike fully covered and secluded Turkish girls, Circassian girls can be seen. They are relatively free to associate with male peers, and have been quick to adopt Western dress. The area's most lauded events are Circassian weddings, which draw men from far and wide to observe the lovely spectacle of pretty Circassian maidens participating in the folk dancing that begins late at night and continues till dawn. Circassian girls also enjoy the traditional right to accept or reject marriage proposals, and today as in the past acceptance often leads to elopement as a way of avoiding excessive bridewealth demands. Once married, however, Circassian women become even more secluded than their Turkish sisters.

The freedom and openness associated with bachelor status is accompanied

Tradition and Change

Neighborhood Children

Town market day

Town market day

the municipality and the national government is one of tutelage: all decisions made by municipal officials can be altered or negated by either the provincial and sub-provincial governments or the Ministry of Interior. For the town, the most immediate controlling official is the assistant governor, who directs the activities of the Departments of Population, Police, Land Registration, Agriculture, Forestry, Education, Religion, Health and Veterinary Services, Settlement, and Gendarmery.

The town of Susurluk possesses a municipal form of government and a sub-provincial seat. Within the Susurluk sub-province there are two districts and 47 villages.

The responsibilities of the town government include inspection of businesses serving the public such as hotels, coffeehouses, restaurants, and cinemas; the enforcement of sanitary regulations in businesses dealing with food; the establishment of maximum prices for certain foods and services; the maintenance of water, electricity, sewerage, and fire-fighting services; the establishment and regulation of a slaughterhouse and wholesale market; the maintenance of the town park and streets; and, cooperation with the national government.

In addition to being administratively integrated into Turkey's hierarchically ordered governmental structure, Susurluk is socially, culturally, and economically integrated internally, regionally, and nationally. The structure of this integration and the mechanisms which promote it vary from level to level.

The Defended Neighborhood

Primary concerns of all Susurluk households are the sanctity of the home and the safety of their women and children. One indication of these concerns is the enclosed courtyard characteristic of older homes; another is the solidarity that members of an immediate neighborhood display to the outside. Many important parts of a family's daily routine are not restricted to the confines of the home. While the men are often away, women and children spend much of their time in the immediate neighborhood, with young ones playing in the streets and women exchanging visits with neighbors, fetching water from public fountains, and walking to and from the bakery and general store. In effect, the immediate neighborhood is a shared extension of all the households whose women and children participate in its use. Consequently, throughout Susurluk groups of neighboring households have united to form what may be termed ''defended neighborhoods'' — spatial units within which neighbors cooperate to maintain a degree of security for their members which is relatively high in comparison to adjacent areas. Given the nature of traditional Turkish society, with its insistence on domestic privacy and the sanctity of women and children, and given that formal mechanisms of social control are unable to guarantee these, informal arrangements become necessary to govern spatial movement and to segregate categories of individuals that might otherwise come into conflict. A defended neighborhood is primarily a response to perceived fears of invasion from the outside. Although its member households may not be related through kinship or have common ethnicity, they share spatial propinquity and a common plight.

It is not uncommon for strangers entering a defended neighborhood to be stopped by male residents and questioned about their business there. In Susurluk there have been numerous incidents of neighbors joining together to beat off would-be kidnappers who invaded their territory to carry off teen-age girls for marital purposes. The sense of territoriality is so strong that on occasion even women group together to drive out adult males who have violated their space or abused their children, and young men take a sibling attitude toward neighborhood girls, safeguarding them to the extent of intimidating outsiders who may entertain romantic notions. The sibling attitudes generated by long-time co-residents become so ingrained that neighbors frequently address each other with kinship terms and sexual relations between them are often regarded as incestuous.

The right and obligation to protect and shelter neighborhood girls has been institutionally recognized in the custom of *toprak basti* (trespass tax), which is enacted during the marriage ritual when the groom's kin fetch the bride from her parents' home. A group of the neighborhood's young male defenders meet the procession at the edge of their territory and demand a trespass tax before allowing it to proceed. In Susurluk and its surrounding villages this demand is commonly met with payments approaching 300 Turkish liras. Denial causes hostility. During my year in Susurluk, regional newspapers carried accounts of three conflicts over *toprak basti*. Two of these occurred in Balikesir villages and terminated with several knifings. The third took place in Bursa and resulted in the murder of one person.

The defended neighborhood is also characterized by a female-dominated network of trust, cooperation and mutual aid linking its member households. When a death occurs, neighboring women look after the mourning household for at least a week, believing that its members are too grief-stricken to care for themselves. When one woman falls ill, others attend to her family until she recovers. Neighbors also contribute materially to the poorer households among them, especially during holydays.

Moreover, neighboring women feel entitled to receive, and under obligation to exchange, private information and gossip. They share in a common pool of facts, half-truths, rumors, and myths about residents of the neighborhood, the quarter, and the town. They also share in the consequences of any member's behavior, as there is a collective pride and guilt over one another's achievements and shortcomings. In sum, each defended neighborhood possesses its unique "sub-culture," and the women and young are its major producers and carriers.

The Quarter — *Mahalle*

After the defended neighborhood, the next larger area into which townspeople are socially integrated is their quarter *(mahalle)* of residence. Susurluk has six residential quarters and each is quite distinct with respect to age and population.

The town's oldest and most homogeneous of these is Orta (Central) Quarter, which is predominantly residential, containing only a few commercial establishments such as general stores, coffeehouses, and bakeries. Most of its homes are old one- and two-story structures with adobe walls and red tile roofs. About 80% of its residents are Manavs, 18% are Balkan Turks (descendants of nineteenth century immigrants), and 2% are of other ethnicities. Orta is the town's most stable quarter, having the lowest turnover of families. Most of its homes have remained in the same lineages for generations, and practically all of its available space is occupied.

The real geographical and functional center of town is Han Quarter, located to the northwest of Orta and ranked second to it with respect to age. Han contains the town's main business district and industrial area, along with the municipal building, court house, police station, gendarmery, post office, bus station, banks, and several hundred homes. It is crisscrossed by the two major streets — Milli Kuvvetler (National Forces) and Çarsı (Market) — upon which much of the town's commercial, governmental, and social activities take place. Here one sees some of the town's oldest wooden frame and adobe buildings peering up at adjoining four-story concrete monuments of the modern age. Çarşı street, as its name implies, is the locus of the town's weekly open market. Every Wednesday it is covered with make-shift canopied stands from which sellers hawk brightly colored textiles, fresh fruits and vegetables, olives and olive oil, dried beans and rice, cheeses, yogurt, eggs, chickens, Qurans. hardware, and other items. Han's residential population is the second most homogeneous of all the town's quarters. About 60% are Manavs, 30% arc Balkan Turks from the nineteenth century migrations, and the remaining 10% are more recent immigrant Turks and peoples of other ethnic groups.

To the east of Orta, on the town's southeast corner, is Kışla (Winter Shelter), a quarter whose name and origin may go back to the time when nomadic Turks used its low, flat land as their winter camp. It is a residential area whose age and location have contributed to its mixed character. Being one of Susurluk's oldest quarters, numerous Manav families are among its residents. But its location on the town's edge has made it an expansion quarter, providing home-sites for diverse nineteenth and twentieth century immigrants from the Balkans and

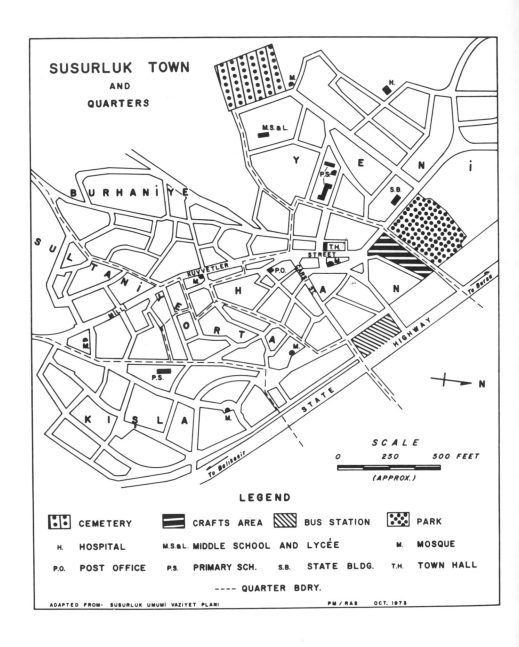

SUSURLUK TOWN
AND
QUARTERS

BURHANİYE

SULTANİ

YENİ

M.S.&L.

P.S.

S.B.

KUVVETLER

MİLLİ

ORTA

T.H.
STREET
M.

P.O.

CADDE

HAN

HIGHWAY
To Berso

STATE

M.

M.

P.S.

KISLA

M.

To Balikesir

N

SCALE

0   250   500 FEET

(APPROX.)

LEGEND

CEMETERY	CRAFTS AREA	BUS STATION	PARK

H. HOSPITAL   M.S.&L. MIDDLE SCHOOL AND LYCÉE   M. MOSQUE

P.O. POST OFFICE   P.S. PRIMARY SCH.   S.B. STATE BLDG.   T.H. TOWN HALL

---- QUARTER BDRY.

ADAPTED FROM: SUSURLUK UMUMİ VAZİYET PLANI   PM/RAS   OCT. 1973

Caucasus. Prior to 1965 Kışla also contained about forty households of Gypsy basket weavers, who were forced out of town that year when their homes were expropriated for a new primary school. In 1970 this quarter's population was estimated to be 46% Manav, 46% Balkan Turk, and 8% of other ethnicities.

Bordering on the southwestern part of Kışla is Sultaniye, a residential quarter established by immigrants and regional peasants in the late 1920s. Since then it has experienced steady growth to the south. For instance, in 1952 one of its uninhabited sections became the site of about 150 homes for new Turkish immigrants from Bulgaria. The quarter still contains the homes of a few families of Gypsy basket weavers. In 1970 about 85% of its population was comprised of Balkan Turks from various migrations, and the remaining 15% were peoples of other ethnic groups.

Established at about the same time as Sultaniye and located on an incline and hill to its west is Burhaniye, an ethnically mixed expansion quarter predominantly occupied by Balkan Turks from various migrations and about fifty to sixty households of Gypsy Musicians. They comprise about 75% and 15% of its 1970 population respectively, with the balance being peoples of other ethnic groups.

Susurluk's most recent quarter is Yeni (New), established in 1950 on the town's northern corner. Functionally it is quite diverse, containing the new town park, two primary schools, the middle school and lycée, the town soccer field, the hospital, the sub-provincial government building, three modern apartment houses built by the sugar refinery workers' union, several hundred one- and two-story homes built in the fifties and sixties, and a small squatter settlement *(gece kondu)* on its western hill. The sugar refinery is also administratively part of this quarter, but being two and one-half miles outside of town, the refinery community is a social world unto itself. The residents of Yeni Quarter represent a wide range of socio-economic backgrounds: from some of the town's leading families residing in the newest and best dwellings, to poor peasants living in shanties they call home. The estimate of its 1970 population composition is 75% Balkan Turk, 8% Georgian, 5% Yürük-Turkmen, 5% Circassian, 5% Manav, and 2% other groups.

Each quarter is an administrative unit of the municipality with a quarter chief *(muhtar)* and a four-member "council of elders" *(ihtiyar heyeti)*, who are elected every four years from among its residents. Candidates may affiliate with a political party or be independent. Once elected, they serve as intermediaries between governmental institutions and quarter residents, with their most common duties being the certification of documents relating to birth, parentage, marriage, death, residence, and ownership of property. They must also supply the army with a list of males in their quarter who are eligible for military duty. Instead of salaries, quarter officials are entitled to small fees for services rendered, however they ordinarily collect fees for the certification of commercial documents only.

Quarter officials also provide numerous informal services to their constituencies by acting as their arbitrators, counsellors, and middlemen. They often settle quarter disputes informally, without recourse to the courts. They read and interpret all sorts of letters and notices brought to them by illiterate or unsophisticated residents, and quite often they represent these humble people before bureaucrats, officials, bankers, the police, and others holding formal positions of authority. Because their quarter officials can help them cope with the mysterious officialdom and bureaucracy infringing on their otherwise intelligible lives, many people have a keen interest in quarter elections and maintain amiable relations with successful candidates. In effect, quarter officials function as important mechanisms of social integration. They promote identification with the quarter, foster better social relations within it, and facilitate the social and psychological adjustment of their constituencies to the town.

Quarter identification is further promoted by government agencies that selectively dispense scarce resources such as schools, water works, finances for road construction, electric power, etc. by quarter within the town. In order to be considered for any of these benefits, a quarter must unite and petition the controlling authority through its quarter chief. In this respect, each quarter exists within a structure of parallel residential solidarities that compete for the limited resources controlled by outside agencies. For example, during the dry summer of 1965 a water shortage coupled with frequent breakdowns of the municipal water pumps left many households outside the town's center without water for long periods of time. The deprived citizens of Sultaniye Quarter reacted to the situation in a united way by executing a barefoot march around Susurluk to the town hall, where they deposited their empty water vessels and petitioned the mayor. This dramatic demonstration of their common plight prompted town officials to give first priority to the solution of the water problem in their quarter.

Within each quarter there are foci of religious, social, and commercial activity that also foster identification with the quarter and contribute to the social and cultural integration of its residents. The quarter mosque provides both a place where residents, especially males, can congregate for communal prayer and companionship and a point from which Islamic values can be disseminated. The mosque's prayer leader *(imam)* figures prominently in quarter life. He attends to the religious needs of his congregation and plays a religious role in the various life cycle rites accompanying birth, circumcision, marriage and death. He tries to promote harmony in the community, and like the quarter chief he sometimes mediates neighborly squabbles. His ultimate objective is to create a spirit of brotherhood among the members of his community.

Care for the mosque is the responsibility of all quarter households, and those residents especially concerned join an association which solicits money', labor, and materials for the mosque's upkeep and repair.

Other foci of quarter life are the coffeehouses, general stores, bakeries, and public water fountains. The first are the exclusive domain of men, and the last that of women, but all serve as places of attachment and companionship. Residents of each quarter like to boast that their mosque is the best attended, that their bakery makes the most delicious bread, that their storekeepers are the most honest, that their coffeehouses are the cleanest and most friendly, and, especially, that their neighbors are the most compatible.

In essence, the last boast makes the others possible. The ability of neighbors to carry on a full round of life in a limited space without arousing one another's culturally dictated anxieties over the violation of home and family is the foundation of harmonious quarter life. The ideal quarter is one whose residents share mutual consideration and a basic agreement on norms of conduct. This condition, which will be termed "normative integration," is not constant throughout the town. Although all Susurluk residents are Muslims, who may adhere to the same abstract Islamic values, their varying backgrounds provide somewhat different bases for social conduct and its evaluation.

The degree of normative integration in Susurluk's quarters is hypothesized to be dependent on two factors: degree of ethnic homogeneity or common background among residents and the amount of resident turnover. That is, normative integration is expected to be comparatively high in quarters whose populations are, relatively, culturally homogeneous and physically stable. This hypothesis was tested by comparing interpersonal complaints (e.g., physical and sexual assault, insult, theft) in the various quarters filed with the police and reported in the local newspapers over a ten-year period: 1961-70. Newspaper coverage of formal complaints is considered near complete.

In Table 4 complaints are divided into two categories: "Intra-quarter" involving residents of the same quarter, and "Inter-quarter" involving a complainant who resides outside the quarter of his assailant. As the population sizes are not widely disparate, each quarter's complaint total may be regarded as a crude index of negative normative integration. The higher a quarter's total number of complaints, the less normatively integrated it is believed to be.

The table evinces that the town's two oldest and most homogeneous quarters — Orta and Han — have the lowest number of complaints. Both quarters, but especially Orta, have been inhabited by the same families for numerous generations and in recent decades have experienced relatively little new settlement or resident turnover, while the remaining four quarters have served as expansion areas, providing homes and home sites for regional peasants and immigrants from foreign lands.

TABLE 4
1961-1970 Complaints

	Orta	Han	Kişla	*Quarters* Burhaniye	Sultaniye	Yeni	*Totals*
1965 population	1518	2074	1768	1984	2026	1898	11,268
Intra-quarter Complaints							
Physical assault	2	1	10	12	15	10	50
Insult	—	—	2	1	6	2	11
Sexual Assault	—	2	2	—	—	1	5
Theft	—	1	5	2	3	4	15
Other Interpersonal Conflicts	—	1	1	5	4	—	11
Total	2	5	20	20	28	17	92
Inter-Quarter Complaints							
Physical assault to outsider	1	3	2	2	1	1	10
Total Complaints	3	8	22	22	29	18	102

Notably, most formally reported conflicts occur between residents of the same quarter. This, in part, is attributable to the strain of residential propinquity and a culture that stresses privacy and sexual segregation.

One may wonder how many intra-quarter conflicts go unreported. The town's chief of police, an outsider from Konya with extensive police experience in Turkey, says Susurluk is one of the most peaceful towns he has known. He maintains that people here successfully resolve most of their conflicts informally without recourse to the police or courts. Formal complaints usually result when informal mechanisms for mediation either have proven insufficient or do not exist. For some of the town's more recent arrivals time may have been inadequate for learning existing norms and informal mechanisms of dispute settlement or for establishing new ones. This may partially explain the greater number of reported conflicts in the expansion quarters.

The Town — Community of Selective Involvement

Although life in the quarters may be very fulfilling, no quarter is autonomous or self-sufficient; each is a partial structure of larger social systems. The foci of quarter activity and attachment — the coffeehouses, general stores, bakeries, and public fountains — are regulated by the municipal government, which sets prices, standards of sanitation, and operating hours. The quarter mosque and its religious personnel are under the supervision of a federally appointed official: the *mufti*. All households have economic and educational interests extending beyond their quarter, such as shopping in the commercial district, banking, employment, and children's education. Kinship and friendship ties also cross-cut quarter boundaries.

While a townsman is able to commit himself to all or most of his quarter's communal activities, on the town level his loyalties, demands, interests, and participation are fragmented. The town presents a widely differentiated set of cultural, social, economic, educational, political, and religious organizations in which townspeople participate selectively to attain common goals, air complaints, or enjoy leisure time. Some of these organizations restrict their membership on the bases of such criteria as political party affiliation, occupation, or sex. Examples are the Women's Branch of the Justice Party, the Retail Merchants Association, and the Chairmakers Association. Others, like the Turkish Music and Cultural Associations, are open to anyone sharing a special interest.

Each association has five to seven officers and a general membership. Usually the officers are the founders of the association, and they continue to provide its thrust, guidance, and identity. About one hundred townsmen coming from the ranks of municipal officials, primary school educators, businessmen, and religious personnel consistently assume leading and supporting roles in many of the town's associations. They mobilize and guide the citizenry in the attainment of selected goals and contribute substantially in terms of time, talent, and money to community affairs. Their personalities, their interlocking associational memberships, together with the institutions they represent provide the town with much of its direction, cohesion, and spirit.

If we were to regard the town as a hierarchical ordering of spheres of identity and involvement, these men and the roles they occupy would represent the highest tier, linking, if not encompassing many of the partial social structures existing at lower levels. The town may be viewed as a "community of selective involvement," with most people participating in a fragmented and partial manner, but with a core of formal and informal leaders whose extensive involvement promotes the town's integration and special identity.

Regional and National Integration

The town is also integrated regionally with the villages in its sub-province and nationally with Turkey's major cities. Since the 1950s the strength of this integration has been increased by Susurluk's new economic prominence.

Having become beneficiary of a major factory and a number of banks, many of Susurluk's important economic activities fell under the control of outside interests. More than ever, the town became the recipient of urban ideas, practices, products, regulations, and people. In turn, this new economic energy made Susurluk a more potent influence on surrounding villages, by importing peasants to advance her own development and exporting urban ideas and products.

Susurluk's position between city and village is exemplified by the disparate life-styles, incomes, and sources of her population. Approximately 40% of the town's 1970 population is estimated to have been born elsewhere, with about half of these coming from Turkish villages and the rest from towns, cities, and Balkan villages. While most of the urbanites were assigned to Susurluk by their employers (e.g., banks, government, the sugar refinery), the villagers, excepting the Balkan immigrants, came seeking jobs.

This interpenetration of people, materials, and culture between city-town and town-village has been facilitated by various mechanisms of social integration, i.e., roles and institutions which promote communication, understanding, and the social and psychological adjustment of villagers, townsmen, and urbanites to each other. As in all developing countries, effective mechanisms have been built upon existing kinship and friendship ties. Many peasants who moved to Susurluk had kin or former village mates already living in town, who helped them with problems of housing and work. Most migrants still maintain contact with relatives and friends in their villages, especially by exchanging visits on holydays and during important life cycle rites accompanying birth, circumcision, marriage, and death. Consequently, Susurluk is linked to all its surrounding villages by kinship and friendship networks which provide the bases for communication, mutual aid, and exchange of news, ideas, and goods.

The weekly market also serves as an important integrative mechanism which operates simultaneously on cultural, social, and economic levels by providing peasants with opportunities to establish face-to-face contacts with townsfolk and urbanites, sell their village products, and thereby acquire needed cash to purchase goods manufactured in towns and cities. Every Wednesday thousands of peasants in their traditional dress travel to Susurluk on a new complex of roads in the trucks, buses, and tractor-drawn wagons, which have replaced their donkeys and oxen, and flood the town's central area. They participate in a market largely consisting of preferential trade relationships. For example, a town family, only one generation removed from a nearby village, sells cloth to all comers, but offers credit only to buyers from their former village. Similarly, when purchasing village products, townspeople seek out sellers from their own or their ancestors' former village, as this connection provides the basis for special treatment in terms of higher quality goods or lower prices.

In addition to their buying and selling, peasants visit briefly with friends and relatives or attend to other personal and business matters. They stroll the main streets, admire new products prominently displayed in store windows, and view amusedly the gaudy posters advertising current and forthcoming films. Amidst the throng and activity of the market young lovers find opportunities to become separated from their elders so that they can meet, exchange soft words, and reaffirm their mutual affections. Once back in their villages, peasants spend much of their free time discussing town experiences and planning for the next market day.

Coffeehouses supplement the market as promoters of integration. Commonly, male peasants from the surrounding villages have their favorite Susurluk coffeehouses in which they can take refuge and from which they can venture to cope with the town's cultural code and its peculiar socio-economic organization. They say the coffeehouse is a place to which their foot has become accustomed *(ayak alışmış)* or to which their foot turns *(ayak döner)*. On market days they deposit their bundles there and meet with friends and kin to discuss news over a hot glass of tea. Townsmen and government officials seeking a particular villager will go to his coffeehouse either to find him or to leave a message. The coffeehouse also functions as an information center, providing those peasants planning to migrate to town with news about jobs and housing.

Another important integrative mechanism is the complex of multipurpose relationships established between villager and merchant. Many village families, and sometimes whole villages, deal almost exclusively with one particular town merchant, whose parents may derive from the same village. The merchant buys from these villagers, sells to them on seasonal credit, and acts as their social middleman, counsellor and broker in town. Being more literate and knowledgeable of urban ways, he keeps their financial accounts and advises them on social, economic, and governmental matters. If necessary, he engages lawyers for them, recommends doctors, and may even act as mediator in disputes and marital affairs. Villagers planning to move to town consult him about jobs and living arrangements. By performing these indispensable functions for villagers and new migrants, the merchant earns their indebtedness and patronage. For the peasants, this is a familiar way of dealing with a strange environment — a personal, face-to-face relationship based on informal oral agreements which permits them to avoid direct, unassisted confrontations with large, formalized, and foreign institutions.

Susurluk is also part of a broader market structure which includes Balıkesir to the south and the cities of Karacabey, Manyas, and Mustafakemalpasha to the north. Each city holds its market on separate days, so that it is possible for a merchant to sell his goods in different cities on five different days. Some merchants from the larger cities actually do this, but for most Susurluk merchants, the effective selling market is confined to Susurluk on Wednesday, Mustafakemalpasha on Thursday, and Manyas on Saturday. The staggered market days in this region create a pulsating flow of peoples and products between and among cities, towns, and villages. This movement derives energy from established socio-economic ties and gains momentum through the creation of new ones.

Another dimension of the town's integration consists of vertical linkages between differentiated parts of the town and their respective extra-community systems. For example, the sub-provincial government is linked to the provincial government in Balıkesir, and from there to the Ministry of Interior in Anakara. Susurluk banks have "branch" status and are under the direction of regional banks in Balıkesir and central banks in either Istanbul or Ankara. In a similar fashion, the town's police, courts, school system, religious personnel, post office, and telephone and telegraph services are all under the supervision of regional officers in Balıkesir and central authorities in Ankara. The sugar refinery is also part of a nation-wide system and is centrally directed from Turkey's capital.

Characteristic of these linkages are their bureaucratic nature and locus of authority. Policy statements, guide-lines, directives, and appointments emit from the central offices and flow to the town. Town agencies respond with acknowledgements, compliances, and performances. The relationships are prescribed mainly in terms of the larger systems, with secondary consideration given to town-specific problems. For instance, production quotas for the sugar refinery are chiefly determined by national and international market estimates, not by local production and employment needs. Likewise, credit levels of town banks are not based on current local demand, but on pre-determined policies of central offices. During the early 1960s many townsmen refused to deposit savings with the local agricultural bank because they claimed it was not giving them needed loans.

The relative lack of local direction and control is associated with an absence of local attachment on the part of agency officials. The managers and executives of all the town-level organizations listed above are out-of-towners for whom Susurluk represents a temporary stop along the promotion route to larger cities. They are vertically oriented men, who conduct their businesses primarily to please and impress superiors in distant cities and secondarily to benefit townspeople. Consequently, the effect of these vertical linkages is predominantly centrifugal: they attach and direct various parts of the town to national systems, but do comparatively little to promote the town's integrity.

This fissionary process is counteracted to a limited extent by the ability of a few town leaders to circumvent the local and regional officials, over whom they have no authority, and to influence informally their superiors in the higher echelons of government. For example, during 1969-70 Susurluk's mayor, a retired colonel and branch president of the national party in office, traveled frequently to Ankara to present his town's case directly to cabinet ministers (fellow party members), who then had directives, corresponding to the mayor's requests, sent down to the bureaucrats of their respective agencies in the town. This circumvention is possible because the mayor belongs to the national party in power and can trade local political support for special favors. The route to the top is an informal one, necessitated by the structural barriers imposed by the formal bureaucracy.

Travel and Mass Media

Modernization involves three kinds of mobility: geographical mobility — the ability to change one's location; social mobility — the ability to change one's social position; and, psychic mobility — the ability to change one's self-image. The three are interrelated; for example, a villager leaves the soil to work in a modern factory, raises his social status, and begins to regard himself as a "progressive" townsman, rather than as a "backward" peasant. The first two kinds of mobility require changes in the economic and social structure; the third necessitates psychological change.

The psychic transformation considered here, has been described by Lerner (1958) as the development of empathy — the expanded ability of a people to identify in an active mental sense with roles, times, and places different from their own. Travel and mass media can be instruments of this change because they introduce their participants to new people, provide them with real or vicarious experiences in different places, and expose them to a wide range of values and opinions. The literate, widely traveled members of a society differ from illiterate, isolated fellow-members in this respect because travel and media exposure have expanded the scope of their empathic ability beyond the range of their firsthand experiences and places of residence. Before people can confidently participate in a new situation, they must familiarize themselves with it psychically.

In developing societies mass media also has important educational and political roles. It contributes to the development of modern skills, to the dissemination of factual knowledge, to the creation of patriotic sentiments, and to the establishment of national identity.

In the 1950s travel potential for Susurluk residents was greatly enhanced by reconstruction of the Izmir-Istanbul state highway which passes by the edge of town, a sharp increase in the number of motorized vehicles, and a decrease in fares. Consequently, many townspeople now make the forty-five minute trip frequently to Balıkesir, the provincial capital, and they have become accustomed to visiting larger, more distant cities also. 93.4% of the adult sample

claimed to have visited Istanbul, Turkey's largest and most advanced city, and
76.4% said they have been to Ankara, the country's capital. Numerous buses
destined for each, pass Susurluk daily. Susurluk also enjoys tri-weekly train
service to Izmir, a modern city of about one-half million inhabitants located
approximately 150 miles to the south on the Aegean. Townspeople frequently
discuss and appraise life in Turkey's major cities with their crowds, modern
products, bargains and expenses, clothing styles, tall buildings, political
demonstrations, etc. Travel experience helps them feel witness to the country's
developments.

In 1935 Turkey claimed literacy for less than 20% of her population, and the
percentage was lower yet for rural settlements like Susurluk which had large
non-Turkish minorities. For the most part, townspeople had to rely on news
transmitted orally by travelers. Not until 1937 did the first radio come into the
sub-province, being placed in the town's military club. A few years later the
second and third radios found places in coffeehouses, where they were more
accessible to the adult male public. By 1967, 4,239 radios were officially
registered in the sub-province, and with the Turkish manufacture of cheap
transistors in the late 1960s, the actual number probably exceeded 6,000 by
1969. 98% of the adult sample said they listen to the radio regularly, preferring
Turkish music, national and international news, and Western music (a new
preference) in that order.

In shops and coffeehouses, the radio provides constant background music,
but when the news comes on, the men perk up and listen in an animated fashion,
offering loud exclamations of approval or condemnation. When the news
finishes, several men present "expert" commentary to whomever listens.
Politics ranks as one of Turkey's national sports, and the radio has helped many
people in small communities feel involved.

An increase in literacy has accompanied greater use of the radio. Official
statistics report that 80% of the town's males and 52% of its females over six
years of age were literate in 1965. Only 4% of my adult sample admitted
illiteracy,[3] and 91% claimed to read a national newspaper regularly. When
asked what part of the paper interested them most, respondents named national
and international news (50%), picture novels (22%), and sports (16%), however almost all read the entire newspaper, which usually consists of only eight
pages. The vast majority prefer papers that either specialize in "sensational"
news (47%) or ones that are politically classified as "right-of-center" (41%).
The remaining 12% read "left-of-center" papers. *Hürriyet* and *Günaydin* rank
as the most popular sensational publications. Although neither adheres to a
consistent political ideology or view, they certainly do not avoid politics, one of
Turkey's most popular topics. *Tercüman,* the most read right-of-center paper,
supports the Justice party.

About seven or eight newspapers have been published in Susurluk over the past twenty years. Most of them were short-lived weekly or tri-weekly affairs that saw light around election times only. *24 Haziran,* a two-page daily with a circulation of about 450 copies, represents the most successful attempt. A local Manav, who actively supports the Republican Peoples Party, has been publishing the paper for the past ten years. In addition to local news items, he carries daily editorials by Republicans and a local leftist teacher, who comments on everything from economics to sex.

Another form of mass media — motion pictures — has become extremely popular since the 1950s. Susurluk boasts one indoor tri-season cinema and three outdoor summer ones. When in season, all four show films nightly to enthusiastic audiences. Turkish love stories, which follow a Romeo and Juliet-type scenario, and American Westerns draw the largest crowds. The cinemas also run European and Indian films. About one-half of the townsmen questioned prefer foreign films to Turkish ones, because they show worlds and life-styles quite different from their own.

The cinema's popularity decreases with age. Many teen-age boys boastfully claim to have seen every film the town has received in the past few years, while some senior citizens have never seen a motion picture and could care less. Women and girls attend less often than men and boys, despite the cinemas' practice of segregating seat areas for families and unescorted females.

The glamour of motion pictures has captured the imaginations of many young people, who adopt in modified fashion the hair styles, dress, and vocabulary of their favorite film stars. The personal lives, especially the scandals, of Turkish and foreign stars provide older women with subjects for excited conversation.

Conclusion

Susurluk's economic development has been accompanied by greater political, socio-cultural, and economic integration with the region and nation. Travel and mass media have promoted psychological integration as well. With the immigration of peasants to town and the emigration of townspeople to larger cities and Europe, the town community has multiplied its interlocality ties. Susurluk's experience conforms to Warren's (1972) "Great Change" model that applies to towns around the world. According to this model modernization entails change in the relative importance of horizontal relations — relationships among individuals and groups within a community — and vertical relations — relationships between local people and regional, national, and international persons or organizations. Through modernization, the vertical axis attains greater increments of political, economic, and socio-cultural power, and consequently subordinates the horizontal one. A contest develops between the forces of local interests, concerns, and traditions and extra-community interests, styles, and fads. The following chapters discuss the economic, social, political, educational, and religious ramifications of this contest in more detail.

Notes to Chapter III

The Town Today

[1] In Turkey's first true open multi-party election, the Democrat Party soundly defeated the Republican People's Party which had ruled Turkey since she became a republic in 1923.

[2] This editorial like others to follow is an abbreviated and edited translation made with the objective of eliminating excessive repetition without losing or altering the author's expressed point of view. Names and exact publication dates will be omitted in recognition of the authors' right to anonymity.

[3] This discrepancy between the census and my sample can be explained by two factors. The first is that illiteracy is greatest among those over 60 years of age and itinerant Gypsies, both of whom were underrepresented in the sample. The second is that the literacy rate most likely increased somewhat from 1965 to 1969-70, the time of the interviews.

CHAPTER IV

Economy and Society

Occupational Structure

Prior to the opening of the sugar refinery, most employment in Susurluk was in the form of family-run farms, crafts, and retail businesses. The functions of these families were diffuse. For instance, members of an agrarian family performed all the operations associated with raising crops and animals; they made and repaired most of their tools; with the help of kin and neighbors, they built their own home and animal shelters; they made their own clothing and consumed the fruits of their own labor. There was little economic differentiation and only a small market for wage labor. For large scale tasks, neighbors and friends helped each other on a reciprocal basis. Interpersonal relationships were multi-stranded: economic ties were interwoven with kinship, neighborhood, or friendship ties. Therefore, norms guiding social behavior were particularistic — people dealt with each other as unique individuals with known backgrounds and long-standing acquaintanceship. This is in sharp contrast to the impersonal, anonymous relationships more characteristic of economic life in large, industrial cities, where, for example, people occupying the roles of clerk and shopper interact primarily on a single-stranded basis: seller-buyer. Norms guiding this form of social behavior are called "universalistic," because they apply to anyone occupying a specific role, e.g., clerk, regardless of his unique background.

Among other things, economic development has meant the creation of many new jobs and the differentiation of economic activities from kinship. The employment activities of the bread-winner have become separated geographically, temporally, and socially from his family. The father is most commonly employed outside the home in either the factory, a small firm, or a government agency. His older sons do not work with him; they either attend school or work somewhere else. He and his family purchase most of their food and clothing in the market place. Both economic and familial functions have become more specific, the latter being largely confined to socialization of the young, companionship, and emotional gratification.

Economic development has also meant a broader, more diversified occupational structure for a formerly agrarian community. In an attempt to index intergenerational occupational mobility, the 182 member adult sample was asked to name their own as well as their fathers' work. While only 3.3% claimed agriculturally related occupations for themselves, 48.8% did so for their fathers. Rather than follow in their fathers' footsteps, these sons of the soil chose other endeavors, thereby enriching Susurluk's economic growth.

With the expansion of opportunities for wage labor in town and cash cropping in the surrounding villages, purchasing power and demand for goods and services have increased, giving a solid base of support to many of Susurluk's small industries, crafts, retail stores, and service businesses.

Today in addition to the sugar refinery Susurluk's main industries and crafts include: a private, locally owned seed oil processing plant and flour mill which together employ about 50 people, and approximately 70 workshops in which furniture makers, iron workers, coppersmiths, and tinsmiths produce their products. These are small private businesses employing from one to fifteen workers each. Among what I will term ''non-industrial'' crafts are about ten shoemaking shops, twenty tailor shops, five confectionaries, and six yogurt and cheese making shops. In the service and commercial categories there are twelve barber shops, three small hotels, nine restaurants, twenty-eight coffeehouses, two taverns, thirteen bakeries, thirty-eight small grocery stores, six fruit and vegetable stands, and six butcher shops. Several hundred small retailers come to Susurluk from other towns and villages on market day.

The Sugar Refinery and some of Its Consequences

The major reason for this development has been the sugar refinery. Construction on this facility began in May 1954 and operations commenced in September 1955. It was designed and built by the Arge Company of Germany and is one of the 12 sugar refineries owned and directed by Türkiye Şeker Fabrikaları A.Ş., a Turkish government enterprise. During 1968 the factory employed a 67-member, full-time managerial staff; 175 full-time service employees (repairmen, firemen, drivers, gardners, maintenance men, etc.); 200 full-time production workers; and 675 seasonal production personnel, who work during the sugar beet harvest and processing months of September, October, and November. All members of the managerial staff were born, educated and trained in settlements other than Susurluk, many coming from Turkey's larger cities. Practically all service employees and full-time production workers and about one-half of the temporary workers are from Susurluk Sub-province and reside in town; the remainder are villagers.

The sugar beet processing period generally lasts about 100 days a year. Because sugar beets can be planted in the same field only every four years, and because of fluctuating weather conditions, the factory's sugar production has varied greatly over the past ten years — from a low of 20,536 tons of processed sugar in 1963 to a high of 51,924 tons in 1967-68.

About 20 Susurluk villages are among the over 300 villages in the combined Balıkesir, Çanakkale, Bursa, and Izmir area which grow sugar beets for the factory. The total number of farmers involved each year often exceeds 10,000. For many of these peasants sugar beets represent their first cash crop.

In addition to supplying the farmers with a market, the factory through its agricultural technicians offers villagers technical assistance. Soil tests are made, proper fertilizers are recommended and often supplied, periodic inspections are made and advice given, equipment is loaned, and so on. Along with raising sugar beets, the factory is engaged in a program to promote improved animal breeding. It operates a model farm and works at introducing better breeds of cattle. Certain residues from the processed sugar beets, such as oil cake (küspe) and molasses (melas), are sold inexpensively to farmers for fodder.

The factory also represents a model community located only four kilometers outside of town. Modern apartments for the managerial staff and their families; modern restaurant facilities for management and labor; a medical clinic staffed part time by a doctor; a new cinema and auditorium where Western films in their original language are frequently shown and where balls and dances are occasionally held; an attractive guest house for visiting personnel and government officials; clean overnight quarters for workers; and tennis and basketball courts along with well-planned streets lined with cultivated trees, shrubs, and flowers constitute a scene very unlike the town or surrounding villages. In essence the sugar refinery community represents a new world to which many townsmen and villagers aspire.

The sugar refinery clearly introduces its workers to a new way of life and resocializes them for it. Bus and work schedules, time cards, a strict chain of command based on technical competence, special dress, cleanliness requirements, and even eating etiquette impose new demands and constraints on employees' behavior. In addition, production workers find that the pace and rhythm of their activity and a considerable proportion of their interpersonal relationships with other workers are technically determined. The modern factory system requires a set of ideal norms for social action which differ markedly from the ideal norms of traditional society. Management and production workers, especially, should deal with each other with primary reference given to duties to be performed, ability to perform them, and specific occupational roles in the productive system. Promotions should be made and new positions filled on the basis of merit, skill and ability. Management-employee relations should be specific, being delimited by terms of a contract. This ideal work complex stressing universal norms and specific functions is contrary to the area's traditional work culture with its particularistic norms, diffuse functions, and differing concepts of time, quality control, and worker evaluation.

While the legitimacy of these modern, ideal prescriptions for social action is never openly challenged, certain compromises or accommodations are ever present. Workers, especially those in the service categories, develop loyalties to their superiors, just as superiors become paternalistic toward them. Such workers make special pleas to help friends or relatives secure employment at the factory, or to gain some other favors. In turn superiors feel free to ask for work which goes beyond the terms of the contract. Thus in some cases recruitment and employment relations are highly particularistic, being based on personal considerations, even as they are in Japan after many years of industrialization.

The relatively high paying, secure and generally attractive jobs at the sugar refinery have been potent additions to Susurluk's socio-economic structure. They have caused a new ordering of social status and occupational prestige. Previously town society was characterized by two socio-economic classes: large landlords on the one hand, and small farmers, craftsmen, and merchants on the other. The factory has created a new middle class of wage earners. In addition, the upper level managerial staff of the factory now vies with local landlords for the top positions in the social strata. Not only are these professionals highly educated and comparably well off, they also control access to many factory jobs, which are highly attractive in a town with an expanding population and a chronic unemployment problem.

The increased buying power of the district's village and growing town populations has permitted enterprising merchants and craftsmen to prosper and join the expanding bourgeois class. Some of the town's new rich are sons of small craftsmen, who invested their family capital in retail businesses and manage them with the acumen of minor Rothschilds.

Employment at the refinery has also provided workers from different social and ethnic backgrounds a strong basis for common identity. Refinery workers have shown a strong interest in joining and participating in the activities of their national labor union. Locally they have formed several cooperatives for the purpose of constructing apartments and a commercial building which they have either sold for profit or rented for a steady income. Workers have also organized a retail food cooperative which offers lower food prices and profit sharing for its members. More recently, in June of 1970, a group of workers formed a local branch of the National Action Party (*Milli Hareket Partisi*), and they planned to nominate a slate of candidates from among their own number for the next local elections. As in Guatamala (Nash 1967) and in other developing countries, the factory provides the situational setting for the formation of friendships between men who otherwise might not know each other. Their lack of common background is offset by their working together and sharing a common interest in their job, union, and cooperatives.

The union also promotes identification with international labor. Local union representatives have attended labor union functions and educational programs in the United States and Israel in 1965 and 1972 respectively.

The sugar refinery has also affected savings and consumption patterns, the movement of goods and services through the market and labor mobility. Most workers make regular deposits into savings accounts either at the banks in town or the branch bank located on the factory grounds for their convenience. They purchase more manufactured goods, such as radios, appliances, watches, and clothing than small farm families in the town or area. The refinery attracts workers from various cities, towns and villages and gives them skills which allow them increased geographical mobility. They can opt either to work for a different company or request transfer to one of the other eleven sugar refineries around the country.

These general changes in the socio-economic structure are, of course, the result of many individual experiences of life's vicissitudes. The case of Aydin, a Turk in his forties who grew up with poverty in a Thracian village, provides a heartening illustration. During the Second World War he was taken by the Army and dispatched to Susurluk where he married a peasant girl. Having no land or means of support in Thrace, he remained in Susurluk with his wife's family after his military discharge. But this decision violated the traditional patrilocal residence rule and caused Aydin to fall into the derogatory category of *iç guveyi* (a groom who lives with his in-laws) and become the object of mockery by fellow townsmen. Such social humiliations complemented his economic plight. Aydin was a humble person, lacking any skill and possessing only the rudiments of literacy. For a number of years he earned a few cents a day by shaving customers on the main street of town. His outdoor "shop" consisted of nothing more than a stool placed on the edge of the cobble-stoned way, two small basins, a towel, and a razor. From there he hawked his services like a common peddler. Later he began earning a few pennies more by waiting on tables in a busy coffeehouse. Eventually, he abandoned his barbering career and waited on tables full time. Although this too was low prestige work, he derived some satisfaction from addressing his customers with deference, serving their orders promptly, and receiving an occasional compliment. Aydin craved his townsmen's respect and hoped to earn it by his diligent service. Waiting, he liked to think, even in a coffeehouse was a recognized skill, a true occupation. When the sugar refinery came, everyone's hopes were aroused, and Aydin was among those whose job applications were accepted. He was hired as a waiter in the refinery's "plush" guest house where he now serves the top echelon of the refinery and visiting dignitaries. Neatly dressed in pressed slacks, white shirt, and tie, he attends to the guests with poise and pride. At home his steady cash income has made him the chief breadwinner and household head. He now supports his elderly in-laws and has exonerated himself from the status of *iç guveyi*. In town Aydin leisurely strolls the main street where he once lathered faces and enjoys relaxing in the coffeehouse with his friends. His dress and demeanor are dignified, appropriate for a respected townsman.

Changing Relations among Craftsmen

Mechanization, modern social and labor legislation, and developing attitudes more commonly associated with the modern, competitive market place are undermining the traditional apprentice-journeyman-master system with its para-kinship relations and religious value system. According to published accounts (Ozer 1963; Bayatlı 1942) and to descriptions supplied by local craftsmen and a *müezzin* (one who calls Muslims to prayer), the nature of this traditional system in Susurluk and the surrounding areas was as follows. The father of a twelve to thirteen year old boy asks a master craftsman to teach his son a trade. If the master has room in his shop for a new apprentice, he may agree to look the boy over; this involves an estimation of the boy's physical ability and moral character. In addition to observing the boy's success at small tasks, the master will assess his honesty. The master might leave a small coin on the floor, to learn whether or not the apprentice will pocket it or turn it in when he sweeps up the shop. The master will be attentive to the boy's friends, believing that good companions contribute to the making of a good craftsman. If the master finds the boy able, honest, and trustworthy, he will keep him on as an apprentice, otherwise he will let him go. During the next three to five years the master will act as the apprentice's vocational and spiritual teacher, giving instruction in the skills and religiously based social etiquette of the trade. The boy will learn that his and other crafts have patron saints (*pir,* sing.) who continue to demand the high standards of quality and discipline that they established in their trades centuries ago. Some of the patron saints recognized in Susurluk are as follows: *Davud* (David) for the metal craft; *Idris Nebi* (sometimes equated with Enoch, eldest son of Cain) for tailoring; *Selvani Farisi* for barbering; *Nuh* (Noah) for carpentry; *Ibrahim* (Abraham) for masonry; *Muaviya* (Muawiyah, Arab naval leader, who commanded an expedition to Cyprus in 649 and became the fifth Caliph in 661) for seafaring; and *Adem* (Adam) for farming. The apprentice will learn to call on Allah and his patron saint to help him with his work. For example, when beginning to cut a bolt of cloth, a tailor says: "In the name of Allah and with the hand of Idris Nebi, I take up these scissors." Work begun in this manner is bound to be blessed and therefore successful.

Coppersmith

Locally crafted copperware

Stove-maker

Enver, the plane-maker (right), and apprentice

The first year mostly comprises watching and learning. The apprentice contributes little to the production of the shop and therefore receives no wage until the second year. His relationship with the master is one of respect and obedience. The master is considered part teacher, part father. He must treat his apprentice with all the kindness and consideration that he would his own son. It is said that a rose grows on the spot where a master strikes an apprentice. The punishment is auspicious; rather than resent it, the apprentice should thank the master for taking notice of his need for discipline.

When the apprentice has successfully completed his training, his master holds a graduation banquet (*ziyafet*) to which he invites the other masters and journeymen of the trade, several local dignitaries, the boy's father, and local religious leaders. After all have eaten, the master rises and announces that the boy has worked by his side for so many years, during which time he has acquired all the necessary skills of their craft and has demonstrated the good moral character necessary to become a qualified journeyman. The master then proclaims the *destur* — permission for the new journeyman to go off on his own and earn an independent living by his craft — and presents him with a set of trade tools. The new journeyman kisses the master's hand, thanks him for teaching a saintly trade with which the journeyman can now earn his daily bread, and asks Allah to accept him. The other masters and journeymen acknowledge this promotion and signify their acceptance of the new journeyman by girding a sash (*peştemal*) around his waist, similar to the way Turkish and Persian Islamic Brotherhoods initiated their members (*cf.* Trimingham 1971:184-85). The occasion is further solemnized by readings from the *Quran*.

The apprentice's gratitude and respect for the master are eternal. Years later, when he is married and has a family, the apprentice will take his children to the master on holydays so that they might show their respect by kissing the hand of the man who gave their father his livelihood.

According to elderly masters, the graduation banquet and *destur* ceremony were common until about "ten years after World War II," or until the middle 1950s when Susurluk began experiencing major economic development. Today they are rare occasions and the traditional master-apprentice relationship is exceptional.

These changes can be attributed largely to three sets of causes. First, new legislation establishing a minimum daily wage for eight hours work with time and a half thereafter now applies to workers sixteen years of age and over. For purposes of this law, Turkey is divided into six districts according to a cost of living index, and the 1969 minimum daily wage varied from a high of TL 19.50 (about $1.95) in Istanbul to a low of TL 15.50 in the poor Eastern provinces. Susurluk was in the third highest district with a minimum daily wage of TL 17 for workers sixteen years of age and over and TL 15 for younger workers.

Unfortunately, this law, applying to all businesses employing four or more people, has proven less beneficial to labor than expected. In order to avoid falling under the law, many small businesses with four or five workers have reduced their employees to three, and those with only three refuse to expand by hiring more. Many master craftsmen now refuse to take on new apprentices, who traditionally receive much less than the minimum wage while learning the trade.

New legislation also requires employers to contribute an amount equal to 12% of their employees' wages to workers social insurance premiums. To avoid this expense many employers fail to register all of their workers or else register them at a wage lower than actual.

A second cause is mechanization — competition from the machine. Many time-consuming hand phases of manufacturing are no longer considered efficient or profitable. New power machinery can perform many operations more quickly and profitably, requiring fewer workers. As the cost of labor rises, the use of machinery becomes increasingly more attractive.

A third cause is the growing acceptance of an economic ideology stressing the maximization of profit and deemphasizing human relationships. In an increasingly mechanized and competitive market, employers pay more attention to costs of production and less to the skill and character development of young workers. Many craftsmen and small industrialists no longer believe it their obligation to train apprentices according to the religiously based ethical standards of their saintly craft. Employer-employee relations are now more commonly delimited by contract and regulated by law. These formal mechanisms of integration have superceded norms of interaction based on kinship and religion. The master-employer is no longer part father, part teacher.

This decrease in para-kinship relations between master and apprentice is paralleled by a decrease in real kinship ties also. In a non-random sample of 29 master craftsmen (plane-maker, carpenters, tailors, shoemakers, etc.) nine learned their trades from their fathers, eight learned from other relatives, ten learned from non-relatives, and two learned in trade schools. However, none of these craftsmen were teaching or had taught their trades to their own sons, and only a few were even distantly related to their current apprentices. Practically all said they wanted their sons to go on to "something better" in life.

The desire to maximize income is also predominant among workers. When members of the adult sample were asked to choose the one criterion from five offered which they believed most important when considering a job or occupation, the majority (65.8%) named "pay," followed by "prestige of the work" (16%), "interest of the work" (12.7%), "ease" (2.8%), and "power of the position'' (2.8%). Most of those who said "interest" were in the higher educational categories. When the married members of the adult sample were asked what they wanted most to accomplish in the forthcoming years, 80% said they either wanted to earn more income or finance something that required more savings than they currently possessed, e.g., educate children, prepare for a family wedding, buy a home, buy a car, etc.

To illustrate the impact of these three sets of changes with an actual example, let us briefly examine Susurluk's furniture-making craft. In the past, a master trained a young boy to the point where he could take an unseasoned log and singlehandedly convert it into several pieces of fine furniture. Today the emphasis is on "mass produced" furniture of simple design. For example, a number of workshops specialize in very simple wooden chairs and tables which are in great demand by coffeehouses and outdoor cinemas. Due to intense competition, the profit margin is very small — 10% to 12%. With new power tools, the master can cut all the parts for about 50 chairs from purchased boards in one day. In another couple of days he can complete all the more complex assembly steps. The rest of the work — simple assembly, sanding and staining — is left to boys under 15 years of age who earn about TL 25 to TL 50 a month. Employers let these boys go when they turn 16 rather than pay them the TL 17 a day required by the minimum wage law.

There is no incentive on the part of the masters to train apprentices as they did formerly. With the new machinery all complex work can be done easily by one person after only several months of practice. What is needed is cheap labor to do the simple finishing tasks. In addition, with competition as intense as it is, training another journeyman amounts to preparing yet another potential competitor.

Certain other trades like shoemaking and tailoring must now compete with factory-made products. Rather than invest a great deal of money in wages and time in training apprentices, many masters in these trades are gradually converting their workshops into retail outlets for factory-made goods. Although they still may make goods on demand, they prefer the quick profit and turnover of simple retailing. Thus, as in many industrializing countries, the competition of manufactured goods makes large segments of traditional artisan activity obsolete and contributes to unemployment.

The training of apprentices is progressively being differentiated out of kinship, religion, and the craft industries and taken over by a newly created, specialized agency — the vocational school, where the training is under the supervision of a new specialist — the full-time vocational teacher.

Trade Unions and Employers Associations

Trade unions and employers associations are formal institutions that function to integrate modernizing socio-economic systems by providing norms for employee-employer interaction and means for handling their disagreements, conflicts, and disputes on a legal-contractual basis.

The development of trade unionism in Turkey is relatively recent. Kemal Ataturk, modern Turkey's founder and first president, opposed the formation of all class-based organizations, believing they would have a divisive effect on the new country. The legal expression of his reasoning was the Associations Act of 1938, which prohibited the creation of trade unions and political parties, other than Ataturk's own Republican People's Party. The situation remained the same until the end of World War II when Turkey's leadership, desirous of imitating the victorious Western Democracies, permitted the formation of political parties in 1946 and labor unions in 1947. However, they withheld the right to strike. Despite this new legislation, unionism especially in the private sector remained undeveloped, partly because employers with patriarchal mentalities and paternal attitudes maintained an anti-union bias (Tuna 1963), and partly because Turkey's "consensus-oriented culture" defines conflict between employer and employee as something bad. "The parties involved believe that their future relationships will deteriorate considerably once they have engaged in defending their interests or views in an aggressive way on a face to face basis" (Dereli 1968:51). With respect to authority, the employer-employee relationship was and continues to be very similar to that between father and son. Norman Bradburn, an American social psychologist, who studied this relationship among Turkish businessmen, says his subjects "almost universally . . . described their fathers as stern, forbidding, remote, domineering, and autocratic. Few of them had ever argued with their fathers, and those who had had done so at the price of an open break. Several men reported that after having argued with their fathers they had not spoken to them for ten years" (1963:464).

To make appeals to the employer-patriarch, Turkish workers, like subordinate kin, have generally worked through a third party, who has close ties with the employer and does not suffer from a great disparity in status. For example, sons often work through an understanding uncle, and employees frequently elected a fellow worker, related to the employer, as their union representative. Such "yellow unions," as the Turks term them, can be seen structurally as an intermediate step in the evolution of work relations based on kinship to work relations based on formal contract.

With greater industrialization and increased competition in the private sector of the economy during the 1950s both labor and management developed a deepened sense of separate class identity and mutual conflict of interests. In July of 1963 the Turkish legislature gave labor the right to strike, and in anticipation of this development, the National Turkish Employers' Confederation organized in 1962 to promote the interests of its members vis-a-vis national labor organizations. Employers' associations, on the local level, had been forming since 1947.

During the time of my field work there were two active unions in Susurluk: the Sugar Industry Union and the Municipal Employees Union. The latter had won its first collective bargaining agreement in 1964, despite resistance from the Republican mayor, and it continued to bargain collectively with the town government thereafter. In 1969, its national affiliate won a long-standing battle for employees' medical benefits on an appeal to the Turkish Council of State.

In addition to these two effective unions, there was a small dormant drivers union and sporadic talk about the formation of a union for agricultural workers.

In the craft industries one local union sprouted, blossomed, withered, and died. Organized in May of 1965, the wood-workers union had gained about 65 members, employed in fifteen different shops, before it attempted to bargain collectively in July of 1965. When fourteen of the fifteen employers failed to attend the first negotiating session, the union enlisted the provincial labor director as mediator for the second session. The employers again failed to participate, so the union called a strike in nine shops involving 45 workers. In an open letter appearing in the town newspaper on September 12, 1965, the union president charged that: 1) employers are paying less than the legal minimum wage and are not contributing their share to workers social insurance premiums, 2) employers have fired three union representatives and are coercing workers to avoid the union, and 3) employers have not acted in good faith with the president of the Izmir Wood-Workers Union, who is acting as legal negotiator for the local. The president ended his letter with a new invitation to employers to meet with union representatives and bargain in good faith.

The employers responded to the union threat by organizing themselves into the Wood Industry Craftsmen Association. Among its seventeen members, eleven were known to be active in the "left-of-center" Republican People's Party and three in the conservative-moderate Justice Party. Apparently economic interest took precedence over political ideology. After 32 days the union ended the strike, and with the signatures of eleven employers to the collective bargaining contract, the workers felt they had a victory. For the first time in Susurluk's history, local labor had organized, openly opposed patriarchal owners, struck, and won. However, euphoria was short-lived. By a combination of lock-outs, blackballs, and coercion, the employers, who themselves are masters of their trades, were able to put union craftsmen out of work and keep younger workers from joining the union. On October 7, 1967 the union's obituary appeared in the local newspaper. In the crafts industries, organized craftsmen-employers, greater mechanization, and the constant threat of unemployment place labor's organizational efforts at a serious disadvantage.

Many craftsmen would rather be employed at low wages than have no work at all.

Economic Cooperatives and Associations

In his 1949 study of the Turkish city of Gaziantep, Robinson (1949 a) noted little evidence of community cooperation in the form of privately organized social and economic organizations, and he attributed this condition, in part, to restrictive government regulations and red-tape. The organization of a private society required submitting a constitution to the central government and notifying the police of all meetings, which they are empowered to attend. During the 1950s, the newly elected Democrat government eased restrictions and encouraged the formation of economic cooperatives and associations by providing technical extension workers and low-interest loans for many cooperative projects. This resulted in a flourishing number of such organizations, but observers such as Dereli (1968:50-51) and Mansur (1972:48) have commented on their ephemeral and relatively ineffective nature, and attributed this to Turkish individualism and mutual suspicion — qualities common to many peoples with an historic background of subsistence agriculture.

On the basis of an extensive review of the world literature, the American anthropologist Foster (1973:34) has concluded that "peasant life is characterized by . . . a bitter quality of mutual suspicion and distrust, which makes it extremely difficult for people to cooperate for the common good." These traits are also prevalent among Turkish townspeople and city dwellers, many of whom are only one or two generations removed from the village, where about 70% of the Turkish population still resides.

During the time of my field work there were about a dozen economic cooperatives and associations in town: the small business loan cooperative, which is sponsored by the Peoples Bank and controlled locally by Republican Party members to the disadvantage of non-members; the oil-bearing seed cooperative, organized with the aid of agricultural extension workers to help small farmers deal collectively with factory owners; drivers gas station cooperative; several sugar refinery workers cooperatives; animal breeders association; apple growers association; musicians association; metal craftsmen association; drivers association; wagoners association; and the wood industry craftsmen association.

Except for the cooperatives of the sugar refinery workers, none of these is especially noted for its successes. Probably the one with the most eventful beginning and lackluster continuity is the Akin Transportation Association, largely created through the efforts of Seljuk Bey, an ambitious man of about 35 years in 1970, who can be described as a local innovator — one who is actively interested in new ideas and methods and who possesses an independence of thought and initiative. Seljuk credits his military experience as the stimulus for much of his innovative thinking. During that time he worked closely with the U.S. Army and American construction firms in Turkey. American work discipline, punctuality, and work coordination especially impressed him. "By contrast," he observed, "in Turkey we don't know how to keep appointments, how to plan time. We don't use time, we pass it (*vakit geçirmek*). We don't understand what is essential to improvement. We want to imitate the best externally, without changing internally." His solution was that every Turkish male be required to work in a modern foreign country for two years, in lieu of military service, to learn work discipline and work culture. He discussed his organizational efforts with the Akin Transportation Association to illustrate local work deficiencies.

The association's history goes back to 1962 when the first five minibuses (*dolmuş*) began to transport people from Susurluk to either Bandirma or Balıkesir and back. Formerly, large buses provided the only public transportation. They kept no firm schedule, but waited in the garage area until at least 30 to 35 passengers boarded. By contrast, the faster minibuses, would leave as soon as they had nine or ten passengers. This competitive advantage helped the minibuses cut deeply into the business of the local bus company, which resorted to a price war. In response, Seljuk helped the independent minibus owners organize to meet their mutual threat. They set competitive prices and established a rotation system so as to provide regular service without competing against one another. They chose the name "*Akin*" ("attack") to symbolize their assault on the bus company. In time, their cheap, faster service proved too much, and the bus company surrendered most of its Susurluk-Balıkesir, Susurluk-Bandirma runs.

Attracted by the success of these independent operators, other townsmen purchased minibuses on credit and joined the Akin Association, so that by 1970 it had 55 minibuses making the inter-city runs. However, to Seljuk's disappointment, the association has improved its organization very little since the threat of the bus company subsided. He describes the present situation as follows:

> The drivers live very narrow lives. They don't think about taking an annual vacation, attending an occasional theater production, going on a relaxing trip with their families, etc. They live for and worry about one thing: making their daily round trip which nets them between TL 500 — TL 600 a month. They rise every morning at about 4:30 and run down to the garage to get their names on the top of the day's rotation list. That way there is the possibility of making two round trips in one day. As the first minibus seldom has enough customers to leave before 6:30 a.m., the drivers sit

around the tea houses, smoking and drinking, while they wait their turn. Once it comes, they take a load of passengers to either Balıkesir or Bandirma and again wait all afternoon for their return trip. At the end of the day they drink some cheap wine in the bus station area and retire to bed early so that they can be up by 4:30 the next morning. This is not living!

I proposed that we reorganize on the basis of a system that has been tried and proven in other towns like ours. For example, all members would be allotted thirty round trips a month. This is about how many they now make. A schedule would be drawn up in advance, assigning members to morning or afternoon shifts. That way they all could sleep until at least 6:00 a.m. and there would be no need to hang around the garage all day and waste time. Tickets would be sold to customers in the garage and the money held by the Association's treasurer. Fares from passengers picked up along the road would be turned in to the treasurer also. At the end of the month, all money would be divided among the members on the basis of trips made. As the schedule would permit all to make an equal number of trips, each would receive his just due.

Unfortunately, the members have voted against this plan. They fear that fares picked up on the road won't be pooled. As several have said to me, 'I would pocket them. Why wouldn't the rest?'

Although the drivers were able to organize and effectively meet a mutual threat in 1962, distrust and lack of competition have prevented their association from achieving further improvement. The drivers are content to complain about their present situation without further attempts at joint cooperation.

Cost of Living and the Desire to Emigrate

People generally considered Susurluk an inexpensive place by comparison to larger cities. They often comment that this made it attractive to retiring government officials and army officers, such as the current mayor, who had served assignments here in the past and return upon retirement to live out their last years quietly and inexpensively. During the 1960s, however, townspeople began complaining that Susurluk, too, has been caught up in the spiraling cost of living. In June of 1969, the vice-president of the town's Cultural Association published an average expense budget for a local family of four (husband, wife, and two school-age children) computed on the basis of August 1968 prices. He cautioned that the total monthly expense figure of TL 835 was lower than actual, because he omitted expenditures for luxury items and major appliances and because the August food prices are among the lowest of the year. Expense categories were divided into the following proportions: food (46.5%); rent, heat, light (22%); clothing (13%); cigarettes (4%); recreation (3.5%); school (2%); other (9%).

The 46.5% food rate is rather high, especially for an "inexpensive" town in a developing country. According to United Nations statistics, the 1962 food rates for countries ranged from 51% and 50% for Ghana and Ceylon to 22% and 21% for Canada and the United States, respectively. As consumption levels and standards of living rise, the food rate generally declines. In Susurluk consumption desires have risen rapidly in the last decade with more and more families wanting refrigerators, kitchen appliances, cars, etc., but food rates have remained high, and probably are rising. The compiler of the family budget warned that the following percentage price increases have occurred in Susurluk from 1967 to 1969: food 40%, rent 20% — 30%, and shoes 10% — 15%.[1] This leaves many townspeople with even smaller proportions of income to expend on newly developed consumption wants. Those without their own gardens, who live on small, fixed incomes are affected most adversely.

The self-estimated monthly incomes of married males in my adult sample ranged from a low TL 300 for a shepherd, a coffeehouse waiter, and a Gypsy basket weaver to a high of TL 3000 for two successful retail businessmen. Sixty-four percent of all monthly incomes fell within the TL 500 to TL 950 range, and fifty-four percent of the sample fell below TL 850, while forty-six percent were above. The average monthly earnings for various occupational groups were as follows: craftsmen owning their own shops TL 1000   TL 1500; other craftsmen TL 500 — TL 900; sugar refinery workers TL 700 — TL 1000; small grocers TL 700 — TL 900; primary school teachers TL 600 — TL 900; town officials TL 550 — TL 750; postal workers TL 550 — TL 1000; wagoners TL 400 — TL 500. Many men have to supplement their main incomes by working at other jobs. For instance, a town accountant does bookkeeping for several local businesses, and two sugar refinery workers operate their vintage family cars as taxis at night and on weekends.

The townsmen's most frequently aired complaint is Susurluk's and Turkey's limited economic opportunities. A typical example is a primary school teacher who showed me his monthly income statement of TL 866 net and asked why a teacher with his twenty years experience cannot earn enough to buy a house and enjoy a decent life with his family. "I would give anything to go to America or Germany to work even as a garbage collector, for they earn enough to live. In Turkey, my education means nothing." Even a young self-declared radical-socialist from a wealthy family, who made it a point of loudly condemning "capitalistic America" whenever he saw me in a group, approached me privately and pleaded for help to get to the United States so he could find a future.

This extreme dissatisfaction with income and consumption opportunities coupled with a compelling urge to emigrate has become generalized in the last decade, when Turkey, as an associate member of the Common Market, began sending large numbers of workers to Germany and other West European countries. The Turkish Labor Minister reported that from 1961 to August 1, 1972 his ministry has placed about 600,000 Turkish workers, including 104, 362 women, in jobs in advanced foreign countries, and one million more Turks were on the official waiting list (*Tercüman* 3 Aug. 1972). At the time of my field work there were an estimated 150 townspeople and another 200 Susurluk villagers working in West Europe. Approximately 25 escorted and unescorted townswomen were among them. The economic motive serves as a strong force to drive men to distant lands and free women from their traditional seclusion.

When these workers return to Susurluk on vacation, driving their newly purchased European cars, loaded with caches of radios, tape and cassette recorders, fountain pens, clothing, watches, even small televisions, they become the envy of the town. Their enticingly detailed narrations of social and economic life in Europe serve to heighten local dissatisfaction among townspeople who increasingly want to become active participants in a modern, consumer-orientated society.

By 1970, only seven men had terminated their employment in Europe and returned to Susurluk. None of them has made any innovative impact on the town. The two men I knew well, confessed that leaving Europe for Turkey was the biggest mistake they ever made. One returnee spends practically all of his free moments half-tearfully reminiscing about his happy days working in Cologne's Ford Plant. His advice to the town's young men is to get to Europe and never return.

Individual Examples of Economic Strategies

The following brief accounts illustrate several economic strategies commonly employed by townsmen attempting to achieve their hopes of economic security for themselves and their families.

Adan, the Grocer

Thirty-five year old Adan is from an established Manav family. He resides with his wife, two children, and mother, and operates a small grocery store that also carries a line of kitchenware (glasses, pots, and pans), but lacks a refrigerator. He works alone, except for the occasional help of his school-age son, and nets about TL 800 in a good month. Adan carries monthly credit accounts for a few government employees and annual accounts for villagers, who pay at harvest time. These villagers also supply him with agricultural products, like eggs, which he resells. He claims there is no difference between cash and credit prices. He offers credit to reliable, known customers to maintain their continuous patronage.

Adan also cultivates 50 *dönüm*s (1 *dönüm* = 1000 square meters or about ¼ acre) of inherited land. In 1969 he planted 28 *dönüm*s of sugar beets and 19 *dönüm*s of sunflowers; the remainder was vineyard. Both sugar beets and sunflowers bring in about TL 500 a *dönüm*. Women, whom he hires for TL 8 a day (versus TL 12 a day for men) do most of the field work. He estimates that his gross annual income from agriculture is TL 33,000 with expenses of TL 10,000.

His future goal is the construction of a new three-story building, with a grocery for himself on the first level, an apartment for his family on the second, and another apartment to rent on the third. He already owns his present home and store, plus two other buildings in town. When I asked if he wanted to expand his store, he answered no. He prefers it to remain a small one-man operation, that requires a minimum of management and bookkeeping and permits him to converse leisurely with friends and wait on an occasional customer.

Adan's assets comprise what many townsmen regard as the three wisest investments: town real estate, agricultural land, and retail business. Apartment houses are especially attractive because they provide the owner with rent-free living, a continuous rental income, and an increasingly valuable capital asset. Rents and real estate values have been rising much faster than the two to three per cent annual interest offered on savings accounts. Farm land has provided solid returns since 1955 because of new cash crops and the special tax advantages of agricultural income. And retail businesses, whether they be groceries, dry goods, hardware, or appliance stores, are advantageous because they can easily be managed by one family, without the "headaches" of social insurance premiums, legal minimum wages, and the management of hired help. There is also an informal tax advantage: one can hide a good part of his income.

Enver, the Plane-maker

Enver, a master plane-maker and Circassian, is married to a Georgian woman, who, like himself, was born in a nearby village. He learned the trade from his own father, and boasts that between the two of them, they have been crafting planes for 60 years. Although he makes a variety of carpentry tools: small hammers, scrapers, and a dozen different planes, his basic products are three standard types of plane, two of which sell for TL 24 and one for TL 18. His per unit cost runs slightly more than one-half the sales price, and to break even he must sell about 300 planes a month. He uses several machines in the productive process: two wood cutters; one lathe, which cost TL 10,000 three years ago;

and a sanding-wheel to sharpen blades. He also employs one apprentice, who often works from 6:00 a.m. to 10:00 p.m.

Enver sells his products to three wholesalers in Istanbul, and his production is solely dependent on what they are willing to buy. He has had difficulty finding other outlets. Although there are possible outlets in Ankara and Izmir, they would order so little, he feels it is not worth his while to do business with them. His Istanbul wholesalers distribute all over Turkey.

When asked about business prospects and his future plans, he complained about five sets of obstacles to the increased success of his business. The first was competition from German imports, which sell better at three times his price because of their guaranteed parts of high quality metal. Such metal is not available to him. Secondly, his sale outlets were few and limiting. Thirdly, he complained about the minimum wage and social insurance requirements, which price labor out of his market. "Formerly apprentices received very little, while learning the trade. Now they want a set salary of TL 150 a month to start. We can't give it. So the trades are becoming less attractive to young people and their parents. Other jobs are easier and more secure. A man who earns TL 700-800 a month at the sugar refinery for an eight hour day with an annual twenty day paid vacation couldn't earn TL 550 a month here even if he worked ten hours a day." Fourthly, he complained about the lack of modern machinery in Turkey. "If good, modern machines were available to me, I could take any unskilled person, show him how to operate the machinery in a short period of time, and then pay on a piece-work basis." And lastly, he saw his Susurluk location as a disadvantage. "I'm here, and my raw materials and markets are in Istanbul. I must spend TL 20,000 a year on transportation expenses. And because I must compete with manufacturers in Istanbul, I can't add this expense to my sales price."

Like many others, Enver does not see a bright future in Susurluk. At 45, he considers himself too old to be accepted for a European job. He sometimes dreams about relocating in Istanbul.

Fahri, the Restaurateur

Fahri immigrated to Turkey from Bulgaria with his family when he was only one. His father died shortly after their arrival, so he was raised by his mother under trying economic circumstances. After attending the local school and performing his military service, he returned to Susurluk and got a job in the new sugar refinery restaurant as a waiter. Although it was a good, secure job, he hoped for something better — a business of his own. Consequently, he seized upon the opportunity of going to Germany in the early 1960s, where he worked at the Ford Plant in Cologne for three years. Originally he planned to work and save every *Pfennig* until he had the equivalent of TL 20,000 — an amount he believed would establish him forever in Turkey. However, at the end of three years he had accumulated TL 60,000, which he invested in a German-made minibus. He returned to Susurluk and operated his minibus between Susurluk, Balıkesir, and Bandirma as an independent. Disagreements with members of the local transportation association resulted, and Fahri found this work unsatisfactory and unprofitable. He sold his minibus for TL 57,000 and decided to reinvest his capital in a local restaurant, relying on his earlier waiting experience at the refinery's dining hall. After a year of unemployment he finally came to terms with the owner of an established restaurant and purchased the business for TL 30,000, two-thirds of which went for equipment and furnishings and one-third for good-will *(hava parasi)* — established patronage and convenient central location. Fahri hired a cook, a full-time assistant, and two waiters. Business went well at first, but then it began to decline. In an attempt to make the restaurant more attractive, he spent the last of his savings on a major renovation. But business only declined further. Not only had the former owner opened a new restaurant a little farther up the street, but two new open-air restaurants in the beautiful town park began attracting much of the summer trade. Moreover, many townsmen — young and old alike — had adopted the custom of frequenting the restaurants at the bus station, where they sit and observe the urban styles of men and women, especially young ladies, traveling between Izmir and Istanbul. Many young men consider this the best recreation the town has to offer.

Fahri was forced to let all his help go, with the exception of one waiter. He took over cooking duties himself, but the resulting diminishment of his menu has made business even worse.

All his dreams of establishing himself in Susurluk are shattered. "We are immigrants, without a known family or heritage. I hoped my savings could help me create a secure and stable place for me and my family. It failed." At 37, his only hope is to return to Germany. "This time it will be for good." But the Labor Ministry's waiting list is very long.

Notes to Chapter IV

Economy and Society

[1] On the basis of "realistic" projections of Turkey's population growth and production and consumption of wheat — the country's most important food staple — Tuncer (1968) predicts that the per capita consumption of wheat may well decrease from 1967 to 2000, and wheat prices will go up substantially. Turkey will have to decide whether to cut consumption drastically or face a very large import bill.

CHAPTER V

Kinship and the Family

The Importance of Kinship and the Family

Many social scientists have confirmed the relevance of the family and other kinship units to the study of social change. But probably Marion Levy makes the most emphatic assertion for the family's central importance in his work, *Modernization and the Structure of Societies* (1966:379). He argues that the

> analysis of the family structures first in the study of any society, in addition to producing information easily marshalled in terms of the life cycle of the individual, is more likely to produce more relevant information about different areas and aspects of social structure than examination of any other single subsystem of any society. In other words, the probability is great that more can be learned more quickly about any new and strange form of society by a sophisticated analysis of its family structures than by the analysis of any of its other forms of organization.

He bases his assumptions on a number of empirical facts:

1) Families and/or other kinship units exist as subsystems in all known societies.

2) Partly for biological and psychological reasons, and partly for socio-cultural reasons, strong solidary relationships often exist between and among kin; these relationships have important economic, political, and social implications.

3) Psychology has demonstrated the important influences that kin, especially familial, relationships have on personality formation.

4) Generally the family and/or kin units provide early socialization for a society's members. Within a kinship context, individuals learn basic roles and basic role differentiation.

5) Most individuals in all known societies are members of one or more familial and/or kinship units throughout their entire lives. This membership always has some degree of influence on their participation in other social groups and networks.

In recent decades numerous studies of social change have reported instances where the range of important kinship ties has been greatly reduced in particular societies. Examples where lineages, clans, or sibs have lost all practical sociological, economic, or political significance. But only rarely has the range of important kinship ties been reduced beyond the nuclear family.

The Analytic Approach

Ideal tools for the study of kinship and familial change would be the concepts, postulates, and operating rules of an accepted body of social theory. Unfortunately, such a theory does not exist, and in the specific area of the family, social theorizing has been badly neglected. At present probably the most prevalent hypothesis of familial and kinship change is that industrialization and urbanization undermine large kinship systems, reducing them to some form of the conjugal system found in Western countries. This crude hypothesis has several theoretical gaps and factual discrepancies:

1) It is not exactly clear how industrialization or urbanization affect kinship. Certain elements in the traditional kinship system may be affected more than others. Some traditional elements may prove functional in the changed setting and be maintained, even stressed.

2) Change is not a mere function of either industrialization or urbanization. Legal, ideological, and value changes can affect kinship independently of either industrialization or urbanization.

3) Even though the kinship systems of various societies may be transforming into a type of Western conjugal system, they may have begun from different starting points and may be taking different paths of development.

4) While industrial systems may be ranked as more or less advanced with relative objectivity, kinship systems may not. The nuclear family represents the predominant kin group in many technologically primitive societies. Conversely, some of the most successful industrial and commercial families in the modern Western countries (for example, the Rothschilds, Rockefellers, and Fords) have attained and maintain their positions through the profitable use of wide range kinship ties.

On a theoretical level, the hypothesis is based on two interrelated assumptions: the "theory of structural constraints" and the "fit" between the conjugal family and the modern industrial system. The first involves the idea that the modern industrial system imposes certain organizational and institutional demands and changes on the economy as well as on the entire social system. According to this theory, social systems are composed of functionally interdependent components, of which the family or kin system is one. As these components evolve in the direction of improved functional fit with the modern industrial system, their structures usually change. In the case of the kinship system, it is assumed that evolvement will eventuate in the conjugal system, as this provides optimum fit. The traditional extended family system with its standards of ascription, particularism, and diffuseness is theoretically ill-suited for the efficient functioning of a modern industrial system in which hiring and promotion are based on merit and one's relationship to his job is functionally specific. It is also maintained that the traditional extended family system inhibits the mobility necessary in a modern industrial system.

This theory conforms to the traditional structural-functional approaches in anthropology which give principal attention to the study of the formal structures of a society's institutions and the ways in which these institutions function as component parts of a single integrated system to contribute to the maintenance of social equilibrium. The recurring complaint about this type of approach to the study of change is that it lacks dynamism: that it is basically a static model of the social system and cannot deal with change in a satisfactory manner. It is also criticized because it fails to account for a spreading Western ideology favoring the conjugal system. In many cases, this ideology is independent of industrialization.

This study employs an orientation which adds useful dynamism to the structural-functional approach. It examines kinship change with a focus on people's goals, the way goals change through time, and the ways individuals interact with kin to attain goals. The "conjugal family" concept employed here and used by many social scientists is an ideal construct whose component elements may not exist in any known society, but which is most closely approximated in societies of the modern, industrial West. Some of the basic elements of the ideal conjugal family construct are as follows:

1) People are relatively free to choose their mates, and love plays an important role in determining choice. Kin have no strong rights, authority, or financial interests in the matter.

2) After biological and legal considerations, the age of marriage is governed primarily by the ability of the couple to be financially independent. This is determined in part by the economic system and the occupational structure of the society.

3) The newly married couple enjoys freedom of mobility; after marriage, they determine the location of their residence.

4) The network of kinship relations is of relatively narrow range and not loaded with reciprocal rights, duties, and obligations. There is a comparatively small degree of participation by other relatives in the everyday affairs of the conjugal family.

5) There is a tendency toward equality between spouses with respect to responsibility and authority in the family. Before the law and in the labor market men and women enjoy equal rights.

6) The socialization of children takes place within the conjugal family during their early years, but later it is shared with formal institutions like schools (Goode 1963).

This ideal construct will be employed as a measure or model in the analysis of changing patterns of family and kinship systems in Susurluk.

Kinship Units, Descent, and Inheritance

Despite the varied ancestry of the people living in the town of Susurluk and its surrounding villages, their kinship systems are similar in many respects. They trace descent through males and pass most property, particularly homes and land, through the patriline. In the past, especially, their ideal household was patrilocal extended. That is, a daughter commonly left her natal household upon marriage, while a son brought his wife into his father's household and extended its membership. Both Manavs and Balkan Turks conceptually divide their relatives into variously labeled categories. However, the boundaries of these categories are not clear; they vary somewhat from informant to informant. Part of this lack of agreement may derive from the fact that the labels were borrowed from Arabic. Because Arab and Turkish systems of kinship differ, the kinship labels of one are often ill-suited for the other. To add more confusion to the situation, the non-Turkish settlers in the area have also adapted these labels to their own kinship units. In order to simplify the matter, I will describe what I believe are central or common tendencies of kinship usage and ignore the innumerable variations.

Probably the most basic kinship unit is the nuclear family, which is labeled *"aile,"* although this word can also be used for "wife." The word *"hane"* is employed for domestic unit or household, which may be either nuclear or extended. Its members eat together and share income and expenses. The next category is the *sülale* or patrilineage. For some Manavs and Yürük-Turkmen known *sülales* may extend over seven or more generations. However, for most people in this area they are shallow — five generations at best. In the past the *sülale* was much more important than it is at present; after the household it was the primary source of aid and mutual obligations, especially during times of major crisis.

Another kinship is the *hısım* which appears to be a bilateral kindred including both the *sülale* (patrilineage) of one's mother and of one's father. The members of both these lineages are referred to as *hısım akrabalar (hısım* relatives). Close affines such as siblings' spouses and parents' siblings' spouses are sometimes included in the *hısım* category also. After the *sülale,* the *hısım* is the next potential source of aid and mutual obligations. The most commonly reciprocated obligation of *hısım* relatives is participation in the various rites accompanying the important status transitions in the life cycle — birth, circumcision, *hafiz duasi* (graduation from Quranic school), marriage and death.

In addition to the *aile, sülale,* and *hısım,* Yürük-Turkmen and Chepnis also identified on the basis of *aşiret*s and/or *kabile*s. In the past an *aşiret* was a "tribe" composed of a number of related and unrelated patrilineages. Each "tribe" had a recognized leader *(bey),* who coordinated migrations, use of grazing and watering places, and organized the tribe for purposes of offense and defense. The word *"kabile"* is sometimes used interchangeably with *aşiret,* but in some cases it may have been a confederation of *aşiret*s effectively organized only during times of war or other emergencies. Turks borrowed these terms from Arabic. While the elderly Yürük-Turkmen with whom I talked identified themselves with various *aşiret*s or *kabile*s, they said that there are no *bey*s today and the tribes no longer exist in any organized way. Many young Yürük-Turkmen did not even claim to know their ancestors' tribal affiliation.

The ideal descent, inheritance, and post-marital residence rules of Yürük-Turkmen are very similar to those of other Turks in the area, with the exception that there is a greater stress on the patriline for purposes of inheritance.

With the establishment of the Turkish Republic, kinship reckoning and consequently the utilization of wide kinship networks have been hindered by the passage of nationalistic and Western inspired legislation. Prior to 1935 surnames in the Western sense were not common in Turkey. Traditionally three devices were utilized to maintain identity with living and deceased kin.

1) A suffix such as *–oğulları* (descendants of ————) was added to the first name of a real or mythical ancestor and ideally the resulting name was used by all agnatically related descendants to denote their relationship. For example, all the descendants of Koca Mehmet Pasha were referred to as Koca Mehmet Pashaoğulları. In the past this type of eponymous designation was also used by large tribal and quasi-tribal groups whose members were not all agnatically related. For example, in addition th the Yürük-Turkmen *kabile*s (tribes) already mentioned in the history section, several Georgian *kabile*s immigrated to this area during the 19th century, such as the Biyikoğulları and the Dursuncanoğulları. In effect this device was employed to identify relatively large groups of "related" people over multiple generations. (Other suffixes were used in a similar manner, e.g., *–oğul, –giller, –lar*.)

2) Another device which indicates intergenerational affiliation, but on a smaller scale, is the practice of repeating first names every third or fourth generation. For instance, a child might be named after either the parent or grandparent of his mother or father. However, it is not proper for parents to name their child after a living relative, less that relative believe the parents are looking forward to his death.

3) On yet a smaller scale, a person was identified in terms of his father by carrying his father's first name after his own on official lists. For example, Ahmet Suleyman is Ahmet, the son of Suleyman. Ahmet's father might appear on the same document as Suleyman Mustafa or Suleyman, the son of Mustafa. In addition to paternal affiliation this practice also facilitated the identification of male and unmarried female siblings. Upon marriage a girl would carry her husband's first name after her own rather than her father's.

In 1934 the Turkish legislature passed a law requiring the use of European type surnames beginning 1 January 1935. All household heads were required to register their surnames with local government officials. Lists of "pure" Turkish names were drawn up and many citizens were pressured into selecting from the list rather than registering Arab, Persian, European, or other non-Turkish names. This practice prevented many from registering their non-Turkish lineage or tribal names. An additional restriction limited the number of households in a single community that could choose the same surname. This prevented a large number of related households from legalizing their traditional lineage appellation even though it may have been Turkish.

From a social point of view this law has had a divisive effect. It has become impossible for people to recognize kinship connections on the basis of surnames alone. To add to the problem, many households which now carry the same surnames are not related. On many occasions citizens who went to register surnames early picked famous traditional names which in fact belonged to other households. Late-comers often found that their own lineage names had already been chosen by strangers, and they were forced to pick something else.

The actual execution of this law varied from town to town with the character of the presiding government clerk. For example, one Susurluk man told me that he wanted to register the name Başağaç (first tree) because his was the first household from Romania to settle in town. However, the clerk did not like this name and said, "I myself chose the name Baron. You'll take Barin." Thus, the humble citizen passively received his present surname. Another local man said that he had to fight for weeks to get his traditional lineage name registered because the clerk did not think it was Turkish enough. The sources for present day surnames are extremely varied. Some people chose names on the basis of their occupations, e.g., farmer, confectioner, gunsmith. Others chose place names such as those of rivers, villages, mountains. And some chose descriptive names like "strong," "happy," and "fearless."

As part of the over-all Turkification program the use of first names has also been affected. For instance, in some circles there is social and official pressure to use Turkish first names for newly born infants. At present the first names of most middle aged and elderly Turks ultimately derive from Arabic, Persian or other non-Turkic sources. As a result, many families perceive a conflict between kinship loyalties (i.e., the desire to name an infant after a grandparent) and Turkish nationalism.

Marriage Prohibitions

All Manavs with whom I talked stressed that marriage with any relative less than three *gömlek*s (literally "shirts") distance is prohibited. Such kin include one's: grandparents, parents, parents' siblings, parents' siblings' children, siblings, siblings' children, children, and children's children. (See Chart A.)

In addition to these prohibited kin, two people who have suckled milk from the same woman become milk siblings *(süt kardeşler)* and may not marry each other. Violations of this rule are unknown here.

The prohibited kinship categories forming Ego's exogamous unit are members of the *hısım* or bilateral kindred. Within this unit, however, the degree of prohibition varies. For example intercourse with grandparents, parents, siblings, offspring, or offspring's offspring is clearly incestuous. Marriage with such categories is strongly prohibited and never has been known here. Sexual relations with other members of this exogamous unit appear not to be incestuous. Although marriages with such kin are not socially condoned, they occasionally occur. To illustrate this apparent inconsistency I believe it best to relate what some Manav informants have said about the rules of exogamy and the reasons for them.

An adult Manav male,

> We don't marry relatives unless they are very distant. For example one can marry his mother's mother's sister's daughter. It is especially forbidden *(haram)* to marry a close relative on the father's side. For instance the father's brother's daughter *(amca kızı)* comes from the same seed *(tohum)*. Therefore one can't marry her. I know of one or two marriages between mother's sister's children, but it is better to marry more distant kin or strangers.

An 18 year old Manav male originally from Yıldız, a village in Susurluk Sub-province.

> Manavs believe it is best to marry a stranger. Our religion forbids us to marry the father's brother's daughter *(amca kızı)*. Occasionally someone will marry a close relative (first cousin) on the mother's side, but this too is looked down upon. By marrying a stranger I get both new relatives and new acquaintances who may help me in the future. The more relatives and friends I have, the better off I am. They are all potential sources of aid.

CHART A

Relatives Within Two *Gömleks* Of Ego

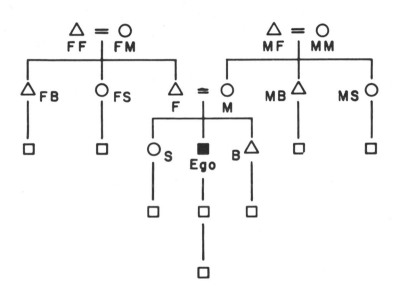

△ = Male   ○ = Female   □ = Either Sex

PM/JOP OCT 1973

An adult Manav male,

> Neither Manavs nor Balkan Turks marry close relatives. [Upon being pressed] I know of a few Manavs who married either their father's sister's daughter, mother's brother's daughter, or mother's sister's daughter, but definitely not the father's brother's daughter. Marriages between close relatives turn out bad. They usually fail. To marry within one's *sülale* is especially bad. The couple never gets along *(geçim olmaz)*. The Laz [by this he meant immigrant Turks from Turkey's Black Sea coast] in Susurluk marry their father's brother's daughter in order to prevent wealth from leaving their *sülale*. Yürüks do the same. [Upon being pressed further] Now that I think hard I can remember only one Manav marriage involving a father's brother's daughter. But this was an unusual case. The boy's father was a tightwad and a no-good. He had no friends. He never spoke to anyone — didn't even drink coffee with neighbors. You can imagine what kind of person he was. Do decent people refuse to be sociable with neighbors? Anyway, he had a son and no local family wanted him for a son-in-law, because of his father. So he married his father's brother's daughter who lived in another town. But this is a sin. If my father's brother's daughter and I were the only two people left in the world, and we had to share the same bed together, I wouldn't even touch her sleeve with my finger like this. [He demonstrated on my sleeve.]

Two adult Manav males who claim descent from Koca Mehmet Pasha,

> Among Manav's, siblings' children *(kardeş çocukları)* cannot marry. Our religion, Islam, prohibited marriage between close kin years ago. Now today we know, from a medical point of view, how wise this prohibition is. Siblings' children come from the same seed; they are of the same blood. Their intermarriage results in degeneration.

Every male and female Manav with whom I talked on this subject agreed with the above statements. Non-Manavs whom I questioned about Manav kinship practices also concurred. In an examination of 183 marriages involving at least one Manav in the town of Susurluk I learned that two were with the father's brother's daughter and six were with matrilateral first cousins (MoSis-Dau = 5; MoBrDau = 1). Over 95% of these marriages did not involve recognized consanguineal kin.

In addition to the repeated abhorrence for marriage with the father's brother's daughter, several other elements are frequently reiterated. The first two involve the concepts of seed *(tohum)* and blood *(kan)*. While all members of the exogamous unit share the same blood, at least in part, patrilineal kin are closer because they also share the same seed. "Man is to woman as seed is to a field."

It is especially bad for close patrilateral kin to marry because they both share the same blood and result from the same seed.

The third recurring element is the use of Islam as the justification for these prohibited degrees of marriage. In fact, Islam does not prohibit marriage between first cousins. According to the *Quran* a single male may not marry his mother, mother's sister, father's wife, father's sister, sister, brother's daughter, or sister's daughter. Therefore, he may marry any female in his own generation except his full or half-sisters. In addition, a married male cannot wed his wife's mother, daughter, son's wife, or two sisters together. While Turks in this area do not violate these Quranic prohibitions, it cannot be said that they acknowledge them. Practically all the Manavs, Muhacirs, Circassians and Georgians with whom I spoke were not aware that their own marriage prohibitions exceeded those of Quranic law. To the contrary, they contended that the two sets of impediments were identical.

The idea that father's brother's daughter marriage is resorted to for the purpose of preventing wealth from leaving the *sülale* is also very common. The immigrant Turks from the Black Sea (especially from Ordu Province), the Yürük-Turkmen and the Chepni in this area do not believe that first cousin marriage is prohibited. On the contrary, many regard it as a preferred form of marriage. A number of patrilateral parallel cousin marriages have taken place within these groups, and general opinion is that they were arranged to keep the family wealth intact. Gypsies in Susurluk claim to observe marital prohibitions similar to those of the Manavs, while Circassians, Georgians, and Bosnians are even more exogamous, regarding marriage with any relative as undesirable. In this area first cousin marriage among these last three peoples is practically unknown.

The Family and Household

The traditionally ideal household for both Turks and Caucasians is typified by male dominance, deference to elders, and the subservience of women. Its actual internal organization varies with such factors as household composition and the personalities and background of its members. Yet there is a common set of expectations about relationships between members which is characteristic of Susurluk. The father is the head of his family; he is an authority figure who demands the respect of all females and younger males. Mothers are also respected, but their relationships with their children are warm and informal. The mother-daughter tie is especially close as daughters commonly spend their entire pre-marital life in close companionship with their mothers, learning domestic skills. Every woman is happy to give birth to a son for the event increases her status in the eyes of her husband, her in-laws, and the community. She frequently pampers her son, who remains close to her until he reaches the age of eleven or twelve. At that point he begins to identify more closely with men and spends much of his time with his male peer group. The father-daughter relationship tends to be rather formal with little display of mutual affection, especially after the daughter has reached puberty. While a daughter may argue or joke with her mother, she commonly is obedient and deferential to her father. During pre-pubescence, relationships between siblings of either sex are free and easy, and siblings spend a great deal of time together in the home. As they grow older, their statuses change, with the older sibling sharing many of the rights and obligations vis-a-vis the younger that a parent of the corresponding sex has toward his child. For example, the older sister, called *abla,* becomes like a second mother to her younger brother or sister. Likewise, the older brother *(ağabey)* is in many respects a second father. Often times, an *ağabey* is near tyrannical in his behavior with a younger sister. As he assumes the guardianship of family honor, he may try to observe, supervise, and criticize his sister's every move outside the home. Several teenage girls told me that an *ağabey* can make a girl's life hell. Relationships with kin outside the family are, in many respects, partial extensions of familial relationships. For instance, the father's brother *(amca)* is considered "half a father" and, like the father, is an authority figure. In general all older kin on the father's side are treated with more formal respect than kin on the mother's side.

The ideal formation of a patrilocal extended household involves a process of dynamic fission. To illustrate this process let us begin with an example of a household which has achieved the ideal. It is composed of a patriarch, his wife, and his two married sons and their families. We will call this T_1. At T_2 the patriarch and his wife die. Now, according to the ideal norm, the two sons establish two separate households, each composed of one nuclear family. Later, at T_3 with the marriage of the original patriarch's grandsons, these two nuclear households are converted into agnatically extended ones. Although the ultimate goal is the attainment of a patriarchal and agnatically extended household, a frequent intermediate step is the establishment of a nuclear one. Therefore, given the demographic facts of real life and this ideal norm involving dynamic fission, we should expect to find a large number of nuclear households even in communities where the ideal household is an extended one. Thus, census data alone are usually insufficient evidence from which to induce norms for ideal household formation and postmarital residence rules. All informants over 35 years of age agreed that about 20 years ago this *was* the generally accepted ideal and goal of most married males of all ethnic groups in Susurluk.

Of the 181 households in my 1970 sample, 71.3% were nuclear, and the average-size household for the total sample was 4.34. Twenty-two percent of the sample appeared to fit the ideal household type, or a variant of it. However, closer examination reveals that half of these forty cases did not result from the ideal process. In these cases, it was not the son who brought his wife into the paternal home, but the parents (usually only a widowed mother) who joined their son's originally neolocal household as dependents. In several cases, parents had moved from the village to town to join their sons who were successfully employed there.

Most of the extended households which resulted from the ideal process were two types. The first were households of poorer families in which a son had recently married and could not afford to live separately. Many of these sons expressed their intention to establish separate households when they were financially able. The second were households composed of kin who were jointly engaged in a family business — either agricultural, commercial, or craft.

An excellent example of these are the Black Sea Turks (called "Laz" locally) who have built up prosperous family businesses on the bases of kinship loyalties and former residential ties. Since about 1900, several groups of families immigrated to Susurluk from Trabzon, a Black Sea province with an insufficient economic base to support its normally expanding population. The men were skilled craftsmen, especially metal workers. They overcame the challenges of survival in a new environment by working hard in mutual support and reinvesting their earnings in real estate and retail businesses. Over the generations these people maintained close bonds by marrying either kin or unrelated Black Sea Turks, and today they commonly live in extended households and operate family businesses. More recently, groups of related families have begun to share new apartment buildings with their retail shops located on the first level.

A typical illustration is that of two young men who are patrilateral parallel cousins (brothers' sons) and who are partners in a flourishing hardware business located on the first level of a new apartment building in which they reside separately with their families and surviving parents. They attribute their business success to hard work, the joint investment of their families' accumulated capital, and personal ties with their Istanbul wholesalers and distributors, who are either kin or Black Sea Turks from Trabzon. The partners boast that because of these preferential relations they get goods shipped to them immediately on credit, thereby giving them a time advantage over their competitors, and they are reliably supplied with products normally in big demand but in short supply. As a consequence, they have been able to win several important supply contracts with factories in the larger cities nearby.

These and other local family firms stand out as counter examples to the general trend of diminishing kinship bonds. In Susurluk, as well as in other parts of the Western and non-Western world, kinship ties and loyalties have proven highly functional in modernizing economies. After examining numerous kinship studies from societies around the globe, Goode concludes that, "considerable data suggest that kin networks are larger, engage in more exchange, and control their children more effectively, toward the upper social strata, and these are in turn the more successful families within an industialized society" (1968:341).

All my informants claimed that extended households were more common in the past when Susurluk was a small, agrarian community. This claim is supported by national statistics. According to the 1965 census, the proportion of village households containing two families or more was 26.9%; for towns (sub-provincial capitals) it was 14.5% and for cities (provincial capitals) it was 9.8%. The average-size household in the small agrarian villages was also larger than in the sub-provincial capitals (which are usually mixed agricultural, commercial, and administrative centers) and cities, being: 6.16 persons per household for villages, 5.22 for towns, and 4.69 for cities. A national survey (see Magnarella 1970) reveals that the proportion of people using birth control devices increases with settlement size: village, town, city, metropolis. On the basis of these national patterns, it seems likely the average household size and the prevalence of extended households in Susurluk decreased as the town evolved from a small agricultural community to an industrial, commercial, and administrative center.

Unfortunately, reliable statistics for the composition and size of households in the past are not available. However, even if they were, they would be of limited help when dealing with ideal goals, as actual household size is also influenced by numerous factors, including migration, occupation, economics, military service, government assignment, education, and longevity. On the level of norms, household types are most immediately determined by postmarital residence rules. For example, a patrilocal, postmarital decision rule leads to the creation of a patrilocal-extended household. An ideal household norm is accompanied by an ideal postmarital residence rule. In order to learn whether there has been any change in this ideal rule or goal, I asked members of the adult sample with whom they believed newlyweds should reside. The vast majority, 82.5%, answered that newlyweds should live alone, separate from their parents. As one person put it: "It's the only way they will find peace." The results also showed that the more educated a person is the more likely he is to favor neolocal residence.

These answers and other data from my study strongly indicate that the ideal postmarital residence rule has changed for many townsmen. The reasons for this trend are undoubtedly complex. It appears that a new, expanded economic structure, improved travel, and an awareness of job opportunities outside the community are making possible a change whose impetus was inherent in the traditional culture. A large number of townsmen explained that newlyweds should live alone if finances permit, since, in part, patrilocal residence exists for economic reasons. In agrarian Susurluk, families were commonly both the units of production and of consumption, and most young couples were financially dependent on their families. Now with increased job opportunities patrilocal residence is no longer necessary for many of them.[1] Another important factor is the great value Turkish men place on masculine dominance and authority. By residing in his father's household, a young man remains in a subordinate position. All of his decisions can be influenced by older kin, especially parents. A married son becomes his own man, so to speak, by establishing his own home. Neolocal residence is also preferred by many young wives who want to avoid domination by their mothers-in-law.

This basic change in the structure of family relations has important implications for the process of goal-directed activity involving kin. In a number of cases I observed that elderly kin, whose status demands deference and obedience, participated less in the day-to-day affairs, decisions, and other goal-directed activities of younger families living in nuclear households than in those living in extended ones. The generality of these observations was tested by asking the younger married members of the sample (n = 120) whether of not (and if so, how often) they consulted elderly kin when making important decisions. The results indicated that heads of nuclear households are less likely to consult older kin for important decisions than married males living in extended households. However, in many cases nuclear households only exercise a new degree of autonomy. For them ties with older kin continue to be important for purposes ranging from emotional to economic support.

These changes in ideal post-marital residence and household composition have important implications for socialization and personality formation. For example, an American psychologist has concluded that in the traditional Turkish extended family the dominant role of the patriarch tends to inhibit the development of achievement motivation in young males (Bradburn 1960). This is supported by McClelland (1961) who has noted that the need for achievement is usually low in any society where the patriarchal extended family is common. However, with the nuclear family in a modernizing context a greater part of socialization occurs outside the family — in schools and among peer groups.

Due to the generally low level of educational attainment among today's adult male population, it does not require much schooling before young boys find that they have already surpassed their fathers and must be relied on to perform tasks requiring literacy. New occupations require young men to learn skills which their fathers never possessed, and having acquired such skills they are soon earning more money than their fathers could realistically hope for. Viewing the total context, it appears that patriarchs have less leverage than formerly, and as a result their dominance is diminishing. Possible implications of these changes might be a greater degree of autonomy on the part of young males as well as increased achievement motivation.

Husband-Wife Relationship

The internal organization of local households is largely determined by the socio-cultural division of labor and the age, sex, and relationships of their members. Ideally women should be obedient and subservient. There is a saying here and throughout most of Turkey that "women have long hair, but short minds." Thus their activity should be controlled. One local man told me that in the *Quran* Allah has said, " 'If you do not worship me, worship your husband.' "Therefore," the informant continued, "a husband is second only to Allah. A wife must heed his every word."[2]

Although supreme authority may rest with the father, the actual internal organization of the household is mother-centered. The mother, being largely confined to the home, manages and directs its internal affairs while the men spend most of their time away. The division of labor is clear-cut: women have responsibility for the internal home, and men provide the income and represent the household in dealings with the external world. Even public shopping has traditionally been a male duty.

The areas covered by male and female roles are almost completely mutually exclusive. Rarely, if ever, does a husband take on wifely tasks. Even when his wife falls ill, in the absence of a mature daughter, the wife's neighbors, friends, or relatives take over her household duties of cooking, cleaning, sewing, etc. This sharp division of labor has contributed to a strong interdependence of the sexes. Men find it impossible to live without women and still maintain their masculine integrity. Likewise, it has traditionally been difficult for women to maintain a household without men, as females in small conservative communities are cultually blocked from most public occupations.

This sharp distinction of sex roles and the division of labor has been symbolically represented in the architecture of traditional Turkish homes, which contain two sections: the *harem* (women's quarter) and the *selamlık* (men's quarter). In earlier times, segregation by sex was even more marked in urban areas than in rural ones.

The external social relations of local Susurluk families most often take the form of individual rather than group networks. That is, the family as a unit rarely engages in social interaction with other social units. Instead, individual family members have their own social networks. For husbands and wives these social networks tend to be highly segregated, with each spouse interacting with a different set of people. These networks are usually close-knit, in that most people comprising a network know each other and frequently interact. Generally, such networks are important to the individual throughout his life.

In most of Turkey and especially in small towns such as Susurluk there has traditionally been an absence of courtship and a segregation of the sexes in most public and recreational activities. For these reasons heterosexual peer groups among young adults are rare. Instead, peer groups are unisexual and their memberships are tightly knit, being composed of relatives and close friends. Very often members think of themselves as being closer to one another than siblings. In such communities, therefore, both husband and wife enter marriage with their own separate close-knit social networks. Each spouse continues to look to members of his or her social network for companionship, emotional support, recreation, and even economic aid. Because these external relations offer so much, correspondingly less demand is made on one's spouse and a rather rigid segregation of conjugal roles is maintained.

While women spend most of their time in the private world of their homes, men are most often outside the home, in the public world. Many men, like the 79.4% of the adult sample, regard work rather than family life as their most satisfying activity. This is partly because most occupations in town are extremely social, allowing for visiting, chatting, and even casual entertainment. Shopkeepers and tradesmen such as tailors, shirt makers, and shoemakers spend a large part of their day conversing and drinking tea with friends as they work. For these men twelve to fourteen hour days are common. Tailor shops, for instance, commonly open at 9:00 in the morning and close at 11:00 at night. Prior to special days orders multiply and even longer hours are required to finish suits in time for the holidays. Tradesmen commonly work diligently while carrying on amiable conversations with visitors seated about their shops sipping hot tea. Many commercial and trade shops have taken on the character of the traditional Turkish *oda,* by becoming daily gathering places where friends meet to discuss all matters of concern. Other tradesmen such as iron and wood workers, whose generally dirty and noisy workshops inhibit friendly visiting, maintain sociability through daily gatherings in their coffeehouses and periodic meetings of their associations. This sociality also extends to banks and governmental institutions where employees work long hours and enjoy the company of good friends and visitors during the day. One of the indispensable employees in such institutions is the *odacı,* or room attendant, who performs the important duty of serving visitors and staff their social tea and coffee.

Social life continues after work hours and on Sundays when most Susurluk men are free. But they spend a great part of this leisure time outside of the home in public places also, — the three most popular being coffeehouses, cinemas, and the town park. While the coffeehouse is an old institution, for Susurluk the cinema and park are relatively recent. Movies, especially outdoor summer ones, became popular only in the fifties, and the town park, beautifully landscaped with trees, shrubs and flowers, was completed in 1961. Scattered among the greenery are small wooden tables and chairs where people relax and sip tea or coffee. The town's casinos, restaurants, and clubs are popular with a restricted segment of the population: members of the town's official and upper commercial classes,[3] who dine and drink raki together in small groups at their favorite restaurants and then repair to the City or Relaxation Clubs to play cards. This kind of entertainment proves far too expensive for the average townsman, who satisfies himself by drinking tea among friends in a coffeehouse or in the park and watching a weekly movie.

In the past, husbands and wives customarily did not frequent places of public entertainment together. However, more recently some changes have taken place. A large number of townsmen now take their wives to the cinema and the town park.

Although it has only been in existence since 1961, the park has become the town's most popular strolling, relaxing, and gathering spot. In addition to a play area for children and a small "zoo" displaying some birds and rabbits, the park contains two tea gardens which double as casinos at night where food and drinks are served to the sound of the latest popular recordings. In part, the town park duplicates the restaurant and outdoor dining area already existing at the sugar refinery where families of the official class sit together for their evening meal. These familial gatherings in a public place by an important reference group offer local families a model to emulate. As local restaurants and coffeehouses are completely taboo for local women, the new park became an extremely important mechanism for change. From the beginning municipal officials stressed that it was designed for family use and named it "Susurluk Family Park." Being new, it was not fully subject to the existing customs and taboos segregating the sexes in other places, and leaders of the town, such as the mayor, are endeavoring to establish familial norms governing park use by taking their own families there daily.

Although the beautiful Sea of Marmara is only 50 minutes to the north by cheap public transportation, few townsmen and only nine members of the sample take their wives to the beach. This is a new form of recreation that can be attributed to the sugar refinery which maintains a large resort for its employees and their families on the Sea of Marmara at Erdek, about one hour from Susurluk. All employees are entitled to spend fifteen days each summer at the resort in rent-free cabins. While few of the local men are willing to let their wives actually swim or sunbathe, an increasing number of them are taking their families to Erdek for a summer holiday or vacation — another concept unknown before the arrival of the sugar refinery. Even cinema attendance has been strongly influenced by official class families attached to the refinery who go to the movies together almost weekly.

Because Susurluk people have traditionally assumed that male and female interests are different, local wives do not expect to spend leisure time together with husbands sharing common interests. By contrast, many of the educated wives of officials demand the companionship of their husbands. In 1965, a group of these women dramatically expressed their expectations in the local newspaper, with an open letter to the sub-provincial governor — their husbands' superior — in which they complained that their husbands were spending too much time in their clubs playing poker, coming home late at night, and generally disturbing familial peace. They wanted the law prohibiting gambling to be enforced and the clubs to close earlier so that their husbands might rejoin their families. These are not the submissive women who make ideal wives in a small community like Susurluk, but they are the kind of women who influence change.

Formerly, the women of Susurluk had little to do with family finances. Men controlled the money and were not accountable to their wives. However, since the establishment of the sugar refinery, this arrangement has been altered. For instance, prior to 1955 women made rare appearances in the market place. But the newly arrived wives of the refinery's managerial staff had been accustomed to public shopping in the cities where they had previously lived, and many continued to shop publicly in Susurluk. These women established an important precedent. Since many of the local men were working days at the refinery, and since young boys were attending school, shopping for daily household needs became a problem. Gradually, more and more families solved it by allowing their women to imitate their "urban sisters" and shop themselves. In this way, women began to handle a larger part of their families' finances and to represent their families more often in external affairs. While this has freed them somewhat from the confines of the home, it also has created problems. Many husbands demand a detailed accounting of daily or weekly expenditures. Because many of the middle-aged and more elderly wives possess only the rudiments of literacy, simple accounting is an extremely difficult and troublesome task, and even small discrepancies may occasionally lead to serious conflict.[4].

Conjugal relationships in Susurluk are not only influenced by the behavior of official class families, but also by greater exposure to a modernizing national society and the Western world. Although many local people are anxious to improve their standards of living through modern technology, they are critical of urban and Western influences on the family, heterosexual relationships, and social life in general. These influences violate the traditional concepts of honor and shame. While these concepts are common throughout the world, their substance is relative to the social systems which they function to preserve. In essence, honorable acts are ones which accord with reigning social norms and values; shameful acts violate such norms and values. In Mediterranean societies like Turkey where the conscience of honor is so highly developed, reaction to social change is often strong.

Critical points of honor rest on a man's relationship to his wife, daughters, or sisters. By maintaining their purity in traditional cultural terms, a man preserves his honor. When his women become tainted, his own honor turns to shame. In Turkey, as in some other Muslim countries, it is traditionally believed that preservation of female purity requires seclusion from other men. Even a minimum of exposure may lead to a state of defilement for a woman and dishonor for her man. As a result, Westernization in the critical area of heterosexual relationships, especially conjugal ones, has been met with stubborn resistance. The following poem, which appeared in a local newspaper in 1969, cogently expresses the concern of many Susurluk people. While the poet makes specific reference to the "pagan" New Year's Eve celebration, which has entered Turkey from the West, and Susurluk via the sugar refinery, his concern is, of course, more general.

New Year's Eve and My Woman

When I won't have you the object of gossip
How can I let you consort with strangers?

Veiled
Your physical and your spiritual beauty
Grows in my heart.
My woman.

You should never be exposed to all.
You should never be the bait of desire.
You should never be without modesty.

But here you stand for all to see, my woman.
What can be the reason?
Has the evil eye looked upon my Ayshe-Fatma?
What person,
What thing
Has pushed you in this mud?

Enough, my woman
Enough of this empty drunkenness.

These fads from Europe –
What have they to do with us,
With our tradition?
With our religion?

Whatever comes out of Europe you grasp,
You take in the name of fashion
Placing it on your head as a crown.

The hemline, sometimes tight
Sometimes narrow, rose.
Mini is less than mini
The hemline is at your thigh.

The bee hive has fallen
Honey mixes with mud.
Show sorrow, my woman
Mother of this generation.
You must not be a carnival clown.

Progressives say
The veil is reactionary
But I say
Primitives are more progressive
Than they.

When members of the adult sample were asked their opinions about the outside employment of women, 56.3% said that single girls should be allowed to work outside the home if their income was needed, but only 34% held the same view for married women. As a result of numerous conversations with local men, I learned that opposition to the employment of married women is commonly based on three fundamental fears.

The first is neglect of home and family. Many men believe that caring for a family and running a household are full-time jobs in themselves, which cannot be done properly if their wives are out working. In Turkish the word for family (*aile*) is also the word for wife. The two concepts are merged culturally as well as linguistically. For many men the argument was not that a woman's place is at home with her family, but that she is the family. The second fear concerns local concepts of honor and shame and involves the idea that outside employment enhances the dangers of promiscuity as such work often entails contact with unrelated men. The third involves a potential challenge to male authority or a threat to male identity. It is believed that with increased economic power, wives might assume a new air of authority in their conjugal relations.

The main motivating forces favoring the outside employment of women are economic necessity and the desire for a better standard of living.

Although the Turkish Republic was established as a secular state, about 98% of her population is Muslim, and for this reason it is appropriate to note that the Muslim *ulema* (theologians) of Al Azhar University in Egypt issued a *fatwa* (decree) on June 11, 1952, which "denied women the right to take jobs in public life 'because of their femininity which makes them likely to quit the path of reason and moderation,' but was prepared to see them exercising certain professions 'where strength of judgment and will are not required'" (Forget 1962:100). We can think of this position as a strong conservative standard against which the attitudes of Susurluk men can be compared. Members of the sample were read a list of occupations and asked which ones they believed women could successfully perform. Ninety percent or more believed women could be successful doctors, lawyers, judges, pharmacists, teachers, nurses, writers, and tailors. Smaller proportions of the sample thought they could be successful engineers (87.4%), laborers (80.8%), grocers (60.4%), military officers (37.4%), and butchers (21%).

These answers certainly make the men of Susurluk appear much more liberal than the 1952 *ulema* of Al Azhar University. However, it is probably no coincidence that one of the respondents who said that a woman could not be successful as a judge claimed that her sex would prevent her from being objective. "A handsome man could influence her. She's a woman first." But most members of the sample agreed with the statement made by one of the young bachelors: "Today women and men are one. Women can do any kind of work."

In the light of this common attitude, one immediately asks why only 21% of the sample said that women could be successful butchers. As several people (both male and female) explained to me, a major part of the answer lies in the realm of traditional religion and the concepts of purity and pollution. A woman is considered ritually impure during her entire menstrual period. While in this state of impurity she should not pray, fast, read the *Quran,* enter a mosque, or go on a pilgrimage. And, unless absolutely necessary, she should not prepare food or cook for people outside her family. From this it naturally follows that women would not make ideal butchers. This thinking may have been extended by some to the occupation of grocer, even though this occupation requires much less direct contact with food.

One of the main objections to women as military officials is that the occupation is basically inconsistent with the idealized female role, no matter how broadly defined it may be. Anything military is masculine. But in spite of this socio-cultural incongruity, slightly over one-third (37.4%) of the sample believed that women could successfully perform this role.

Along with the spread of a more liberal view of women and a changing economic and occupational structure have come greater opportunities for female employment outside the home. For example, a new cannery in the neighboring district of Mustafakemalpasha employs many more women than men because the management finds them more dexterous and efficient workers. These women come from small conservative communities where this kind of employment goes against traditional social mores. However, material want, optimum working conditions, and good pay have proved sufficient to overcome the obstacles of honor and shame. For these same reasons about twelve Susurluk families have allowed their single daughters or wives to leave the country and work in Germany unescorted by either their fathers, brothers, or husbands.

In Susurluk the sugar refinery employs only a few local women in low level cleaning jobs. However, two of the banks have hired local girls as secretaries and a few local high school graduates are employed as teachers in the elementary schools. In addition, two or three local girls work as clerks in the post office, and about 100 young women from the town's poorer families work during peak seasons as day laborers in the farm fields. The town also boasts a female pediatrician and two female pharmacists, all of whom have come to Susurluk from larger cities.

In order to obtain some general data on husband-wife decision making, married members of the sample were asked how frequently they consulted their wives when making important decisions concerning their families. Of 127 respondents, 29.1% claimed they always consult their wives; 55.9% said they do so sometimes or often; and, 15% said they never do. Significantly, degree of consultation rose with the respondents' levels of education. These results, coupled with other observations, give us a basis for prediction. Given the growing ideal of the neolocal nuclear household, the increasing levels of education in the community, and the spreading jural and social ideology (discussed below) of equality in conjugal relations within the context of a modernizing economic and occupational structure, I believe one can assume that family decisions are progressively becoming joint ventures with wives playing more active public and private roles in the goal-directed activities of their families.

Fathers and Sons

The father-son relationship, which has important implications for social stability and change, was also examined with respect to decision making. As demonstrated, an alteration in this relationship has contributed to the dissolution of the patriarchal extended household as an ideal norm. Generally speaking, when sons conform to the values of their fathers as conveyed through parental advice they act to maintain the traditional socio-cultural system. On the other hand, as sons, especially educated sons, begin to make progressively more of their important decisions on the basis of their modern education and seek the advice of their fathers less, they promote change.

The 55 young bachelors in the sample were asked if they consulted their fathers (or, in the absence of their fathers, other elderly kin) when making important decisions. Only three (5.5%) claimed not to consult their fathers (or other elderly kin) at all, while over half of the sample (58.2%) said they always do. The remaining 36.4% consult with varying frequencies. Their answers indicate that in spite of changes in the community's social and economic structure, the father-son relationship remains close.

Observational evidence strongly supports this conclusion. Fathers display a great deal of concern about their sons' education, vocation, and general future, and most fathers want their sons to attain an occupational status higher than their own. Sons attending institutions of higher education rely on their fathers for financial support for longer periods of time than do sons entering a trade immediately after primary school. While advanced education may contribute to intellectual autonomy, it results in prolonged financial dependence.

A father's concern for his son derives in part from the idea that his son will eventually replace him. Traditionally the son carries the family name, inherits his father's wealth, and represents the continuity of the male line. When a man dies, he leaves behind his name and his son. Together, they represent his living being — his social legacy. To a great extent, this remains true today. To obtain a current measure of this concern, the total sample was asked if *they* wanted to choose their sons' occupations. A high proportion, about one-half of them, answered yes, and no significant differences between the various educational groups emerged.

Assessing the degree of change here presents a difficult problem. One might assume that traditional patriarchs were more common in the past, and most of them would have strongly influenced their sons' vocational choices. However, such an assumption should be treated as a hypothesis to be tested, not as a baseline for comparison. Hoping to gain comparative data for a past generation, the total sample was asked if their fathers had influenced their selection of an occupation, type of work, or education. Fifty respondents (28%) answered yes, while 129 (72%) said no. Many informants felt that fathers today show more active concern for their sons' vocational futures than their own fathers did about theirs. In the past, a narrow economic and occupational structure, coupled with limited educational opportunities, created a situation in which few occupational choices existed. This limiting situation determined one's occupation more than parental influence. Today by comparison a confusing maze of opportunity channels exists, and many fathers feel the necessity of guiding, even pushing, their sons in the right direction.

The father-son relationship is also central to the topic of intergenerational conflict. During February of 1970, Professor Ozcan Koknel of Istanbul University's Medical School treated this topic in a series of articles appearing in a major Turkish newspaper. He was especially concerned with the ''generation gap'' as manifested by continuous and often violent student unrest and the fact that people under twenty-five commit about half of the common crimes in Turkey. One of his main conclusions centers around the idea that most of today's youth were socialized in a traditional Turkish setting, typified by patriarchal households and conservative communities. He believes this kind of upbringing is proving dysfunctional in a modernizing society with accelerated change, causing many young individuals to experience a state of anomie.

In Susurluk interviews with local police, teachers, and citizens and a content analysis of two local newspapers covering the 1961-70 period lead me to conclude that juvenile delinquency and serious intergenerational conflict are not prevalent here. On the contrary, in my observations I was greatly impressed by the respect adolescents and young adults show their parents and the understanding and concern parents manifest toward them. For instance, on many occasions I witnessed young men refuse to enter places of recreation such as coffeehouses, casinos, or taverns if their fathers were already there. This is because respect demands refraining from smoking, drinking, playing cards, or carrying on in a free and easy manner in the presence of one's father. However, if a man knows that his son is already in such a place, he will avoid it also, and not spoil his son's good time.

In an attempt to learn more about intergenerational conflict within the family I asked those married members of the survey who had adolescent or older children if they had any reason to complain about their children's behavior toward them. Only a few gave positive replies: two said their sons did not study enough, and one complained that his daughter had abandoned traditional norms and had become European in her dress and behavior.

Hoping to see the other side of the coin, this same question was reversed and asked of the 55 bachelors in the sample, but the results were practically the same. Only four complained about their parents. One claimed that his father did not understand him; another answered that his father lacked concern for him;

and two said their fathers restricted their freedom. It should be pointed out that the father charged with lack of concern is a stepfather, and one of the fathers who restricted freedom did so by not allowing his son to grow long hair. Only two members of the sample complained about their mothers. One said his mother lacked understanding, while the other said his mother, like his stepfather, lacked concern.

All in all neither the fathers nor the young adult bachelors offer evidence of serious intergenerational conflict within their families.[5] Yet, in the light of our knowledge about the dissolution of the ideal patriarchal household and the strain on young people trying to work out new codes of conduct in a rapidly changing social context, it may seem inconsistent to conclude that serious intergenerational conflict is absent in this community. This conclusion becomes more understandable when we examine two elements in the traditional culture. One element restricts deviance, while the other facilitates it.

Unlike large cities in which anonymity is possible, small Turkish communities tend to be tightly knit in that almost everyone knows everyone else, and all members have the right and duty to be concerned with one another's public behavior. In public places every adult takes it upon himself to curb the improper behavior of younger people. In this respect the community resembles a large kin group. In fact, young people and elders customarily address each other with kinship terms, whether they are related or not. Even young Turks, like their elders, have a highly developed sense of honor. To misbehave in public places immediately invites cries of "shame" and "disgrace" from older observers. This kind of public chastisement creates extreme embarrassment.

But in spite of public and familial social control, deviant behavior is inevitable. Turkish society has not only recognized this fact, but has even institutionalized tolerance for various kinds of abnormal conduct. For example, traditional Turkish society regards the contrary behavior often accompanying adolescence as natural. Society has acknowledged the inevitability of such behavior by labeling an adolescent boy a *"delikanlı,"* which literally means "mad blooded." *Delikanlı*s are notorious for their "mad," "nonsensical," or "ridiculous" actions. Adult men commonly explain away the antics of their adolescent sons by merely saying, "He's a *delikanlı."* Although adolescent girls have no corresponding label and their anormative behavior is not as readily condoned, parents do believe that they, too, can be seized by a madness during this period.

This culturally prescribed explanation for youth's anormative behavior buffers a great deal of potential conflict. On the one hand, it allows adolescents to trespass the normal boundaries of propriety without seriously threatening the authority of their fathers, and on the other it supplies potentially threatened or concerned parents with a culturally accepted explanation for deviant behavior.

Parents are also fortified with the belief that their children will outgrow this *temporary* condition. In small modernizing towns like Susurluk, cultural mechanisms such as these have been able to temper potential intergenerational conflict resulting from change.

Notes to Chapter V

Kinship and the Family

[1] The Turkish social scientists Erdentuğ (1959) and Yasa (1957) believe that a changing economic structure is contributing to the dissolution of the traditional patrilocal household in their research villages also. They report that sons establish separate households as soon as they are financially able.

[2] The Turkish sociologist Yasa writes that "family misunderstandings in Hasanoğlan [his research village] are short-lived because the woman nearly always submits to the man's absolute authority" (1957:119). And the female social scientist Abadan states that "the great bulk of Turkish women still conform to the old image of the tradition-bound, obedient, submissive, religious female" (1967:99).

[3] People employed in some official or managerial capacity by either the sugar refinery, the banks, or the government are regarded as members of an "official class" *(memur sinifi)*.

[4] The Turkish social scientist Şahinkaya found that 27% of the urban wives and 15% of the village wives in her sample from Hatay Province (n = 200 each) said that money management problems constitute the most serious cause of conflict in their marriages (1970).

[5] Similarly, the Turkish sociologist Kiray (1964) did not discover serious intergenerational conflict in a small Turkish town on the Black Sea coast.

CHAPTER VI

Law, Kinship, and Society

Prior to the establishment of the Turkish Republic in 1923, Islam and the Ottoman State had never been separate. Islam existed as an all-embracing ideology providing Muslim citizens with a framework of meaning with which to interpret their personal distresses and successes, their past histories and present circumstances, and the future directions of their lives. In addition to providing a moral code for private life, Islam's domain included government, law, and all bases of authority. The Ottoman Sultan was the head of state and simultaneously Caliph — recognized leader of Sunni Moslems.

According to Turco-Islamic practice, parents or guardians had the right to contract a marriage for their child or ward. Thus, with qualifications, marriage by compulsion was acceptable. A woman was bound to monogamy, while a man was permitted four wives simultaneously under certain conditions. The husband enjoyed the discretionary right of unilateral repudiation, and in regards to inheritance, male agnatic kin, especially sons, were favored.

As part of his master plan to create a modern, progressive Turkish State, Mustafa Kemal, Turkey's founder and first president, made secularism one of his uncompromising principles. Considering Islam a prime source of Ottoman retardation, Kemal endeavored to eliminate the major institutions and to reorient the minds of his people. He abolished the *Shari'a* (Islamic law) and adopted legal codes which were regarded as the epitome of Western Civilization. Since 1926 a modified form of family law embodied in the Swiss Civil Code has been applied in Turkish courts. Unlike the various systems of ethno-Islamic law employed in traditional Turkey, the new code greatly improved the position of women. They gained equal rights to private property and inheritance, their consent became necessary for a legally binding marriage, and under specified conditions they could sue for divorce and demand alimony. By contrast, men lost their prerogatives of verbal and unilateral divorce and polygynous marriage. A noted female professor in Turkey believes that the adoption of the Swiss Civil Code represents the most important step ever taken in the advancement of Turkish women (Abadan 1967:94).[1]

The new law also grants young people more freedom. For instance, at eighteen years of age both boys and girls can marry without parental consent, and all marriages require the expressed consent of the two persons involved.

These legal changes represented a bold attempt to create a new national morality and mentality by legislation. It is generally believed that changing law reflects changes in society, that law responds to existing morals, customs, and traditions. Has the modern Turkish experience been the reverse? That is, has legislation succeeded in displacing Turco-Islamic tradition? In 1955 a group of Turkish and foreign scholars examined this question with reference to the adoption of the Swiss family law and answered with a qualified "No" (see *International Social Science Bulletin* 1957). However, I believe the new family law has been gaining acceptance more recently because it is proving functional in a changing cultural and socio-economic environment. Since the 1950s Turkey has made major advances in industry and education. A large proportion of her population now lives in modernizing towns and cities. Even her large village population has more favorable contact with urban centers and Europe via travel and communication than ever before. They are increasingly adopting urban and Western ways. In such a setting many Turks feel that certain traditional Turco-Islamic norms governing marriage and family relations are proving dysfunctional, and they see the norms embodied in the new family law as viable alternatives.

This chapter assesses the influences which legal, cultural, and socio-economic changes have had on the selection of spouses, the marriage ceremony, inheritance, polygyny, and divorce in Susurluk.

The Selection of Spouses and the Marriage Ceremony — Traditional

In Susurluk both the selection of spouses and the marriage ceremony were highly routinized and embedded in the wider kinship system. The responsibilities for and the symbolic ritual of these important socio-cultural events were group- rather than individual-oriented. Change has involved a process of individualization — the emergence of the individual from the kin group. This process can best be illustrated by first describing certain aspects of the traditional procedure and then making comparisons with the newer one. At present both the traditional and the modern systems of selecting spouses and conducting marriage ceremonies exist side by side. While tradition is in the process of change, or even possible dissolution, it is still very much alive today.

The traditional method of selecting spouses was functionally consistent with the ideal patrilocal extended household. Because a new bride joined the household of her husband's parents, her selection was important to all its members, not just to the groom. Final authority over the admission or rejection of this new member rested with the patriarch.

When a daughter marries she leaves her natal household and joins that of her

Village wedding

in-laws as a very subordinate member. The first few years of marriage may be the most trying period of her entire life cycle, and her parents carry the responsibility of seeing that she is not given to a family that will make her life wretched.

These two important considerations are accompanied by a third one involving the interfamilial alliance or acquisition of relatives that marriage entails. Because honor and shame are of paramount importance and are shared by relatives, it is vital to choose in-laws who will not dishonor one's offspring as well as one's household and lineage. Therefore, marital decisions could not be left to young individuals. Although family patriarchs had final word, young men usually enjoyed a degree of authority in this matter, but daughters did not.

Normally the boy's family initiates the search for an honorable and reputable family with a marriageable daughter. They prefer an established family with a known genealogy whose members are free from gambling, excessive drinking, or other vices. After finding an acceptable family, a series of contacts is made, with the initial steps of the negotiation falling on the women of the two households. Only after consent for the marriage has been informally given through women will the men of both sides meet to cement a formal agreement. The preliminary steps protect the men from the loss of honor which a face-to-face refusal would bring.

The first formal meeting of the women is called *görücülük* (seeing). The boy's mother and one or two female relatives and friends visit the girl's home to inspect her and to discuss the proposal with her mother and the other elderly female relatives present. If they are generally satisfied with the girl and the attitude of her family, the boy's side will send *dünürcüler* (intermediaries) — male relatives and/or reliable, influential friends — to ask formally for the consent of the patriarch. This given, agreement on the size of the bridewealth, value of the trousseau, and other financial particulars must be reached.

Many adult males in town told me their wives had been selected in this manner. They said that even after the marriage parental authority is strong in the extended household. For example, one informant confided that his mother made him divorce his first wife because she disliked the girl's "excessive sociability."

The next major event in the marital process is the engagement ceremony *(nişan merasimi)*. It, too, takes place in the home of the future bride. The boy's mother and several of her female relatives arrive with part of the bridewealth — items such as gold bracelets, earrings, and clothing. The girl's mother and elder female relatives welcome the visitors and direct them to the sitting room. After they are seated, the young girl enters and kisses the right hand of each guest as a sign of respect. Then she leaves and the women talk among themselves. At an appropriate time the girl reappears, serves the guests tea, and again leaves the room. (If tea is served too soon, the guests feel their visit is being rushed.) After tea the girl is called back, and the boy's mother places the engagement ring on her finger saying: *"Hayirli, uğurlu, mesut olunuz"* (May you be blessed, fortunate, and happy). The girl expresses her gratitude, respect, and subordination by again kissing the woman's right hand. Her mother then gives the boy's mother a package to be taken home and opened there. It commonly contains three handkerchiefs — one each for the father, mother, and son. This is only part of a complex exchange of gifts between members of the two kin groups.

The kin-group symbols in this ritual are clear. The boy is absent during the engagement, and the main actors in the ring ceremony are his mother and future wife. Because in traditional Turkish society the mother-son relationship is so intensely emotional, a mother usually holds an important intermediate position between her son and his wife.[2] The ring ceremony symbolizes the critical importance of the mother/daughter-in-law relationship both to the smooth functioning of a patrilocal extended household and to harmony during the early years of marriage. The prominence of the elderly women and the absence of the daughter (except during the greeting, serving, and ring ceremony) symbolizes that an important part of this event is the union of two kin groups.

The third event to be described is the religious marriage ceremony *(dini nikah)*. Depending on the particular agreement or circumstances, the marriage may follow the engagement by one week or by as much as a year or more. It commonly culminates seven days of activities. Formerly it took place on Friday evening, the Muslim day of congregated prayer. Today, with Turkey's acceptance of the Gregorian calendar and the institution of Sunday as the weekly holiday, the whole marriage week has been shifted and terminates with the *dini nikah* on Sunday evening.

On Sunday afternoon the parents and relatives of the bride bid her farewell in their home. The groom's side provides a vehicle (formerly a horse-drawn carriage, now a taxi) to transport the bride to the home of the groom's parents. Normally only a sister-in-law or another young female relative or close friend, all of whom must be married, accompanies the bride on this journey, offering her emotional support. The bride's parents and senior kin stay home. The groom's male relatives and friends walk in front of the vehicle and the bride's female peers follow it. When the procession arrives at the groom's home the bride is taken inside where she is welcomed by the groom, his parents and other close relatives. After kissing their right hands she is taken by the groom to the bridal chamber where she remains with her female companion while the *dini nikah* takes place.

The religious marriage ceremony in this district does not require the bride's presence. Commonly the participants include an *imam* or *hoja* (religious leader), the groom, two witnesses, and the *vekalet* (representative of the girl's kin), who normally is one of the groom's male relatives (e.g., father's brother, mother's brother, or older brother). In addition to reading appropriate passages from the *Quran,* the hoja first asks the *vekalet* three times if he gives the girl to the groom. The *vekalet* answers positively three times. Then the *hoja* asks the groom three times if he accepts the bride. He too replies positively three times. This constitutes the ceremony.

Even in this incomplete and skeletal description of this marital *rite de passage* a number of interesting symbols loom large. The bride's farewell at the home of her parents is the rite of separation. When she leaves her parental home she simultaneously exits her former social status and enters the marginal period, an interval during which she is in a state of transition. This state is symbolized by a movement through space in the company of a friend or affine. She has been separated from her blood kin and is encapsuled by the male relatives and friends of the groom in front and by her own female peers at the rear. This transitory state terminates with her arrival at the home of the groom's parents. The bride's entrance into the home of her in-laws and her acceptance by them constitute the rite of admittance into a new social status. Even when post-marital residence is to be neolocal, the bride is transported to the home of the groom's parents. These customs further demonstrate that marriage traditionally involves the transference of a girl from one kin group to another.

The religious marriage ceremony appears to be a sanctification of what has already happened. Neither the presence of the bride nor of one of her blood kin is required. The transference of the bride from one kin group to another is reaffirmed verbally by the groom and one of his own blood kin, who speaks for the girl's side. This reaffirmation is consecrated by readings from the *Quran.*

The Selection of Spouses — Modern

More recently the individual has enjoyed much more freedom in the selection of a spouse. Co-educational schools offer many youths opportunities to meet, become friends, and even to fall in love. The concept of romantic love has from times past held a central place in Middle Eastern poetry. However, only recently, largely because of Western contact through films, magazines, novels, and travel, has love become more generally associated with interpersonal relationships and marriage. This change has not been without serious conflict. As a Turkish professor observes:

> One of the most delicate problems arising from the rapid social and cultural change which Turkey is undergoing at present is that of behavioral norms in interpersonal relationships. The transition from marriage by parental arrangement to one by individual choice, and from social segregation to an intermingling of the sexes, creates endless conflicts. Wherever the old

and the new live side by side, the dilemma of the younger generation reveals itself in an acute form. The quick charge of promiscuity, so easily pronounced in Muslim countries, and the urge for more freedom, often produce severe emotional crises. Due to the absence of generally agreed-upon behavioral standards, the role of peer groups among young people is increasing, while the opposite influence of family bonds and parental authority diminishes [Abadan 1967:92].

The situation described by Abadan mainly applies to Turkey's larger cities. In Susurluk, by contrast, changing attitudes towards marriage have not yet led to any abnormal degree of conflict. Although a number of individual case studies show that youthful love affairs frequently result in conflict between parents and young adults, or between two families, mechanisms within the traditional culture have usually resolved this conflict successfully. Not only does the traditional culture provide modes of reconciliation, it also supplies a "culturally appropriate" way for marriages based on love to come about in the first place. This mechanism is called *kız kaçırma*. While it means both kidnapping and elopement, I refer primarily to elopement when speaking of a "culturally appropriate" mechanism for exercising individual choice in the selection of a spouse. Although kidnapping for purposes of marriage is an old custom in Turkey, it is not a generally approved mode of acquiring a wife. For instance, in Susurluk Sub-province forced abduction commonly leads to violence and the arrest of the guilty party. The penalty has been as high as 15 years imprisonment. Elopement, by comparison, has been at least marginally acceptable. It is the traditional way for a young couple to exercise free choice despite opposition from their elders. If in reality patriarchs always exerted the authority which is theoretically attributed to them, social life might be unbearable for subordinates and the entire social system might break down. In reality, cultural mechanisms do exist which allow subordinates to oppose successfully the will of the patriarchs. Culture also supplies the affronted patriarch with a standard reaction. First he manifests his righteous indignation. Then satisfied that all parties to the affair have acknowledged their violation of his traditional authority and have demonstrated repentance, the patriarch is in a position to be magnanimous. Reconciliation with the girl's father commonly occurs when the the first child is born.

Among Circassians and Georgians elopement is extremely common. It was a traditional means of obtaining a wife back in the Caucasus and its continued practice in this area has contributed to its greater acceptability by Turks.

The elopement procedure can best be illustrated by some actual cases from Susurluk.

The Case of Mehmet

Mehmet is a Georgian, born and raised in a village about 7 miles outside of Susurluk. Below is a paraphrased narration of his elopement in 1950.

I first saw my wife at a Georgian wedding. Though she was the descendant of a Balkan Turk she joined in the folk dancing. This impressed me, for usually only single Circassian and Georgian girls will dance. I danced opposite her for a while and we expressed our interest in each other. During the next year and a half we exchanged notes through friends. Sisters of my friends would take messages to her, brothers of her friends would bring me replies. Every time I went to Susurluk I would pass by her house several times hoping to see her. Although we wanted to marry, our parents would not permit it. Her father was a town official and did not want his daughter to marry a villager. My father wanted me to marry a Georgian. In the face of this opposition we decided to elope. Some of my friends in the village sympathized with me and offered to help. One night, according to plan, my wife slipped out of her house while her parents were sleeping. I met her and together we walked twelve kilometers to a friend's house in my village. The next morning the elders of this household went to my wife's parents to explain what had happened and to assure them of their daughter's honor and safety. They also tried to assuage her father's anger by saying that we were young and in love and couldn't help ourselves, we meant no disrespect to anyone, and so on. Because they were effective, my father-in-law didn't go to the police. But he refused to talk to either of us for several months. At first my own father also showed his anger by ignoring me, but he soon came around.

About a year after our marriage we moved to town. When our first child arrived parents from both sides heaped affection on it. All worked out well in the end.

The Case of Ali

Ali is a 32 year old Manav who owns his own tailor shop in town. At the age of 20 he eloped with a Circassian girl who was also 20 at the time.

I met my wife shortly after she moved to town to live with her older brother and his family. We liked each other and after several meetings I asked her to elope. She consented.

This type of proposal is in accord with Circassian custom. Unlike Turkish girls, Circassian girls are free to discuss marriage with boys. However, no sex play is ever involved. If some *delikanlı* should try to take advantage of the girl, he would be killed.

We decided not to tell our parents because complications might result. For one thing, Circassians always ask for too much bridewealth *(bashlık)*. For another, I didn't think my father would agree. He wanted me to marry a girl from a local, known family. My wife's kin were from the village.

My wife's brother and I were friends and he knew that we might elope, but he kept it to himself. One night, after everyone was asleep, my wife slipped out of her house and met me. We went to my sister's and brother-in-law's home where we spent the night. Next morning my wife's brother went to my home to search for his sister. This is the custom. It was then that my father learned that I was missing too. A little later my brother-in-law went to both sides to explain what had happened and to vouch for the honor and safety of the girl. My wife's side accepted the fact and held no grudge. It was my father who strongly protested. But he soon gave in, and we took up residence in his home. After the normal fifteen day waiting period we had our civil marriage. It took us another month to prepare for the traditional wedding gathering *(düğün)*. Since then we have lived together in harmony.

There are certain ideal rules which constitute an acceptable elopement procedure. The first is that the girl be considered mature enough to give her consent. The second is that she should steal away from her home unnoticed; there should be no confrontation with parents. The third involves refuge in the home of an upstanding family. This family assumes responsibility for the honor and safety of the girl. Preserved honor is of critical importance to the girl's parents. The fourth rule requires prompt (usually next morning) notification of what has happened, and sincere efforts at reconciliation.

Prior to the adoption of the Swiss Civil Code in 1926 a Turkish patriarch's right to demand the return of his daughter was sanctioned by both law and custom. The new code, however, limits the legal sanction by giving girls 18 years of age and over the right to marry without parental consent. I know of several cases in the area where girls used this law very wisely to their advantage. The following episode is a dramatic illustration. A love affair was developing between two young people in a village outside of Susurluk. The girl's parents became alarmed and decided to marry their daughter quickly before this disgrace became public knowledge. As is customary in such cases the family refused to marry their daughter to her lover; instead, they engaged her to a young man whose family was ignorant of the affair. The girl protested, but in vain. She and her lover would have eloped, but she was underage. As part of the legal preliminaries to the proposed marriage, the girl's fiancé took her to the town court to have her legal age increased to 18. As soon as this legality was successfully completed, the girl managed to excuse herself for "a minute". While her fiancé waited on the courthouse steps, she eloped with her lover in a waiting taxi.

Frequently the initiators of elopements are girls, not boys. In a male dominated world, the elopement custom is almost the only means whereby girls,
themselves, can choose a spouse. I had knowledge of several such elopements
while I was in Susurluk. One of them involved a good acquaintance. Upon my
entering his workshop one day his employer jokingly said, "Congratulate
Recep. He got himself a girl!" Upon inquiring, 19 year old Recep told me the
story. About five or six months ago he had attended a nearby village wedding.
There were several girls there, but he claims not to have paid an inordinate
amount of attention to any particular one. About a week later a male friend from
that village brought him greetings from Sunru, a girl who had eyed him during
the celebration. At first he was not sure who she was, but after his friend
supplied a careful description he remembered. He returned the greetings, and in
this way a stream of communication began to flow between the two via friends.
He got to see Sunru once or twice on market days, but they never had a long
conversation. Finally she wrote Recep a letter instructing him to hire a taxi and
drive to the edge of her village late on a certain night. He rounded up two of his
most trusted friends and followed her instructions. With the help of her sisters
Sunru was packed and waiting. As soon as she spotted the headlights she
quietly left her home and joined Recep in the taxi. Together they returned to his
home. Recep had already disclosed his plans to his parents and they agreed to
support him. The family along with a few relatives and friends witnessed the
religious marriage ceremony. This done the couple was united in the eyes of
Allah and the community. The next day news was sent to Sunru's father.
Reportedly he was extremely angry, but powerless to do anything as his
daughter was 19 and had gone voluntarily.

About a month later I attended the couple's civil marriage ceremony. Sunru's
father was still indignant, but Recep was happily married and confident that all
would be forgiven. (Both Recep and Sunru are third generation Balkan Turks.)

Residents of the district and several local newspapers claim that elopements
have been increasing in recent years. This same observation has been made by a
Turkish expert for other areas of Turkey.

> In recent years, as the village began to rise off the subsistence level, as
> improved communication made the villagers increasingly aware of Western
> society, and as village women began to realize that they were not intellectu-
> ally and spiritually man's inferior, the traditional system of marriage began
> to break down. One measure of such a change has been the increased number
> of elopements reported in the village [Robinson 1963:57].

Elopement is part of the traditional culture. It is one type of normative
patterned behavior which can appropriately be employed under certain sets of

conditions. All parties directly involved — the eloping couple, the assisting friends, the indignant parents — have culturally prescribed roles. Everyone knows the behavior appropriate to his role. The whole sequence of events can be seen as a play which is acted out over and over with different performers. What has traditionally been an extremely common form of mate selection among Circassians — i.e., freedom of choice — is increasingly being accepted as the modern way by the district's younger generation. Because the local people have had this traditional cultural mechanism to employ during a period of change, a great deal of potential conflict has been avoided.

Before leaving the topic of mate selection and elopement, the following cases demonstrate that variation from the norm does exist. All took place in villages near Susurluk and were reported in local newspapers.

Gölcuk Village (Jan. 1969): Ahmet, a young man from this village, eloped with a girl under 18. Her family filed a complaint with authorities and had her returned. In spite of several marriage proposals and pleas by Ahmet, the girl's parents decided to marry their daughter to another. This decision angered Ahmet, and several months later during his loved one's wedding he made a daring attempt to kidnap her. However, his efforts were frustrated by wedding guests and the gendarmes were called. Upon arrival they tried to take Ahmet into custody, but this proved no easy feat. In the ensuing struggle Ahmet shot one of the gendarmes in the leg and escaped. At last report he was still being sought.

Karagöz Village (April 1966): Proposals to marry the same girl had been made on the part of three of the village's young men. The girl was very pretty, and the young men were very much in love. This situation created a great deal of tension in the community, and the elders decided something should be done to prevent the violence which generally results from such competition. They concluded that some kind of random selection was the best way to decide the matter without loss of honor to the losers. The names of the young men were written on slips of paper and placed in a bag. In the presence of the village chief and the council of elders the pretty maiden drew one name. All waited anxiously. The lucky male reportedly fainted when he heard the good news.

Köseler Village (Dec. 1967): A boy named Ahmet was in love with a young girl whose father had refused a traditional marriage proposal made on Ahmet's behalf by his widowed mother. However, the young couple waited until the girl was 18, and eloped. With calculated anger the girl's father — who was a widower — abducted Ahmet's mother in retaliation. After the ensuing commotion subsided, the two parties got together and a double ceremony was held.

Çam Village (Aug. 1969): A young man enlisted help from his father and two brothers to kidnap a girl who had repeatedly rejected him. They overpowered her while she was milking goats outside the village and took her to the woods where the young man forced himself on her. (Deprived of her virginity, a girl and her family lose honor and find it difficult to arrange a satisfactory marriage. Thus, they often consent to the proposal of her abductor.) To prevent her from screaming, one of his brothers held his hand tightly over her mouth, accidently causing her to suffocate. The men were arrested by the gendarmes.

Kircalar Village (April 1970): As it is customary for siblings to marry in order of age, a young girl with three older, single sisters found her desire to marry her lover of six years frustrated by her parents. She wanted to elope, but her lover refused, fearing the consequences. One evening after dinner she added sleeping pills to her parents' coffee. When they were sound asleep, she took a prepared bundle of her belongings and ran off to her lover's home. Once inside, she sat down and refused to leave, telling her lover's parents that she wanted to marry their son and if they sent her away after what she had done, her honor would be lost and she would not be worth five cents to anyone. (This less common form of "elopement" is called *"oturakalma"* [sitting-staying].) The final outcome of this case is not known.

The Susurluk newspapers cover only those elopements and kidnappings which result in formal complaints, usually made by the girls' parents. Coverage of these events is close to complete. A content analysis of two local newspapers from 1962 to 1969 produced information on sixteen elopements in the town of Susurluk. Practically all involved either an underage girl or the prior refusal of a proposal from the boy's side. For villages in Susurluk Sub-province 71 elopements and 40 kidnappings were reported. In 44 cases the girl was underage. With respect to ethnicity, two facts are interesting: Yürük and Turkmen males participated in a much higher proportion of kidnappings than their population percentage, and although elopements are common and customary among Circassians, very few result in formal complaints.

During this period the newspapers also carried numerous editorials, headlines, and statements by village officials exclaiming the increased number of elopements in the sub-province. For instance, the press reported on the commotion in one village which had experienced three elopements in a single week. A noisy meeting of the village community was held to discuss the serious situation.

The papers also reported a number of elopements involving underage girls whose parents were not fully convinced of their lovers' intentions. In these instances the parents had the young men arrested and refused to withdraw charges until a civil wedding was conducted in the Susurluk jail.

The trend toward greater individual initiative in the selection of a spouse has been accompanied by a change in the role of the matchmaker. This respected and trusted woman knows all or most of the families in her community, and traditionally parents with a marriageable son or daughter consult her about good families with marriageable offspring. The matchmaker is often enlisted as an interfamilial go-between who plays a prominent role in the marriage proposal and more importantly works to convince the reluctant side that the marriage will be good. My own Turkish landlady — Şükriye — was a matchmaker who claimed to have arranged hundreds of marriages in Susurluk. While discussing these activities with me she noted that since the early sixties, more young men and girls have been secretly coming for help than ever before. Being a good-hearted woman, Şükriye rarely refuses to help young lovers, although this usually embroils her in conflicts with parents who are ignorant of their off-springs' actions. In the past this matchmaker viewed her role as arranging marriages which primarily satisfied families, and secondarily the marrying couples. Now her priorities are often reversed. In addition, instead of acting as a mediator between two families, she now often performs that function between the young couple and their parents.

The following episode occurred in 1970 while I was living in Şükriye's home. It illustrates the important new role the matchmaker plays in a changing socio-cultural and legal setting.

Thirty year old Ahmet was a native of Susurluk who left town for employ-ment as a hospital custodian in the city of Izmir. He wanted to find a wife, and as both his parents were deceased, he relied entirely on Şükriye, Susurluk's beloved matchmaker. Normally, arranging a marriage would not have been too difficult, but Ahmet, a divorcee, was intent on marrying a young virgin. Şükriye approached several families, but they refused to give their daughters because of Ahmet's divorced status. However, a girl of seventeen from one of these families knew Ahmet and was quite willing to marry him. About six months after her father's refusal, Ahmet came to Susurluk and had Şükriye help arrange a secret meeting with the girl, Oya, who was then eighteen. The couple reaffirmed their desire to marry and concluded that elopement was the only way. They decided that Ahmet would return to Izmir, and about a week later Oya would slip away from her family and, accompanied by Şükriye, travel to Izmir to meet him. Oya was anxious to elope soon, because her older brother was about to be discharged from the military. If they waited until he returned home, her chances for escape would be nil. Even if she got away, her brother would surely follow her and attack Ahmet. They had to present both her parents and her brother with a *fait accompli*.

On the appointed afternoon Oya stole away from her home with her birth certificate and identification papers. She wanted to take extra clothes, but was afraid to arouse the neighbors' suspicions. So she wore an extra set of under-wear, but otherwise dressed normally. She went to Şükriye's house, and from there with the old woman they walked through back streets down to the main highway, where they waved down a passing minibus heading for Balıkesir. From that city they bused to Izmir, and then taxied to Ahmet's two room apartment, where the beaming young man met them with profuse gestures of welcome. After a period of excited conversation, Şükriye had Ahmet fetch an *imam* and two witnesses so that the religious marriage ceremony could be conducted.

As Şükriye later explained to me, she had two obligations to Oya, her parents, and the Muslim community: one was to accompany the girl to Izmir, thus ensuring her safety and reputation; the second was to see that the couple was "properly" married before they began living together alone. The civil ceremony could not be conducted without a fifteen day waiting period, but the religious one could be performed immediately. The sacred nuptials were completed that evening, and Şükriye returned to Susurluk the next day.

Upon learning of his daughter's absence, Oya's father suspected what had happened and immediately went to Şükriye's home. Finding that she, too, was gone, he filed a complaint with the police. The next evening Şükriye returned and the police took the 74 year old woman to the station for questioning. They claimed that witnesses had seen Oya and her at the Susurluk bus terminal and demanded to know where she had taken the girl. Easily recognizing this bluff, Şükriye denied any knowledge of Oya's whereabouts. Then the police began to play on her religious sentiments, arguing that the Prophet wants all Muslims to tell the truth and that lying is against the command of Allah. This tack found Şükriye's conscience, but she still would not tell them the full truth, for she feared the police might break in on the newlyweds during their first night alone. So she admitted that she did accompany Oya to Izmir at the girl's request, acting as a guardian. Ahmet met them at the bus terminal and took them to his apartment by taxi. She never learned Ahmet's address, and before they arrived at his place she felt lost. The police released her, but called her back the next day for further questioning. This time Şükriye gave them Ahmet's work address, saying it just turned up at home. This information was immediately forwarded to Izmir, enabling the police there to find the couple and question them.

It was important to establish whether Oya had been coerced in any way, so the police questioned her alone. She insisted before them and later before her parents, that she chose Ahmet of her own free-will and argued that she was eighteen and had the right to make her own "nest." Legally the parents could do nothing, but the prosecutor warned Ahmet to have the civil ceremony performed as soon as possible or he would be arrested for vice.

At last report the couple was legally married and getting on well. Oya was supplementing her husband's meager income with wages she earned as a cleaning woman, and Şükriye felt she had earned *sevap* (Allah's reward for a pious act or good deed) by being instrumental in the establishment of a new family. ''I only did what any good Muslim should.''

Not only are young people exercising more initiative in their marriages, but parents are now stressing achievement rather than ascriptive criteria when evaluating potential spouses. In the past, according to informants, a person was usually assessed in terms of his family, because in a rural agrarian society with few avenues for social mobility, one's ability to rise above his parents was indeed limited. In a modernizing society, the opportunities for advancement — education, industry, new services, and technical trades — are much greater. Thus when evaluating a future husband or son-in-law, individual ability, education, and potential as well as present wealth and family status must be considered.

In an attempt to assess the comparative emphasis on ascriptive and achievement criteria for purposes of selecting a spouse, the married members of the sample were asked what kind of son-in-law they wanted. In addition, bachelors were asked to state the qualities which a potential groom should possess. Practically all respondents said familial and personal reputation and morality were important considerations. However, in addition to naming these very basic criteria, 40.5% of the sample said the potential groom should be ''hard-working'' and 34% said he should be ''educated.'' Notably, 5% simply said that they wanted someone their daughters loved, and only 1% maintained that ethnicity was important.

The married sample was also asked what kind of daughter-in-law they wanted. Again, almost all asserted the importance of personal and familial morality and reputation. The majority added that knowledge of the homemaking arts was essential. About 16% (n = 120) mentioned education as an important consideration, while only two said that they preferred a girl of like ethnicity. A large proportion, about 30%, of the respondents said they wanted someone their sons wanted or loved.

At least two of these responses — education and ''son's choice'' — are clearly modern in terms of the ideal conjugal construct. By an educated girl, most of the respondents meant at least a primary school graduate. As minimal as this level of education may seem to some Westerners, up until a few years ago it was an achievement beyond the realization of most Turkish girls. The fact that public education, especially above the elementary level, has only recently become a practical, realizable goal for most townspeople enables us confidently to assume that this emphasis on the education factor evidences a recent trend toward the greater use of achievement criteria in the evaluation of potential spouses. The ''son's choice'' response evinces the fact that marriage is more and more becoming an undertaking of two individuals.

While the above evidence indicates a deemphasis on ascriptive criteria, a more valid test of change requires an examination of actual behavior. This was done by examining a large number of marriages with respect to ethnicity, an ascriptive element which has traditionally been important to the people of this area. Evidence was gathered by interviewing formally and informally, collecting genealogies, and consulting key informants. The marriages have been divided into three "generations" by age of husband in 1970, and the ethnic units used are those which the members of the community themselves employ: Manav, Balkan Turk, Yürük-Turkman, Circassian, Georgian, Other Province Turk, Albanian, Kurd, Bosnian, Pomak, Nogay, Dagistani, and Crimean Tatar.[3] Because of their special status in the community Gypsies were excluded.

A marriage was included in this test if it met any of the following conditions: 1) at least one spouse was born in Susurluk; 2) the couple was married in Susurluk and presently lives in Susurluk; 3) at least one spouse was born in Susurluk Sub-province and both spouses are living in town. By confining the data to those who meet one of the three conditions we can see the concomitant variation between Susurluk's economic development and increased national integration on the one hand and the proportion of interethnic or mixed marriages on the other. I hypothesized that the proportion of mixed marriages increased with economic modernization. Because the modernization of Susurluk began to accelerate after 1954, there should be a great increase of mixed marriages by males under 35 years of age. The data are contained in Table V.

TABLE V
Susurluk Marriages

Age of Husband	Ethnically Non-Mixed	Ethnically Mixed	Totals
18-35	71 (54.0%)	61 (46.0%)	132 (100.0%)
36-50	203 (72.5%)	77 (27.5%)	280 (100.0%)
51 +	120 (91.6%)	11 (8.4%)	131 (100.0%)
Totals	394 (72.6%)	149 (27.4%)	543 (100.0%)

The results strongly support the hypothesis. The proportion of mixed marriages has increased steadily over the generations to the point where today almost one of every two marriages is mixed. As a result of the town's economic expansion and the large peasant migration to town, today members of the various ethnic groups find themselves working and living side by side, sharing the same dreams for material improvement, and committed to the same means of their attainment. This situation has functioned to reduce preexisting social barriers.

Numerically most interethnic marriages take place between Manavs and Balkan Turks, the two most numerous groups both in town and in the district. Unlike Circassians, Georgians, Dagistanis, Arnavuts, etc., both Manavs and Balkan Turks identify themselves exclusively as sedentary Turks. There is less social distance between Manavs and the descendants of the 19th century Balkan Turks whose families have lived in town for three generations or more than between any other two groups.

The Marriage Ceremony — Modern

Social and legal changes have not only affected the selection of spouses, but the form of the marriage ceremony as well. The traditional marriage rituals, which consecrated and publicly announced the creation of an interfamilial alliance, were necessary for a morally and socially acceptable marriage. However, with the adoption of the new civil code and other attempts at secularization, the traditional marriage ceremony lost its legal standing. In its place a brief civil ceremony in which a government official marries the couple in the presence of two witnesses, has become compulsory. [4] In contrast to the traditional religious marriage ritual, the civil ceremony requires the presence and freely expressed consent of both the bride and the groom. Not only are kin group symbols absent, but in practice the parents of the marrying couple rarely attend the ceremony. This ceremony must precede any other marriage ceremony. That is, it is illegal for an *imam* or any other person to conduct a marriage ceremony involving a couple who has not already been legally married by the government.

But law and practice often differ. In effect, the secular government of the new Turkish Republic endeavored to legislate a morality which was, in many respects, foreign to its citizens. The group of Turkish and foreign scholars who evaluated the reception of the Swiss Civil Code in 1955 concluded that the new civil marriage ceremony had not gained general acceptance as a mechanism for morally and socially sanctioning marriage. This lack of acceptance was especially prominent in villages and small towns, where the vast majority of the population lives. A Turkish law professor who compared the number of civil (legally recorded) marriages in Turkey during the 1950s with the number of marriages in other countries of similar population, concluded that less than one-half of Turkish marital unions for that period had been conducted legally (Timur 1957). Most marriages conformed to tradition, not reform.

The reasons for this lack of acceptance are multiple. In addition to traditional socio-cultural considerations, there are many practical problems of administration:

1) As the first step in the official marital process a couple must apply to the competent official and submit their birth certificates. Generally such certificates are possessed only by those whose parents are entered in the civil registers and who have their own certificates. Consequently, many couples necessarily become involved in the long process of obtaining certificates for parents and even grandparents.

2) Because villagers often registered children five to ten years after birth in order to evade the road tax and postpone their military service, twenty year old men are commonly registered as less than fifteen, which makes them too young to marry legally.

3) Men and women, who want to marry, must undergo a thorough physical examination. But since most doctors reside in cities, villagers find it difficult to meet this requirement. Besides, young men disapprove of male doctors examining their fiancées.

However, on the basis of personal observation and numerous interviews I believe that the great majority of marriages in the sub-province of Susurluk are legally registered. I knew of a few exceptions, but they usually involved very young couples and important practical considerations. For example, in two different cases one of the spouses was attending middle school. Because regulations require students to terminate their studies upon marriage, the parents decided to postpose registration until after the completion of their children's education.

Peasant women impressed me with their understanding of the law. One 75 year old illiterate woman, for instance, told me that the civil marriage amounted to a financial guarantee. If the husband dies, his wife and children automatically inherit his estate. If he is negligent in his duties, his wife can sue for support. If he ejects his wife, she can get alimony. According to her no wise woman should marry without it.

Certain conditions have facilitated the acceptance of the civil marriage in this sub-province. With improved transportation, most villagers find it comparatively convenient to go to town. On market day they can complete the preliminary marriage formalities and still have time to conduct their normal buying and selling. The government doctor, being an understanding person, rarely subjects female applicants to a complete medical examination. The municipal marriage hall, where most of the town's civil ceremonies are conducted, is fairly attractive by local standards and contains chairs for over 100 spectators. The town's marriage official comes from a well respected local family and makes every effort to add dignity to the event. On occasion he even agrees to conduct the ceremony in private homes.

In an attempt to gain further data on townsmen's attitudes toward the two rituals, the married members of the sample were asked the following question: When marrying your children, in your opinion, which ceremony (ceremonies) should be performed? Bachelors were asked to specify which ceremony (ceremonies) should be performed at their own marriages. Table VI contains their responses.

TABLE VI
Preferred Types of Marriage Ceremonies

	Single Men		Married Men	
	Number	per cent	Number	per cent
Religious only	3	5.4	19	15.2
Civil only	27	49.2	33	26.4
Both religious and civil	25	45.4	73	58.4
Totals	55	100.0	125	100.0

These answers require some elaboration. Most of the nineteen husbands who answered "religious only" were born in villages and had attained very low levels of education. This response decreased sharply with rising educational levels. Of the combined samples, 88% claimed that the civil ceremony should be performed. But probably most striking is the fact that about half of the bachelors and one in four of the husbands contended that a civil ceremony alone is sufficient for a morally and socially acceptable marriage. These attitudes indicate a trend toward full acceptance of the civil ceremony and a gradual secularization of the wedding process.

Inheritance

Because a social complex is more or less integrated we should expect other changes in the kinship system to be concomitant with alterations in the ideal household structure and the post-marital residence rule. The traditionally practiced form of inheritance in which sons received more than daughters was functionally consistent with the traditional patrilocal extended household in a simple agrarian economy. Because married daughters left the household, the ownership of any family lands which they might inherit could easily fall into the hands of strangers. To prevent such an occurrence, sons usually received the land, while daughters inherited a portion of the movable property. Although Islamic law entitled a daughter to one-half of what a son receives, in actual practice she generally got far less.

During my field work in the sub-province of Susurluk, I found villagers keenly aware of their daughters' inheritance rights under the new law. However, they employed a variety of flexible means to fulfill this obligation. Some claimed to give their daughters a share of the family wealth in the form of a trousseau upon marriage. Other villagers explained that upon the death of a patriarch the entire estate normally goes to the mature sons, who then carry the obligation of supporting their mother and younger siblings and of eventually paying their sisters' shares out of income and movable property. Villagers generally stressed need and practicality, rather than equality.

Legal authorities in Susurluk believe most townspeople accord with the spirit, if not the letter of the law. The townsmen surveyed support this opinion. When members of the adult sample were asked how they thought a man with both a son and a daughter should divide or bequeath his estate, the vast majority (88.4%) said the estate should be divided equally, explaining that there should be no discrimination between offspring on the basis of sex.

The townsmen who favored the son gave the traditional reasons for their position. They contended that a daughter leaves the paternal household and becomes her husband's obligation. By contrast, a son needs the family wealth to support his elderly parents or to set up his own household. I found this reasoning more common in villages, where it is functionally consistent with a simple agrarian economy in which the family is often the unit of production as well as consumption, and the paternal lands represent the most important capital good. However, a modernizing, industrializing town or city represents a markedly different kind of situation. Most families' incomes consist primarily of wages and salaries. A major portion of their wealth is in the form of cash, household furnishings, homes, or income-producing real estate. The nature of this wealth facilitates its division.

Polygyny

Although Western influence during the late nineteenth century helped create an aversion to the institution of polygyny among Turkey's urban elite, it failed to penetrate to the small town and village levels where men continued to exercise this prerogative with approbation. Estimates of the proportion of polygynous marriages in rural areas during the present century range between 10% and 2%. According to a study sponsored by the Turkish Ministry of Justice in 1942, almost all polygynous marriages involved two wives, and the two most common reasons given for these bigamous unions were need for another female helper and the suspected sterility of the first wife.[5] A third reason for polygyny was the institution of the levirate or widow inheritance by married kin of the deceased.

The belief that wives must be able to satisfy the sexual desires of their husbands and provide them with children is still common throughout Turkey, as it is in much of the world. During my stay in Susurluk, a popular Turkish newspaper gave front page coverage to the story of a 42 year old mother of six and grandmother of five who found her 47 year old husband a younger second wife because she herself could no longer engage in the sex act. Using this article to stimulate responses from local people I learned that sentiments fell into two major categories. The more traditional position was that a wife who has lost her ''womanhood'' should either allow her husband to take a second wife or leave him so that he may remarry legally. By contrast, my more educated informants argued that a man whose wife had already given him children and years of sexual companionship had no right to either a divorce or a second wife.

In general I found that today polygyny is practiced rarely and regarded unfavorably by most townspeople. Polygynous marriages did exist before the new code was adopted, and elderly informants claim that even after the new law a few such unions were secretly entered and socially approved. But in recent decades monogamy has become the ideal norm.

Divorce

Members of the legal profession in Susurluk assured me that divorce, especially by the husband, is no longer an easy matter. The new code recognizes only six grounds for divorce: (1) adultery; (2) plot against life, grave assaults, and insults; (3) crime or dishonorable life; (4) desertion; (5) mental infirmity; and (6) incompatibility. According to local authorities, women have been more successful in finding acceptable grounds to sue for divorce than men. In additon, one legal expert notes that ''the Turkish courts have developed the practice of allowing the wife petitioner considerable maintenance even if she is the guilty party'' (Belgesay 1957:50).

This may represent an attempt by the courts to compensate for certain elements in traditional Turkish culture. The dominant, authoritarian male customarily has enjoyed the right to verbally or physically abuse his spouse. In regard to sex, a marked double standard exists. While premarital and extra marital sex are strictly taboo for women, they have been customarily tolerated for men. A wife can easily arouse gossip and scorn merely by talking with another man. It is no coincidence that one of the most common grounds for divorce in this area is adultery.

According to local informants, newspaper articles, and editorials, another common reason for divorce — incompatibility — largely derives from family conflicts over money or the lack of it. It appears the new economic structure, characterized by wages and a cash economy has contributed to a situation where family income and its disposition have an increasingly strong bearing on marital success.

Males still exercise their traditional, though not legal, right to eject their wives from the home. But today, unlike previous times, wives can, and many do, seek recourse in the courts. Local lawyers and court officials claim that women initiate about as many court cases involving family matters as men.

Summary

The traditional relationship between kinship and the community in Susurluk can be described in terms of a simple two level model. One level is comprised of a group of patrilocal, but female-centered households — each a distinct socio-economic unit. On the second level these households are firmly tied into the larger community by a series of male dominated social networks. Each household is an individual domain with its patriarch acting as king and minister of external affairs. The system is characterized by a marked division of labor by sex and functions in a technologically simple agricultural and limited market economy.

However, with change in the community's economic and occupational structure, increased integration with Turkey's modern urban centers, closer contact with the West, and the adoption of a Western civil code, alterations in this system were inevitable. Because of the new economic structure, very few extended families continue to be both units of production and consumption. This, along with ideological influences, has contributed to the nucleation of the household and the dissolution of the extended family as an ideal goal, with the further consequence that "participant" kinship is becoming increasingly confined to the nuclear family. There appears to be an intensification of internal household relations, with the frequency of consultation between husbands and wives on important decisions increasing while the frequency of consultation with elderly kin outside the household is decreasing. Aided by the new family law and the example of the urbanized official class families, local women are emerging from the confines of their homes and the barrier of masculine protectionism. They are making more of their own decisions and are participating more in the social and economic life of the community. Male attitudes concerning the employment of women outside the home and the kinds of occupations which they can successfully perform are generally favorable to further change.

The social norms prescribed by Turkey's new family law are gaining wide acceptance. In many small communities, like Susurluk, which were once considered the strongholds of conservatism, civil ceremonies have become important social events (see Magnarella 1973). Announcements are made, invitations are distributed, and the official marriage halls are often filled to overflowing with guests and spectators. Not only have civil weddings become important social events, they represent a manifestation of a new morality in the process of creation. However, it is not the law alone which is responsible for this.

Since World War II the Turkish government, the Army, and the many government industries have been quite strict in their requirement that civil marriage certificates be produced before employees and their families can qualify for medical aid, dependents' allowances, financial assistance, and other benefits. There are also provisions in the tax laws giving relief to legally married taxpayers. Factors such as these have made observance of the family law a practical necessity for many citizens. Many villagers and townsmen regard the marriage of their daughters without a civil ceremony as a form of disfranchisement. Another significant development is the extent to which young people have become more aware of the family law and use it to their advantage.

Change has also involved the process of individualization — the emergence of the individual from the larger kin group as evidenced by the increased exercise of individual initiative in the selection of a spouse and the greater emphasis on achievement criteria in the evaluation of potential spouses. This has further contributed to the progressive elimination of sociocultural barriers, which formerly separated the district's various ethnic groups, and has promoted a closer integration of the community.

The Swiss Family Law was more appropriate for the type of family systems found in Western industrial countries. However, the law is gaining acceptance in Turkey because the structure of Turkish society is changing. Under the impact of new industry, and westernizing economic, governmental, and educational systems, the traditional ethno-religious norms governing intra-familial relations are being challenged. There is an increased stress on individual equality, individual achievement, and individual physical and social mobility. These social, cultural, and economic changes are helping to promote a greater acceptance of the new law, and in turn this acceptance is facilitating further change.

Notes to Chapter VI
Law, Kinship, and Society

[1] In the area of women's legal rights the Turks have since progressed beyond the Swiss in some respects. For example, while Turkish women received the right to vote in municipal elections in 1930 and national elections in 1934, Swiss women did not receive similar rights until 1971.

[2] Commenting on two Central Anatolian villages Stirling writes: "The fact that a woman's relation with her son is more important to her than that with her husband, and that a man's relation with his mother is more important, as a rule, than that with his wife reflects the stress in the society on procreation as the end of relations between sexes, rather than sexual attraction and satisfaction" (1965:115).

[3] For the purpose of this comparison each person was assigned the same ethnicity as his father, for two reasons: first, this is socio-culturally valid as people here are identified in terms of their

fathers primarily; and second, to do otherwise may have biased the test in favor of the hypothesis. For example, if a person has a Balkan Turk father and a Circassian mother, unless he marries someone of the same ethnic background (which has low probability) his marriage would have been treated as a mixed one. This practice would have compounded ''mixed'' marriages over the three generations.

[4] In 1925 Turkey's urban elitist controlled central government attempted to legislate a complete change in the traditional wedding celebration also. A law was passed limiting the groom's bridal gifts to two dresses and restricting feasting to one day. It also forbade the public exhibition of the trousseau and the employment of dancing girls. The legislators charged that high wedding expenses often prevented marriages, thereby driving Turkish youth to elopement, illicit relationships, and other immoral activities. This legislation was repealed on May 8, 1967. Opponents to the law claimed that it unconstitutionally restricted personal freedom and proved unenforceable because the practices it proscribed are deeply engrained in Turkish village society (*Daily News* 9 May 1967:1).

[5] The search for sterility remedies in this area and throughout Turkey is perpetual. For instance, during the time of this field work a leading national newspaper carried the story of a 70 year old man who reportedly regained his sexual potence by eating carob beans (St. John's bread, *certonia siliqua*). The news caused a stir in the market place. One merchant in Balıkesir, who normally sells only three sacks of carob beans a week, claimed that within a week after the story appeared in the press he had sold 50 sacks at a price 30% to 40% above normal.

CHAPTER VII

Politics and Society

Because politics in Susurluk have been influenced and often determined by events on the national level, this chapter begins with a brief discussion of Turkey's recent political history.

National Politics

Under the charismatic leadership of Kemal Ataturk, the Turkish Republic was constructed on the crumbled foundations of the multi-national Ottoman Empire, which had suffered dissolution and partition after World War I. Mustafa Kemal (later Mustafa Kemal Ataturk) — the most impressive military officer in the defeated Ottoman army — refused to surrender Turkey to the will of foreign powers. His inspiring personality and unswerving determination revitalized the defeated Turks into a military force that drove the Greek occupation forces from Anatolia and secured an independent Turkish homeland. Kemal then embarked on the ambitious project of remaking the country into a modern nation-state in the image of the leading European powers.

This challenge required the creation of a new identity and symbol of loyalty for the peoples of Turkey. Unlike many of the new African leaders who must educate their citizenry to transfer loyalties from particularistic social units, like tribes, to a very general one, like a state, in Turkey Ataturk had to achieve the opposite. Loyalty and identity had to be shifted from the general to the particular — from a wide multi-national Islamic-Ottoman Empire to a uni-national, secular Republic. This entailed the attainment of a new socio-cultural and political integration on the basis of secular values and norms which alienated many people and undermined their sacred symbols of collective identity. According to the program of Ataturk's Republican People's Party (RPP), "religion, being a matter of conscience, [was to be] separated from the affairs of this world and the state as well as from politics" (as quoted in Rustow 1957:86). Given the pervasiveness of Islam in Turkey, this goal was revolutionary, if not unrealistic.

Ataturk accused Islamic-Ottoman institutions and culture of responsibility for the fall of the Empire and the miserable conditions of the Turks, and he decreed that the new Turkey would be based on the principles of nationalism, secularism, statism, populism, and reformism (see Karpat 1959). Among his many revolutionary acts were numerous secular reforms: the abolition of the Caliphate and Sultanate, the disestablishment of Islam as the State religion, the closing of the religious schools and brotherhoods, the replacement of Islamic law with European codes, the abolition of the Faculty of Theology, the replacement of Arabic script with Latin letters, and the prohibition of the fez — the customary Muslim headgear. In addition, it was required that the Muslim call to prayer be made in Turkish, rather than the traditional Arabic, and Istanbul's Aya Sofya mosque — a symbol of Muslim victory over Christian Byzantium — was converted into a museum, while at the same time numerous mosques throughout the country were turned over either to the RPP for political uses or to the military for temporary barracks and supply depots. New mosque construction was strongly discouraged and in some places prohibited.

From 1923 until his death in 1938, Kemal Ataturk ruled Turkey through a single party system as a benevolent but firm dictator, who allowed no opposition to stand in the way of his reforms. He had an indeterminate number of *hoja*s (religious leaders) hung for preaching against the hat law (G. L. Lewis 1965:94), and two experiments with multi-party politics "failed" when he quickly lost patience with opposition that he felt only impeded the country's rate of progress.

Ataturk's successor, Ismet Inonu, continued the secularist policies with equal vigor, and for numerous reasons, including the desire to fulfill Ataturk's ultimate ambition — the establishment of Western democracy in Turkey — Inonu announced in 1945 that he would permit another experiment in the formation of opposition parties. Dissident members of the RPP, who opposed the government's rigid stance on religion and the economy, immediately organized the Democrat Party (DP). This new party found support among businessmen disgruntled by strict wartime economic controls, consumers suffering from the high cost of living, Christians and Jews who had to pay a discriminatory tax *(varlık vergisi)* in 1942, elitist groups whose ambitions were not being promoted by the RPP, and millions of malcontent peasants who resented the RPP's neglect of agriculture and suppression of religious expression (Rustow 1957).

As expected, however, the rigged election of 1946 deprived these people of an opportunity to register their complaints. After over twenty years of strict compliance with RPP directives, the government officials and bureaucrats responsible for the election's supervision could not remain neutral: many acted as though their patriotic duty was to ensure an RPP victory. To correct this situation, parliament passed a new election law which required secret ballots, public accounting of votes, equal broadcast time for each party, and the supervision of elections by the judiciary. In 1950, the first open and honest election of the Turkish Republic gave the DP a resounding victory. Surprisingly for many, the Republicans honored the will of the people by stepping down. "Turkey thus became perhaps the only country in modern history in which an autocratic regime peacefully gave up the reins of government" (Tachau 1972:382).

The Democrats created an atmosphere of religious tolerance by allowing the Arabic call to prayer and including Islamic instruction in the regular primary school curriculum as a voluntary course. Religious expression, long forced to remain secret or dormant, asserted itself openly once again. Nevertheless, neither the DP nor the majority of Turks favored the reestablishment of a religious state; most people preferred a combination of secularism in government and religious freedom in society. The DP accepted Ataturk's principles and acted against religious extremism.

The political divisions manifested during Turkey's multi-party era grew out of the country's dichotomous socio-economic structure. Until 1950 the RPP existed as a fascist-like totalitarian party, which claimed to be the supreme instrument of society. It was and continues to be an elitist organization whose leaders doubt that a party responsive to the people can solve the country's pressing economic and socio-cultural problems. The RPP rested on a supportive alliance of urban elite, civil bureaucrats, military leaders, and large landowners, who through their affiliation with the party were able to reenforce their domination over the peasantry, who together with the urban poor comprised about 75% to 80% of the country's population.

The DP, having found support among the disinherited and the RPP's own disenchanted, took a number of social and economic measures during its period of rule (1950-60) which altered this dichotomy. It gave more attention and benefits to rural areas: roads, electric projects, farm credits, aid for building construction, new industry (such as the sugar refinery in Susurluk), and more educational and medical facilities. These contributed to the villagers' and townpeoples' new capacity for political awareness and involvement, and their greater integration with the country. In the cities, DP support for private industry and commerce facilitated the development of an urban elite that rivaled or surpassed the high bureaucratic and military echelons in terms of wealth and status. Accompanying these changes and compounding them were an economic boom and inflation that favored many DP supporters, but penalized people living on fixed salaries, such as civil bureaucrats and military officers.

Turkish citizens who profited from the DP's socio-economic measures and/or who valued the greater freedom of religious expression returned the party to power in 1954 and 1957. These events served to increase frustration and resentment among RPP supporters who were suffering from withdrawal of status.

To compensate for their impotence at the election polls, the frustrated urban supporters of the RPP began expressing their anti-government sentiments in the press and through public demonstrations. However, the political tradition that the DP inherited from the RPP was intolerant of vigorous and vociferous opposition. Following the model of the previous regime, the DP became repressive: it silenced the opposition press and legislated against public anti-government demonstration. By legal definition, most adverse expression became criminal.

Significantly, unlike former Generals Ataturk and Inonu, the DP leaders — Prime Minister Menderes and President Bayar — had never been professional military men, and the period of DP rule is the only time in modern Turkish history when a general has not occupied at least one of the two highest governmental offices. This fact contributed further to the military's lack of confidence in the DP. In 1960, when the government increasingly relied on the army to quell the "illegal riots" of political protest by university students in Ankara and Istanbul, the military leadership decided that civilian politics had failed.

Headed by General Cemal Gursel, the military carried out a bloodless coup, arresting Democrats holding national office and replacing most Democrats in municipal offices with either military officers or RPP members. During the ensuing period of martial law, the military permanently outlawed the DP and purged its own officer ranks of DP sympathizers. Former DP Prime Minister Menderes was accused of violating the constitution, and after litigation he was condemned to death along with his Foreign and Finance Ministers. A new constitution was prepared, containing safeguards against political extremism and protecting Ataturk's reforms, "which aim at raising Turkish society to the level of contemporary civilization" (Article 153).

During this period of purge and reform a cleavage developed within the ruling junta between officers who wanted an extended suspension of democratic procedures and those who favored a return to democratic politics as soon as practicable. The latter faction prevailed, and the 1961 multi-party elections resulted in a coalition government and the selection of General Gursel as Turkey's new President.

The early sixties witnessed the birth of numerous parties that vied for the support of former Democratic voters. Eventually, most of the DP men who were allowed to reenter politics reorganized under the banner of the Justice Party (JP), which soon became heir to the DP. On the basis of broad support it won electoral victories in 1965 and 1969.

This new political force is directed by moderate men who favor individual liberties and private enterprise. Unlike their DP ancestors, they realize the necessity of sound economic planning and lack a personality cult. They are mostly people from small towns and villages who have taken advantage of educational and economic opportunities during the DP era. One political analyst has concluded that the JP's popularity and representativeness qualify it as the first truly grass-roots party in the Middle East (Sherwood 1967).

By contrast, the RPP has been forced to continue its role as minority opposition party. Hoping to win support among radicalizing elements of the urban intelligentsia, it altered its political idology in 1965 and moved "left-of-center." This new orientation alienated moderate-conservative elements within the party and among the general voting public.

Throughout the 1960s deteriorating relations with the United States, deriving largely from the Johnson administration's handling of the Greco-Turkish conflict over Cyprus, facilitated the spread of left-wing radicalism in Turkey. Violence between right and left elements became frequent in labor strikes, student protests, and urban demonstrations, and in 1971 the senior military commanders, who had maintained an authoritarian eye on events, became convinced that direct intervention was again necessary to stabilize the country. The commanders executed a "coup by communique" when they called for the resignation of the JP government and the formation of a non-partisan coalition. They also disbanded the Turkish Workers Party (a Marxist organization) and arrested many of its leaders. While the JP continued to be the majority party in parliament, real political power was once again in the hands of the military.

The founders of the Turkish Republic planned to bring the country to a state of Western democracy through the authoritarian rule of a single party, but their long period of unrivaled political control set a contradictory precedent. Subsequent multi-party politics became the kind of zero-sum game played by leaders of many new African states in which a win all or lose all attitude prevails (see W. A. Lewis 1965). While occupying the seat of power both the RPP and the DP resorted to extreme measures to maintain their positions. The political system's corrective mechanism has been the military, rather than the voting booth. True democracy requires all citizens — urban and military elites, intellectuals, bureaucrats, businessmen, laborers, and peasants — to accept willingly the results of fair elections. It further requires the party in power to periodically renew its popular mandate by resubmitting to fair elections. Turkey has yet to achieve true democracy, instead its government is still characterized by the authoritarian means to this desired end.

Susurluk Mayors and Local Politics

Throughout the period of RPP dominance (1923-50) Susurluk mayors rep-

Voter and election observers

resented the establishment: all were RPP members, and with one exception all were wealthy Manav landowners married to Manav women. The exception was a wealthy bachelor of Albanian extraction, who worked as town clerk and succeeded to the office of mayor upon the death of his predecessor in 1944. All mayors resided in either Han or Orta quarter and had higher educations than the average townsman: two were primary school graduates, two were high school graduates, and one had received a degree in theology from Darülfünün Shahane (later known as Istanbul University). This last mentioned mayor had entered office during the late Ottoman period and continued to serve during the early years of the Republic. According to elderly informants, most of these mayors were popular men, who had the town's interests at heart even though they may have used their office and party influence to protect or improve their already dominant positions as landowners.

During this period communications through government channels flowed one way, with local officials transmitting orders from the leaders in Ankara to the townspeople. While the townspeople may have been satisfied with their mayors, they developed a bitterness toward the central government and the RPP. Among their complaints were the government's expropriation of local mosques for the military; the arrogance and high-handedness of appointed governors and assistant governors; the arbitrary and ruthless behavior of the gendarmery; and the special privileges enjoyed by some party influentials. As one local craftsman stated: "The people of this town suffered a great deal under one-party rule, especially during the First World War. While bread, food, and fuel were strictly rationed for the poor, rich party members received the same in abundance. People here don't forget." Nor did they forget. When offered a choice in the 1950 election, most townspeople voted for the newly organized Democrats, as did much of the country.

The first DP mayor, like his predecessors, was a wealthy Manav, but he differed from them in his resentment of the RPP and its anti-religious stance. He was a pious man, respected for his moral character and generosity: he made large donations in land and money to such town projects as the construction of mosques, schools, and the hospital. In 1954 he stepped aside, and the people elected another Democrat.

Although the new mayor and his wife were Manavs, this man represented a departure from tradition in two respects: he was a tailor of moderate means, and he resided in Burhaniye — one of the town's ethnically mixed expansion quarters. Consequently, both the Manav "blue bloods" and the town's common people could identify with him. During his tenure and the national rule of the DP, government channels opened to a two-way communication flow; for the first time local officials were relaying community demands to Ankara, and the town experienced an economic boom: a major new highway, the sugar refinery, farm and small business loans, government aid to education, new banks, and an improved water supply represented some of its major gains. But local euphoria was abruptly ended by events in Ankara and Istanbul.

The 1960 coup came as a shock; most townspeople viewed it as an unjustified violation of their democratic rights. The junta deposed the popular mayor and replaced him with a new Ataturk — a paternal army colonel, determined to transform Susurluk into *the* model town. The officer held extraordinary powers, as he simultaneously occupied the positions of mayor and assistant governor during a period of military rule. His grand design consisted of three major objectives: the construction of a new town square with a giant statue of Ataturk, where the community could gather periodically to perform patriotic rituals; the construction of a town park — a beautiful showplace with flowers, shrubbery, and strolling paths, where whole families could promenade as they do in "civilized" countries; and the establishment of an annual holiday that would permanently infect the citizenry with a spirit of development and improvement that would ultimately earn the town and himself immortality.

To raise money for his projects, the officer imposed an "Ataturk Statue tax" on cinema tickets and sold several pieces of town property. He decided to locate the park in Yeni (New) Quarter on a tract of land already functioning as a cemetery, that contained the remains of previous generations and the grave of an unknown holy man *(dede)* over whom local believers lit candles and prayed for health and good fortune. Despite local protests, the officer ordered townspeople to transfer the remains of their ancestors to a newer cemetery on a hill to the town's west. He then had the unclaimed remains deposited in a common grave on the same hill. To the satisfaction of the town's "enlightened" elements, the bones of the holy man were intentionally obliterated and lost.

With money collected and preliminary preparations completed, he ordered local contractors to complete the square and park by June 24, 1961 — the date of the town's first "Development and Improvement Holiday" *(Onarim Bayrami,* which many townspeople sarcastically referred to as *Onlarin Bayrami* or "Their Holiday"). He proudly invited members of parliament and the region's generals, governors, and mayors to the planned holiday celebrations, and paternally instructed townspeople to clean up their homes, shops, and restaurants and greet the holiday guests with smiling faces and sweet tongues. This was the initiation of a new era. "By 1970," he predicted, "everyone will have heard of Susurluk!" To mark the new epoch and provide the people with a daily reminder of their assigned mission, a local RPP member launched a newspaper, christened "24 June" *(24 Haziran).*

Under the officer's command, the contractors labored at a quick cadence and by June 22 they were near finished. On the eve of the new holiday, the town's anxious anticipation was met with an unexpected and tumultuous downpour that caused the Han River — ordinarily an innocuous brook that gurgles through the town past the site of the new park — to become transformed into a deluge, flooding lower sections of town, but especially the park with up to three feet of water. While the baffled officer viewed the catastrophe in disbelief, the pious visitors to the grave of the now lost holy man nodded knowingly that a just punishment had been dispensed.

The holiday celebration was held three weeks later, but the excitement had vanished, and today, so too, has the memory. By 1969 only a few close friends of the newspaper owner could recall why their town's daily is named "24 June."

During the years immediately following the 1960 coup other incidents occurred in Susurluk Sub-province that evince the political sentiments of many townsmen and villagers. The following were abstracted from the town paper favoring the RPP which began publication in 1961. On Sept. 18, 1961, the day after former DP Prime Minister Menderes was hanged, a townsman was arrested for speaking disrespectfully of General Gursel — leader of the ruling junta — and summarily received a two month sentence. Shortly thereafter, a group of former DP supporters began a successful campaign to financially aid the Menderes family. On Oct. 24, 1961 — the holiday commemorating the birth of the Republic — eight store owners were fined for not flying Turkish flags.

Throughout the 1961 political campaign townspeople gave warm welcomes to former DP members and tumultuous applause to any speaker who dared intimate his dissatisfaction with the ruling junta or the political trials. Meanwhile, in several villages RPP posters were smeared with animal excrement. During 1961-62 several peasant groups complained about the "revolution" chiefs assigned to their villages by the military, and petitioned for their replacement with elected men. These petitions were subsequently denied.

But the ultimate expression of dissent was recorded in July of 1961 when the majority of townspeople and villagers rejected the new constitution in a special referendum, despite its strong support by local RPP leaders and the ruling military, who later interpreted its national acceptance as a vote of confidence in the revolution. With 81.1% participation, the Susurluk Sub-provincial vote was 7,559 "in favor" and 9,865 "opposed." In the reigning atmosphere of military rule, this act required substantial courage.

These and other events of a similar genre have been followed by limited and unenthusiastic town participation in the annual May 27 celebrations commemorating the 1960 revolution. On this day, as the town's RPP supporters gather in the new town square before Ataturk's statue to observe the ritual drills of an army unit and listen to the patriotic poetry of school children, the majority of townspeople go about their ordinary business. Hoping to stir up public spirit for the occasion, the soldiers spend the remainder of the holiday futilely marching up and down and around the town, singing patriotic songs and yelling out cadences until they are hoarse and exhausted.

Not until three and one-half years after the coup were townspeople and city dwellers allowed to elect their own municipal officials. The 1963 Justice Party candidate for Susurluk mayor had the backing of former DP members. He, like his DP predecessor, was a common man — a sugar refinery employee whose Turkish grandparents had immigrated from the Balkans. The RPP candidate was also the descendant of Balkan Turks, but his family had earned wealth and success in animal husbandry, and his membership on the board of the small business loan cooperative provided an additional source of economic power.

Although both men made the same, usual campaign promises: improved park, streets, sanitation, and municipal facilities; more and better drinking water; and fair hearing of all citizen complaints; the JP candidate won by better than a two to one margin. But an unexpected turn of events denied the people their choice: immediately after the election, the RPP filed a protest, claiming the JP candidate was unqualified because of his criminal record. The election board (members of the judiciary) upheld the protest, thereby giving the office to the candidate with the second highest vote — the Republican.

This decision stunned most voters. They all knew their candidate had been charged with a minor discrepancy in bookkeeping at the sugar refinery when he violated regulations by allowing a peasant farmer to take animal fodder with the promise to pay within the next few days. During the interim, the irregularity was discovered in a surprise audit, and factory regulations required that the candidate be taken to court where he received a small suspended sentence. Because townspeople understood the circumstances of the situation, the candidate had lost no respect; in fact, his consideration for the peasant farmer at the risk of personal loss was admired. Prior to the election, as required by law, the JP had submitted the names of its candidates to the election board, which then approved them. Now, after the election, the board reversed itself. The townspeople reconciled themselves to what they regarded as another example of the RPP-bureaucracy alliance.

The 13 JP men, who, along with 7 Republicans, made up the new town council, instituted a series of actions calculated to make political life difficult for the new RPP mayor. They boycotted the first town council meeting, leaving the Republicans without a quorum. At the next meeting they elected as assistant mayor, a JP councilman who had designs on the mayoral office and who ran for the post in the next election. They succeeded in removing an RPP leader from the post of town attorney, and in the Feb. 1964 town budget meeting, with a 10 to 9 vote, they reduced the mayor's salary from TL 750 a month to TL 350 a month. These events stirred up a good deal of controversy with the RPP paper running daily editorials attacking JP councilmen. In the end, all the changes stood, except the salary reduction which the assistant governor, who reviews the budget before it becomes effective, denied.

The post-coup period was bitter for local Democrats, but beneficial to Republicans who wanted to reconsolidate their political strength and diminished status. In 1963, during one of the national coalitions headed by Prime Minister Inonu — RPP President — the government announced that it would establish a small business loan cooperative *(Esnaf ve Kefalet Koop.)* in Susurluk which would be instrumental in helping small businessmen expand, invest in new machinery, etc. at interest rates below those of banks. The cooperative's local board of directors and voting membership was made up almost exclusively of Republicans, and they have remained so down to the present (1970). Over the years townsmen have frequently complained of the Cooperative's partiality for RPP members, and some joke that it is wise to feign support for Inonu when applying for loans. This cooperative has had the consequence of increasing some Republicans' economic power and of compounding the town's political divisions.

Town Republicans also took advantage of the sympathetic attitude of local bureaucrats, like the assistant governor, by publicly criticizing the town's and villages' religious leaders. One local teacher wrote a series of editorials accusing them of preaching against Ataturk's reforms. When the town's highest religious official, the *müfti,* complained to the Ministry of Education the teacher countered by formally charging the *müfti* with sermons against the state and constitution. Although the court acquitted the *müfti,* the case reminded the townspeople of earlier years of religious oppression.

In 1965, national events again had an immediate impact on local politics. When RPP policy makers declared that their party had moved left-of-center, a Republican split developed in Susurluk between middle-of-the-road Inonu supporters and leftists who backed the party's emerging national leader — Bulent Ecevit. Internal conflict led to the resignation of many old time RPP leaders, who were replaced by younger, more radical men with grand designs for remaking Susurluk's and the country's social structure. The 1965 national election, however, proved a great victory for the JP and frustrated the new RPP leaders, who by their education and elitist status believed it their right and duty to govern.

Local leftists decided, much as Ataturk had done before them, that the only way to make the country safe for democracy was by educating a new generation of Turks to think as they did. They planned to use the town's previously non-political Education and Culture Society as the instrument of this plan, but were effectively stifled at the Society's 1968 general meeting by the president

— a political independent — and the general membership who held that the organization should remain non-political. They then resigned and formed their own Cultural Society with two lawyers, the owner of the local newspaper *(24 Haziran)*, and five university students as its officers. In cooperation with a radical teachers union, the Cultural Society sponsored leftist speakers and plays, and the "enlightened" university students offered the town's school children special summer courses in language, math, and history, which were designed to help pupils make up school deficiencies and open their minds to the problems of Turkish society.

To counter these efforts and the now left-leaning newspaper, *24 Haziran*, a group of JP members formed their own cultural association, called the "Nationalist Society" *(Milliyetci Derneği)* and began publishing a newspaper named *"Susurluk 5 Eylul"* ("Susurluk 5 September," the date the town was liberated from Greek occupation following WWI), which carried on its heading the following quote from Ataturk: "Do not forget that the Turks' greatest enemy is Communism. It must be crushed wherever it appears." Hoping to outdo the leftists, the JP members formally inaugurated their society with pomp and spectacle. The Ministers of Finance and Communications as well as several JP members of parliament attended the event, and after a series of political speeches in which the JP was described as a nationalist party, the crowd paraded with the town band to Ataturk's statue where they culminated the ceremony with the national anthem.

During the ensuing months, some of the town's Republicans and leftists criticized the JP organizers for choosing a society name, i.e., "Nationalist," which they contended best described themselves. The critics insisted that they, more than the JP, had the nation's interests at heart. In response, one JP leader wrote an editorial entitled: "Why Take Offense?"

Since the Nationalist Society was established, several people have asked why it was necessary and have accused us of denying that they are nationalists. Brothers, no one is saying that others are not nationalists; this each person must decide for himself. A nationalist is one who is loyal to his country, its language, its religion, and its traditions. If we are all nationalists, why do we stand divided? Why don't we all join together to improve our country?

With two rival newspapers in existence, the 1968-69 period was one of excited and emotional policital dialogue. *24 Haziran,* which claimed to be politically independent, acted as the media for the left, and *Susurluk 5 Eylul* served moderates and conservatives. Editorials printed by one were promptly answered by the other, and the tone of the exchanges gave the impression that no common ground existed between them. For example, editorials on the "Meaning of Ataturkism" appeared in each, the first by a town moderate in *Susurluk 5 Eylul:*

> Ataturk wanted to make Turkey a Western nation; he was both a nationalist and a westernist. He was not against religion, but against religious exploitation. He opposed all who want to limit Turkey's international rights and the rights of her citizens. Those who desire such limitations are primarily the communists. An Ataturkist is bound by and loyal to the nation's customs, traditions, and religion. All true Ataturkists, regardless of your party affiliation, let us join together for a great Turkey.

The counterpoint was written by a leftist teacher in *24 Haziran:*

> Ataturk did not want religion and the State to be tied together. He knew that religion was being used to exploit the people. The exploiters (Muslim clergy) hold that Islam is the most modern religion, the best religion for all nations. If this is so, why are all Islamic countries so backward and underdeveloped? This is because in the hands of the exploiters Islam has become a religion of superstition and myth. It was from this superstition and myth that he wanted to free the people. Did the people want the anti-clerical reforms that Ataturk carried out? The answer is, "No!" But he still carried them out in the name of the national will, because he knew what was good for the people. A true Ataturkist is a secularist.

Other editorials in *24 Haziran* argued that the government salaries paid to religious officials (i.e., *müftis, imams,* and *müezzins)* amounted to bribes and should be discontinued; that Christianity may need a clergy, but Islam certainly does not; that the best state and society are secular; that villagers should use their money for roads and education, rather than for mosques; that the wealthy and the Muslim clergy fear modern teachers, who are enlightening the exploited masses.

Responses in *Susurluk 5 Eylul* countered that local socialists ironically live much better than common townspeople and therefore constitute the "exploiting class." Several editorials, such as the following, contended that those who oppose Turkey's religious tradition are neither nationalists nor Ataturkists, but communists, allied with Moscow.

> Everyone knows that the calamity called communism rejects religion along with the family and private property. Communists display their stupidity by claiming that religion is opium for the people. Those in our country

who sympathize with or serve this loathed ideology are carried away with the idea of cursing religion and its followers. They appear terrified by the strengthening of religious institutions.

We believe religion should not be exploited. We oppose those who use it for personal gain. But we believe it is the fundamental right of the Turkish nation to respect its religion and its ancestors. We will never give those dogs, who have sold themselves, the opportunity to drown out the Muslim call from our minarets with their howling. We throw down a challenge to those who think otherwise. May Allah protect the Turks and Islam!

1968 found additional excitement in the town's municipal campaign and election. The JP selected a newcomer as its mayoral candidate — a retired colonel, who had gained local fame in 1962 when he was arrested (but later acquitted) for speech counter to the 1960 revolution. During the early 1950s, the colonel had commanded the military detachment in Susurluk where he met his present wife, and after compulsory retirement in 1960, he returned to town permanently and actively engaged in local politics. He served diligently on the town council from 1963 to 1968 and impressed most townspeople with his leadership ability.

During the campaign, both mayoral candidates repeated the 1963 promises, but the JP won the election, and this time all the victors assumed office. The new mayor thanked the townspeople in an editorial and also explained that the kind of leadership the people want is in sharp contrast to what the "revolutionaries of the left" offer:

We prefer those who know our past and our accomplishments; who respect our laws, customs, and traditions; who will serve the nation in good faith; and, who favor the intelligent and cautious road upon which to lead our caravan.

With both the local and the national government in the hands of the JP, Susurluk politics resembled the 1950s: government channels were open to two-way communication. The community's chosen representatives could call on the national leadership in Ankara and extract rewards for the town's loyalty. The new mayor — a dignified gentleman with recognized military status — proved an ideal person to lobby in the various ministries for his town's interests. He successfully obtained financial commitments for the improvement of the town's schools, streets, slaughterhouse and meat storage facilities, and water supply. By 1970, the water problem, which 37% of my adult interview sample named as the town's top priority, was virtually solved.

Another achievement of the town's new leadership was the replacement of the lycée principal with a man of their choosing. Because the community has no direct control over education, this feat had to be accomplished through the Education Minister — a JP man from Balıkesir. The townspeople supporting the change charged that the principal was incapable of maintaining discipline and he encouraged leftist teachers among his faculty, who promoted partisan socio-political views to the detriment of the students' general education. They hoped that the new principal would put order into the school and would discipline his faculty to devote their full energies to teaching subject matter necessary for university entrance exams, rather than politics. When the new principal arrived, however, a fission developed between him and the teachers and the educational atmosphere probably worsened.

As of August 1970, three political parties maintained local headquarters in Susurluk; the moderate and the right-of-center JP, the left-of-center RPP, and the conservative National Action Party, which had just been formed by a group of sugar refinery employees, who felt that their political expression had become ineffectual in the large JP. In addition, one local leftist sat on the board of directors of the Workers Party, a Marxist organization with branch headquarters in Balıkesir. Because politics involves basic disagreement over the ideological foundations of society, political divisions in the town, as in the country, extended to economic, social, and educational spheres.

An issue central to national and local politics is the place of religion in society. Most left-of-center Republicans argue that religion should be reduced to a purely individual concern, and more extreme leftists and Marxists claim it should be completely eliminated for the good of the country. On the other hand, JP supporters argue that religion, i.e., Islam, is part of the national tradition and continues to provide the moral basis of Turkish society: therefore, it must be respected. Dialogue between these positions is hindered because each tends to depict the other in extreme dimensions: those favoring respect for Islam are accused of opposing Ataturk's principles and favoring the reestablishment of the caliphate; those espousing socialism are identified with Moscow and considered atheists. Fortunately, leaders of the two major parties are moderate men, capable of more objective evaluation of political positions. A local JP leader with this ability confided to me that he found some of the Workers Party's objectives quite attractive, but he correctly predicted that the party's anti-religious stance would prevent it from ever becoming popular.

Marxism has had little general success in Turkey, partly because of its association with Russia — a traditional Turkish enemy — but also because the Marxist ideology of class conflict contradicts the Islamic ideology of class interdependence, of responsibility of rich for poor, of alms and voluntary giving as the means for redistribution of wealth. Muslims believe that private ownership and material are not evil, provided that the rewards of success are shared with the poor. Sharing is a religious obligation, and there is strong opposition to making it a secular one.

For Susurluk, government has alternated between totalitarian and democratic regimes. During the period of single party rule, the town was largely ignored, except for tax collection and military recruitment, and local participation in the political process was limited and ineffectual. With the advent of multi-party politics, government activity in the town expanded, and so did the town's participation in the political system. Most townspeople favor a multi-party system in which the majority rules, because they are part of the majority. However, while they value democracy and individual freedom, they believe that their inability to give priority to community and national goals over individual ones is a character defect, which hinders Turkey's development. Therefore, they favor strong leaders, like Ataturk, who can carry out their programs, despite petty disagreement and bickering at lower levels. Still, they refuse to give up the right to elect these leaders.

Social Backgrounds of Local Office Holders

Working primarily with key informants, I was able to collect information such as occupation, education, ethnicity, marital status, quarter of residence, and party affiliation for all members of the 1963 and 1968 town council, and for almost all quarter chiefs and officers of the major parties' youth and women's organizations. The data are more clearly conveyed in writing, rather than in tables.

Town Council. As many of the town's most active party men are elected to the town council, we can learn a good deal about each party's representativeness by examining this body. I collected background information on the 34 men (21 JP and 13 RPP), who constituted the 1963 and 1968 town councils. (Six members of the 1963 council were reelected in 1968).

The two parties are quite similar with respect to education and quarter of residence. Each has a majority of primary school graduates with one university degree holder, and each has a majority residing in Han and Yeni Quarters with one or two members living in the other quarters.

However, in terms of occupation and ethnicity, the JP emerges as the more representative of the two parties. While the DP and later the JP attracted the support of peasants and medium-scale farmers, the RPP has enjoyed the affiliation of wealthy landowners, who now reside in town where they manage their new town-based businesses. This economic difference is reflected in the town council: whereas the RPP membership includes no farmers, the JP has five (24% of its total membership). Almost all Republicans and the remainder of JP members are businessmen — either retailers or artisans, who own their own shops and sales outlets.

The JP council membership is also more ethnically varied. Manavs and descendants of Balkan Turks predominate in both parties, but only the JP has a Circassian and a Georgian member. In addition, almost half of the JP councilmen (48%), as compared to only 31% of the Republicans, are married to women whose ethnic backgrounds differ from their own. Such a marriage may broaden the base of a politician's support, by permitting him to appeal to two different ethnic groups.

Women and marriage ties are becoming increasingly important for Susurluk politics. Each of the major parties has a women's wing, whose officers are the wives of the mayor and the town councilmen. These women work behind the scenes to build up support for their husbands. Marriage may also cause kin groups to change party allegiance. For example, in 1963 a JP councilman and his entire family changed party affiliation to the RPP when his son married the daughter of the Republican Mayor. Several years later, another of his sons became an officer of the RPP Youth Wing and a Republican delegate.

Party Youth Wings. Both the JP and the RPP have political youth organizations, called wings, composed of male party members between twenty-one and thirty years of age. Each wing elects eleven officers, who act as delegates to the party congress, as well as perform other important party functions, like campaigning with older members, educating younger voters, doing clerical and administrative tasks, and watching voting boxes on election day.

In 1970, I collected background information on all eleven of the JP and ten of the RPP wing officers. In general, the JP officers were more ethnically mixed and experienced men, better acquainted with the community and more active in its political affairs. While the age range of both wings was the same, the JP had more officers over 25 and more married officers than the RPP (7 versus 2). All JP officers were from local families, and all but one (a student studying in Istanbul) were currently employed in town in either craft, retail, or service occupations. By comparison, two RPP officers had recently moved to town and were considered "outsiders," and four were currently residing outside Susurluk: one was away at school; two were in the military; and another was working in Germany.

The average education of RPP officers was higher than that of their JP counterparts, who were mostly primary school graduates. But this difference, attributable to the few RPP officers who pursued studies out-of-town at the lycée or university level, operates against the RPP by increasing the physical and intellectual distance between youth officers and townspeople. Furthermore, young RPP politicians who study in the big cities tend to acquire political ideas considered too radical for Susurluk.

The fathers of most officers were or had been active in the same party, and some had acquired places in Susurluk history with their deeds. The father of the JP Youth Wing President was among the original organizers of the DP in Susurluk in 1945, and continued to play a leading role in that party's affairs until 1960, when he suffered a fatal heart attack upon hearing the news of the military coup. The father of the vice-president of the JP Wing immortalized himself in 1950 when RPP leader Ismet Inonu came to Susurluk to campaign for that year's national election. As Inonu began his campaign promises before a small crowd in the town square, this townsman took off his shoe, lifted it in the air, and shouted to the speaker: "Look at these holes! For years you've been promising this and that, but you've done nothing!"

With respect to occupation and socio-economic status, most fathers of JP youth members were craftsmen and retailers of medium wealth. Most RPP youth officers also came from families of medium status, which have tradition-ally favored the RPP, even though a few fathers held government positions — bureaucrat, teacher, gendarme officer — which prevented them from being *officially* active in politics. Only one RPP youth officer — the president — descends from a prominent and wealthy Republican, but the relatives of several other officers have important links with RPP influentials. For example, the father of one was employed by the RPP youth president's grandfather, and the brother of another is married to the daughter of a former Republican mayor.

Quarter Chiefs (Mahalle Muhtarları). An examination of the social back-grounds of seventeen quarter chiefs — a sample covering all the town's quarters, from 1923 to 1970 for the oldest and from date-of-origin to 1970 for the newer ones — produces the following conclusions. First, on this level the man can be more important than the party. Quarters favoring the DP or JP in national elections have elected RPP candidates as their chiefs. However, these men tend to limit their involvement in town and national politics, and conse-quently lack strong Republican identification, whereas other chiefs function for their parties as grass-roots organizers.

Second, although most chiefs are members of their quarters' dominant ethnic group, there are sufficient exceptions to support the townspeople's claim that they do not vote primarily on the basis of ethnicity. For instance, Han quarter, with its large Manav population, has had a Circassian as its chief for about seventeen years (1950-60, 1964-70). (Military appointees replaced most DP quarter chiefs from 1960-64). Importantly, however, this man is married to a Manav woman of the same quarter.

Third, chiefs rarely have more than a primary school education, and fourth, they most frequently are local craftsmen or small retailers, whose businesses or places of work keep them in touch with their constituencies and available when needed.

As there are no courses or guide books available to quarter chiefs, a new man must learn either by trial and error or from the experience of others. Regardless of party affiliation, experienced chiefs willingly help inexperienced ones, as it is considered to be for the quarter's good.

During the period of one-party rule quarter chiefs were considered servants of the assistant governor (then called *Mülkiye Amiri),* but today they are more independent. As one long-term chief explained: ''In the past we went humbly to the assistant governor to receive his directives, and then we were forced to follow them. Now, with the multi-party system, the assistant governor can advise, but not coerce.''

In 1969-70, five quarter chiefs were members of the JP, and one belonged to the RPP.

This historical and sociological analysis reveals that Susurluk duplicates the national political pattern in microcosm. On both the national and local levels, the party best facilitating popular participation through a relatively open communication system and avoiding the kind of doctrinaire approach that alienates many segments of the citizenry has proven the most successful mechanism of political integration as evidenced by its broadly based support comprised of diverse regional, occupational, and cultural groups.

Conclusion

Turkey's political system has evolved from a relatively simple to a relatively complex form. From 1923 to 1946 the government, civil bureaucracy, military, and RPP constituted a highly unified and, for most practical purposes, undifferentiated political structure integrated by the person and ideals of Kemal Ataturk. The multi-party era witnessed the differentiation of this structure into separate components with legally defined boundaries and spheres of authority. A wide spectrum of political parties from left to right now compete for votes with the RPP, the party which had previously enjoyed exclusive power and claimed to be everything to everyone.

Turkey has yet to resolve her historic problem of elite-mass cleavage. The populace will no longer tolerate totalitarian governments that direct change without popular input or feedback. Due to gains in literacy and communications technology, the people of Susurluk and other small towns have increased their awareness of the political process and its determination of their destinies. They have experienced not only a revolution of rising expectations, but a political revolution marked by new activism. Voter participation nationally and locally has been extremely high — frequently exceeding eighty per cent. People demand participation in the political process and a degree of self-determination. They rejected the RPP because it denied them this involvement, and they are loyal to the Justice Party, because its ancestors, the Democrats, did not. However, their loyalties are not immutable. They will vote for those most responsive to their social and economic struggle, who actively involve them in the design, implementation, and fruition of programs.

CHAPTER VIII

Education and Ideological Conflict

Educational Facilities and Curricula

The past several decades have witnessed the expansion not only of Susurluk's economy and population, but of her educational facilities as well. In 1931 the town had only one complete primary school (grades one through five) with a total enrollment of 297 students (two-thirds of whom were boys) and a staff of one principal and eight teachers. The small number of students (all boys) who were able to continue their educations beyond grade five did so by taking up residence in either Balıkesir, Bursa, or Istanbul and attending middle schools there. Peasant children were especially disadvantaged, as only eight villages in the sub-province had primary schools. All told, less than one-fifth of the children in the sub-province eligible for primary school were actually attending (Dundar 1933).

By the 1969-70 school year this situation had improved immensely: all but three small villages had primary schools, and one village (Demirkapı) had started the first class of its new middle school. Susurluk boasted three primary schools, one middle school (grades six through eight), a vocational school for girls (post-primary), and a new, but yet incomplete lycée (grades nine and ten). (Grade eleven, the final lycée class, was added in September of 1970.) The town's primary schools had 45 teachers and 1,680 students, with a boy-girl ratio of 9:7. The middle school and lycée had a combined enrollment of 913 students with 25 teachers, while 106 girls attended the vocational school, which is popular with parents who disapprove of co-education for daughters after puberty.

With the single exception of the girls' vocational institution, the school curricula heavily emphasize academic subjects. Primary school studies include:Turkish language, history, geography, civics, natural sciences, mathematics, writing, music, drawing, and physical education. Islamic religion, offered in the last two grades, is not compulsory. The middle school and lycée continue these subjects (except for religion at the lycée level) and add English, physics, and chemistry. Within the primary and middle school curricula students have practically no options; only at the lycée level may they choose to stress either literature and humanities or science and math.

Study loads in the middle school and lycée are rather heavy, as students must carry ten or more subjects simultaneously. Instruction in each course centers around the Ministry of Education's prescribed text book, which provides the basis for teacher lectures and student homework assignments. To succeed in tests students feel they must literally memorize these texts, because verbatim responses to formal, book-specific questions receive full points. Rote memorization in Turkey — a feature so common to many Third World educational systems — can be traced back to the pre-Republican period when children's formal education consisted primarily of memorizing and reciting the *Quran*. Today, in the "modern" schools children are taught to be patriotic Turks who can recite their text books. Teachers do little to integrate the diversity of material in any practical or applied way; even physics and chemistry classes are conducted without the benefits of experimentation.

The middle school and lycée curricula are designed to prepare students for higher education, even though only about 5% and 2% of the town's primary school students can be expected to go on to lycée and university respectively. Despite the fact that most male students will have to drop out along the way to earn a living, there is no vocational education in Susurluk for boys.

Ideological Conflict

Education played an exceedingly important role in Ataturk's program to transform "Oriental" minds and the traditional Islamic basis of society. Shortly after the establishment of the Republic in 1923, the governing revolutionaries, members of Kemal Ataturk's Republican People's Party, designed a nationwide system of compulsory secular education which they hoped would socialize a new generation of Turks in accordance with principles of modern Turkish nationalism. "Since the emergence of the idea of a Turkish national state, Turkish leaders have conceived of the schools as prime agencies in developing national consciousness, ideologies, values, and behaviours different from what had existed before and aimed at the over-all transformation of the political ethic of the country" (Kazamias 1966:220). The major agents of this transformation were teachers. The political scientist Lenczowski has concluded that "the secret of Kemal's success may largely be attributed to the strict enforcement of educational reform. The new generation of village and high-school teachers constituted — with the People's Party members — a zealous cadre which spread Kemalist ideas and trained the minds of Turkish youth. Teachers became Kemal's most devoted propagandists. . . ." (as quoted in Frey 1964:223-24).

As a result of this revolutionary program the residents of Susurluk are experiencing anxiety over the very ideological foundations of their society and culture. The vast majority of townspeople are devout Muslims who fear that their belief system is being threatened. They believe the primary instruments of this threat are certain teachers, especially those in the middle school and lycée, and the immediate objects of the threat are their children.

Because the town lacked post-primary schools in the past, it now has few indigenous citizens sufficiently qualified to staff its new middle school and lycée. Therefore, practically all of its post-primary teachers are outsiders from Turkey's larger cities. They are mostly young people, newly graduated from teachers colleges and universities, whose radical political ideologies, philosophies of education, and definition of the teacher's role differ markedly from those of the townspeople. These teachers have openly expressed their contrary views orally and in editorials published by the town's left-of-center newspaper.

The local president of the left wing Turkish Teachers Union *(TÖS)*, himself an avowed atheist and socialist, wrote these ideas in 1969: "Religious leaders have been the brake to Turkey's progress. Religion has been used to exploit the people materially and mentally. As teachers our duty is to teach students that Turkey is a democratic, republican, and secular state. It is our duty to oppose any persons or political parties that oppose Ataturk's principle of secularism." A similar editorial written by another local teacher concluded with an expression of puzzlement over the fact that the very exploited people the teachers were striving to awaken were the ones who opposed revolutionary ideas most stubbornly.

The president of the Teachers Union also penned the following editorial which depicts local townspeople opposing advances in science and technology because they alter the divine plan.

Let's See What They Will Say Now!

Ever since I can remember I have witnessed that whenever some scientist announces that he has set out to make a discovery, a certain group of people immediately raise an outcry: "Impossible! Whatever is necessary in this world, Allah has already created. Those presumptuous persons who try to discover what Allah has left hidden are irreligious.

When man was trying to invent the automobile, they asked: "What will pull it? an ass?" Upon being told that it would be powered by its own engine, they stood in disbelief. They reacted in the same way to electricity, the radio, and the airplane. However, when these things became realities, they simply said: "Of course. It has been written in the *Quran* that these things would come to pass."

When it came to the subject of moon exploration, they said: "Man has done many things, but he will not go to the moon. The moon is fire; those who go will burn.''

They reacted to the early set-backs in the Apollo program with ridicule. ''Ha, ha, ha. So they're going to the moon, are they! Look at those infidels. May Allah cure them of their insanity.''

But now moon exploration, too, has become a reality. Man has set foot on the moon and has erected the flag of his earth country. What will they say now? Very simple. ''It was written in the *Quran*.''

This editorial, written in the tradition of Mahmut Makal, the famous Turkish reformer who portrayed his fellow villagers as ignorant reactionary Muslims, appeared in a local Susurluk newspaper in July of 1969, a few days after Neil Armstrong made man's first footprint in moon dust. Like Makal, the author is a primary school teacher, self-styled modernist, and secularist. In my conversations with him, his anti-religious bias seemed so strong that he could not conceive of modernization and Islam co-existing. He contended that his editorial accurately describes the reaction of most Susurluk townsmen to the Apollo program.

The rivalry between the family and the modern educator over the minds of students has also been the subject of several teacher editorials. One such statement in 1963 began by praising the Village Institutes, the products of an admirable experiment in teacher training begun in 1940 during the single party rule of the People's Party, but abolished in 1954 during the term of the popularly elected opposition, the Democratic Party. ''They [i.e., the Institutes] were accused of sins ranging from incompetence, through partisan support for the People's Party, to Soviet Communism'' (Frey 1964:221-22). The teacher-editorialist boasted that the 17,000 Village Institute graduates would have more influence on the ideas and thinking of Turkish children than even their own parents, who generally oppose the teachers.

These and other editorials along with ideas expressed to me by teachers show that many of them regard the townspeople as religious and fatalistic reactionaries opposed to Ataturk's reforms and the scientific advances of the modern world. These teachers accept the educational philosophy of the Turkish revolutionary Sadrettin Celal, who advocated that:

The influence of the family and the society on education is constructive in countries already developed, but dangerously destructive in underdeveloped and rapidly developing societies. Perhaps the greatest harm against society in the underdeveloped countries would be to have the schools emphasize the same education which is stressed by the family and society. The first duty of educators in newly developing countries is to separate the influence of the family and society from that of the schools, and to lessen their relationship to one another. Traditions and institutions which are foundations for value judgments are not logical and untouchable . . . . The pedagogue's duty is not to help harmful traditions to survive, but to destroy them [as quoted in Başgöz and Wilson 1968:26-27].

Many teachers hold these firm convictions despite the fact that most of them are not in a position to understand the townsmen. All but one of the middle school and lycée teachers are outsiders, who came to the town neither by choice nor invitation. Their assignments here were the result of a lottery, and they hope to be reassigned to larger cities as soon as possible. Socially they remain an aloof and isolated group spending free-time together in their union clubhouse and avoiding cordial interaction with the townspeople. This isolation is reinforced by their open praise of the radical Turkish Workers Party, which is opposed by the majority of townsmen who favor the right-of-center Justice Party. By contrast, most of the primary school teachers (who are educated at the pre-university level) are either indigenous to the sub-province or else have chosen to settle here permanently with their families. These teachers are fully integrated into the town community, and represent no threat to the townspeople. Most of them are members of the moderate and right-of-center Nationalist Teachers Union.

The results of my own studies of the townspeople's religious attitudes, loyalties, self-perceptions, views on education, and aspirations for their children, differ substantially with the radical teachers' portrayal of the townspeople.

One question presented to the quota sample of 182 townsmen asked each to name the two persons in the world he admired most. The most admired figure proved to be Kemal Ataturk, the architect of modern Turkey, named by 81.4%; next came John F. Kennedy (31.5%) and then Adnan Menderes (24.3%), the leader of Turkey's first democratically elected opposition party. Only 11% of the respondents named Muhammad, the Prophet of Allah. When asked to justify their choices, most of the townsmen explained that the admired figures were either military heroes (55%), persons who contributed greatly to Turkey's development (79.5%), or persons who contributed to world peace and the good of mankind (27.2%). This last justification was most commonly given by those who chose Kennedy. These results show that rather than opposing Ataturk, most townsmen admire him. However, they do differ with the teachers over the interpretation of Ataturk's views on religion and his goals for the Turkish nation.

In an effort to learn something of the townsmen's self-perceptions, members of the sample were asked to name two attributes which they believe best characterize the Turkish nation. They responded that Turks are strong and heroic (52.6%), religious (50.4%), hospitable (45.7%), and patriotic (27.7%). In an analysis of Turkish children's stories David McClelland noted that loyalty and bravery are usually treated in a patriotic context (1963:176-77), and in my conversations with townspeople I found the same to be true for heroism. They believe that one commonly becomes a hero by serving his country in war. Thus, in their characterization of the Turkish nation, and consequently of themselves, the townsmen see the distinctive qualities of patriotism and religiosity combining harmoniously with a cordiality in interpersonal relationships.

One may wonder whether the townsmen's religiosity embodies the excessively fatalistic attitude which the teachers condemn. Responses to three items in the interview schedule help answer this question. The first item asked respondents to choose the prerequisite they believed most important for success in life. Of the four answers offered, 76.4% chose "industriousness" and 14.8% opted for "skill," while only 5.5% picked "fate," and 3.3% selected "pull." The second item asked townsmen to agree or disagree with the following position: "If we have sufficient determination and will power, no difficulty can prevent us from reaching our goals." This strongly non-fatalistic statement found full agreement with 94.4% of the sample; only 7 of 180 respondents disagreed. The third item asked respondents whether or not they had control over their own futures. Seventy-one per cent said they did.

These responses and my own observations during a year in the town lead me to conclude that for the vast majority of townsmen, religiosity and fatalism are not concomitants. A noted Turkish expert, who studied this problem on the village level in 1949, reached the same conclusion: "That concept [i.e. fate] is fast weakening . . . Other than ritual lip service, it is my impression that predestination, supposedly one of the basic tenets of Islam, is not a very real factor in directing the life and thought of the Turkish villager" (Robinson 1949b:2).

Apparently the phenomenon recognized as fatalism in Turkey, the Middle East, and throughout much of the developing world is less a barrier to change than an *ex post facto* rationalization that provides individuals with a psychological and cultural adjustment to situations with numerous perceived and real obstacles to an "improved" way of life. However, once presented with convincing evidence that they can affect their destinies, they often act with surprising spontaneity. Witness the flood of Turkish men and women to West European jobs, and the million more aspiring to experience life and work in the West.

At least two major events in Turkey's recent history have significantly attenuated any hold fatalism may have had on the minds of common Turks. The first event followed World War I, when a defeated country and people, torn and exhausted by war, revitalized themselves, drove out the foreign occupation forces, and established their present nation-state. The second event occurred in 1950 when the common man from small towns and villages witnessed his voting power displace what he perceived to be a repressive and authoritarian government with one more responsive to his needs, desires, and opinions. Both these events affected the common Turk's perception of his world and his capacity to change it.

Two additional items in the interview schedule were designed to learn what values townsmen hoped to pass on to the next generation. They were asked to state the two things they most wanted to teach their children. The major responses were: the value of Islam (57.1%), patriotism (31.3%), morality (29.2%), and the importance of the family (27.8%). The second item asked respondents to choose the two loyalties they believed most important for children. The possibilities offered were: loyalty to either religion, kin, friends, town, or nation. The predominant choices were religious (87.4%), national (69.3%), and kinship (20%) loyalties. Several townsmen explained that family and kinship loyalties are bound up with the loyalty to religion.

Research findings also contradicted the editorial on the townsmen's opposition to moon exploration and scientific discovery. The people of Susurluk impressed me with their knowledge of moon exploration in general, and of the U.S. Apollo 11 and 12 missions in particular. Old and young, literate and illiterate spoke with excitement about the exploits of the astronauts. About 85% of the quota sample and about 90% of the people with whom I talked informally said moon exploration was a useful endeavor. Some of them, like four members of the sample, regarded it with a vision commonly associated with the most far-sighted of modern men: they saw the moon and planets as potential homes — the lands of future migrations. The majority were somewhat less visionary, but still very positive. For instance, 62% of the sample believed moon exploration would expand knowledge, and 19.3% said it would render important material benefits to mankind, such as new sources of energy and medical cures. Altogether, only six people associated space travel with the *Quran*. This reliance on the sacred book as a universal truth to explain what might otherwise seem incomprehensible was clearly not common among townsmen (see Magnarella 1972).

In summary, data derived from interviews and observation evince that most townsmen are religious, but not fatalistic: they believe that individuals can control their destinies and succeed in life by hard work, and they do not oppose scientific advancement. In their value systems, devotion to Islam, patriotism, and love of kin occupy dominant positions, and townsmen hope the same will be true for their children.

But given their strong religiosity, how do townspeople regard modern education? All evidence indicates that they value it highly. The construction of the present schools can be attributed largely to the sacrifices which many local people made in terms of time, labor, and money. Associated with all the schools are active parent organizations which provide aid to needy students and contribute to the upkeep of the schools. Interviews show that townsmen have high educational aspirations for their children: the overwhelming majority of sample members (93.4%) hope their sons will attain a university degree, and fifty-six percent want the same for their daughters. With regards to occupational aspirations for sons, 76.5% of the sample specified the professions, with technology ranking first, followed by medicine and law. For daughters, the occupations of doctor, teacher, and pharmacist (total = 46.6%) were the most popular choices after housewife.

Throughout the history of the Ottoman Empire and the Turkish Republic education has helped people from lower classes achieve higher status. It was and continues to be an ''achieved'' element of central importance to one's place in the system of social stratification. Therefore, the great desire for education in Susurluk may not be totally new. Instead, it might be interpreted as the expression of a people to have their children attain a goal which has generally been valued and desired, but until recently unavailable to the general public.

What does appear to be new is the desire to educate daughters as well as sons. In the past, Turkish educators complained that many parents in small communities refused to send their daughters to school. By contrast, today we find these parents complaining when either their sons or their daughters do not have educational opportunities. While the desire to educate daughters to the university level was very common among educated parents, many of the more humble townsmen were equally emphatic in this wish, although they believe it had low probability of being realized. The following four statements are representative of this group; they were offered by townsmen with primary school educations or less:

A 39 year old Circassian farmer: ''Today girls can be many things. Let my daughter have a university education and benefit herself, her family, and her country.''

A 48 year old Manav janitor and peasant's son: ''I want my daughter to study so that she can be an independent person.''

A 37 year old Balkan Turkish janitor and peasant's son: ''So that instead of being ignorant, she can contribute to her people and her country.''

A 43 year old Manav gas station attendant and peasant's son: ''So that she will be knowledgeable, respected, and useful to those around her.''

The townsmen obviously want their children, especially their sons, to assume prominent roles in the development of a modern Turkey, and they regard the modern educational system as the main avenue of social mobility. However, while they want the vocational components of the educational curriculum to be modern and dynamic, keeping pace with the technologically advanced Western World, they strongly desire that the moral and ethical aspects of education remain close to tradition. As one townsman — the only indigenous member of the middle school and lycée faculty — stated in a 1968 editorial appearing in the local right-of-center newspaper: "We want to educate a generation of Turks who respect Allah and his institutions and desire the perpetuation of the Turkish nation. We want our children to be bound by Turkish traditions, customs, and practices." The majority of townsmen believe that Islamic values and cultural tradition have a place in the educational system — that they do not impede the process of modern vocational education. They want the teacher to be a safe-keeper of moral tradition and a transmitter of modern knowledge. They regard many of today's educators as itinerant invaders with offensive ideologies and compare them unfavorably with the teachers of the pre-Republican era, who participated fully in the social and religious life of the community. But despite their dissatisfaction, there is little they can do to change the present situation, because teacher placement, educational policy, and school curriculum are all determined by the Ministry of Education in Ankara.

The division between the town community and the "revolutionary" teachers was sharpened in late 1969 when two radical teachers' unions called an illegal national strike — the first in the history of the Turkish Republic — to dramatize their demands for higher salaries, improved working conditions, more authority in the formation of educational policy, freedom to advocate social change, and the expulsion of Peace Corps Volunteers and other foreign experts from educational posts. (In an attempt to win support for their demands, some teachers appealed to religious sentiment by claiming that the Peace Corps Volunteers were engaging in Christian missionary activities.)

In Susurluk those teachers who joined the strike were mostly "outsiders" on the middle school and lycée faculties. By contrast, most primary school educators conducted classes as usual. The townspeople reacted to the situation by accusing the strikers of violating a sacred trust and obligation to educate their children. While they signed petitions requesting the Ministry of Education to replace the "irresponsible ones," they visited the working teachers in their homes and in their classrooms to express appreciation in words and with gifts of sweets or specially prepared foods.

The strike lasted only three days, ending on December 19, 1969, with neither the teachers' demands nor the townspeople's petition being satisfied. The two factions continue to regard each other with greater enmity.

Projections

Who will win this struggle to determine which values will be transmitted to youths — the family or the revolutionary educator? Many students of personality development regard the family as the most important agent of socialization. However, while this opinion may be valid for certain kinds of learning, it is inadequate for the formation of political attitudes and behavior. In a comprehensive study of the development of political attitudes among American children Hess and Torney concluded that "the public school appears to be the most important and effective instrument of political socialization in the United States" (1967:101). They also found that the teacher represented an efficacious model for the identification and imitation of political attitudes. In a comparison between the political cultures of Turkey and Iran, David McClelland suggested that the acute differences between the two can be attributed to the Turkish school system, since the family systems of the two countries appear to be remarkably similar (1963).

It is difficult to assess the degree of influence that teachers in this town have had on students, because the middle school and lycée are comparatively new. However, results of a questionnaire administered to seven of the town's nine first year middle school classes and to the only middle school class in a nearby village provide a basis for prediction. The 307 students (238 boys and 69 girls) were asked to write down their occupational goals. Almost half of the students (45.2%) specified "teacher," and the second highest proportion (24.1%; all boys) named "military officer." These are probably the two most revolutionary roles in Turkish society. Some psychologists believe that a child's occupational preference is indicative of what person or persons have strongly influenced him. As in many other developing countries a very large proportion of students clearly identify with their teachers and aspire to imitate them. This will enable the teachers to have a substantial influence on the development of student attitudes. In fact, practically all the male lycée students with whom I talked claimed they and their classmates were in agreement with the social and political philosophies of their teachers and described themselves as leftists. These students also admitted that their views were quite contrary to those of their parents.

Although the ideological fissions plaguing this town are in a nascent state, they are fully developed in Turkey's major cities and often manifest themselves in student violence which many people find incomprehensible. In an address to the nation on April 23, 1972 Turkey's moderate President, Cevdet Sunay, attributed part of the problem to the elimination of parental influence from the schools: "The extremist youth movements and painful incidents which have taken place in our country have shown clearly how families should be vigilant over and interested in their children. I invite all parents to watch over their children responsibly and maintain close and constant cooperation with their schools" (as quoted in *Turkish Digest* 1972:1).

The West has continually applauded Ataturk's efforts to transform Turkey from an Oriental-Islamic nation into a Western scientific one. The educational and ideological conflicts described here are the result of this revolutionary process. Have we been too ethnocentric in our evaluations? Have we endorsed change primarily because we represented the desired model? By agreeing that Turkey should strip herself of her traditional ideological foundations are we unwittingly encouraging her self-destruction? Probably so. The Western model void of religion leaves a moral vacuum. As one American psychologist has wisely noted:

> Our immense success in the development of the physical sciences has not been particularly successful in formulating better philosophies of life, or increasing our real knowledge of ourselves. The science we have developed to date is not a very human science. It tells us how to do things, but gives us no scientific insights into the questions of what to do, what not to do, or why to do things . . . . much of the current crisis in our culture today can be traced to a breakdown in the functioning of our old religious systems, and the inadequacy of a scientific life to replace them with something more functional [Charles Tart, as quoted in Schul 1972:80].

Education in Turkey, especially at the higher levels, has not only provoked a serious conflict over societal values, but also a revolution of expectations that exceed the capacity of the country's economy. In an assessment of Turkey's high-level manpower requirements, Robinson (1967:50) has concluded that unemployment will continue to pose a grave problem (1.5 million Turks were unemployed in 1962) because Turkey's population is growing faster than her economic opportunities. Turkey's State Planning Office estimates that the number of lycée graduates in the 1970s will seriously exceed the number of available jobs. Although Turkey needs technically skilled workers, most students and their parents still operate on the basis of Ottoman prestige values and pursue academic educations which qualify them to enter the mass competition for a comparatively few, underpaid white collar positions. Consequently, a growing proportion of Turkey's educated population will suffer from under- or unemployment and denial of pursued status. They, like the disillusioned educated elite of other Third World countries experiencing grave social and economic problems, will most probably constitute a growing revolutionary element.

CHAPTER IX

Religion and Society

The process of modernization involves changes in the value system as well as in the economic, political, and social systems. The all-encompassing, traditional value system of Islam provides specific rules and guide-lines for practically every human action and thought. These religious values were thoroughly integrated with all other aspects of society. The disintegration of religious values from economic, political, and other social spheres of action is known as the process of secularization. This process produces two basic alterations in human thinking. First, it removes the sacred element from attitudes held towards certain persons and things. Secondly, it creates a rationalization of thought. People begin to think about the world and their activities in it on logical, empirical grounds without reference to sacred symbols. They believe that worldly objects can be manipulated to their benefit on the basis of scientific principles unencumbered by religious prescriptions. This secular world view becomes the mode of thought in the public sphere and relegates religion to the private sphere of individual conscience.

Secularization in Turkey received its main impetus from a revolutionary government, and its gradual continuity from the infusion of Western material and intellectual culture. This experience is best understood as an historical process.

Historic Background

The origin of Islam traces back to the sixth century A.D., when the Prophet Muhammad lived in the city of Mecca on the Arabian Peninsula. According to tradition, the same God (Allah), who previously had made revelations to the Judaic and Christian prophets, chose Muhammad to receive His final instructions. His messages were conveyed through the Angel Gabriel and later recorded by Muhammad's followers to form the *Quran* — the sacred book of all Muslims (adherents to Islam).

Through war and voluntary conversion the Arabs spread the religion, culture, and polity of Islam so rapidly that by the eighth century Islam's domain extended from Spain and Portugal in the West, east across the entire length of

North Africa, throughout the Middle East, and into Central Asia. During succeeding centuries Islam provided a unifying force that brought together people from various ethnic backgrounds — Persians, Jews, Circassians, Georgians, Armenians, Kurds, Turks, Berbers, African Negroes, Spaniards, Portuguese, Arabs — to exchange ideas and contribute to the creation of an Islamic civilization rich in architecture, science, literature, jurisprudence, and theology. The terrible Mongol invasions of the thirteenth century extinguished this cultural effervescence temporarily until the Turks, not the Arabs, restored and revitalized Islam in the long-lasting Ottoman Empire. The Turks remained the primary protectors and propagators of Islam until the end of World War I. Turkish history has been so inextricably tied to Islam, that even today many Turks do not differentiate between things Turkish and things Islamic.

Presently more than 500 million people, or about one-sixth of the world's population, profess to be Muslims. Islam has a special appeal to Third World peoples, showing the greatest growth of all the major religions in the underdeveloped countries of Africa and Asia.

Religious Change

In order to analyze systematically the processes of secularization and differentiation within the religious realm, Islam will be treated in terms of five interlocking systems: the power-authority system, the regulative system, the socialization system, the value system, and the ideological-ritual system (*cf.* Ismael 1970:43-48). The first three will be discussed briefly, and the last two more extensively.

Power-Authority System. During the dawn of Islam, Muslims formed a theocratic state under the direction of the Prophet Muhammad. After Muhammad's death, a series of Arab caliphs or "successors" succeeded him in office. Religious judges administered Islamic law, which was considered so complete that no further legislation was deemed necessary. The Seljuk and Ottoman Turks elaborated the governmental structure of this theocracy somewhat, but retained the principle that all officials should conform to the doctrines of Islam — the source of their legitimation, power, and authority.

This polity was dismantled in Turkey after World War I when the Republic was established with a completely secularized authority-power structure, employing a profane constitution and legislature to define and legitimize all military, governmental, and judicial offices. Consequently the broad authority and influence of religious personnel was negated, and their formerly diffuse roles have been considerably narrowed.

Regulative System. In the theocratic states ruled by the Muslim Arabs, Persians, and Turks the regulative system rested upon the divinely inspired and theoretically immutable *Shari' a* (Islamic law), which was interpreted by religious courts. The *Shari' a* not only functioned as constitutional, civil, commercial, and penal law, it also provided a comprehensive code of ethics to regulate private life.

The revolutionary leaders of the Turkish Republic disestablished the *Shari' a* and replaced it with legal adoptions from Western Europe, causing the regulative system to be differentiated into man-made, secular laws which govern civil, commercial, penal, and governmental activities and the divine code of ethics which still regulates much of private life.

Socialization System. During the era of the Ottoman Empire, Islamic culture was transmitted formally through the schools and informally through the family and community. The Islamic polity authorized and legitimized formal education, most of which was devoted to Quranic studies.

Formal education in Republican Turkey has become greatly differentiated, and the formal component of Islamic socialization has come under secular control. Today Turkey has an impressive array of academic and vocational schools teaching non-religious subjects. The government compels Turkish children to attend secular elementary schools which stress instruction in mathematics, science, the humanities, and citizenship. Although practically all formal Quranic instruction was banned during the early years of the Republic, it is now permitted. The secular government authorizes religious education, finances many of the religious schools, certifies religion instructors, and regulates religious curricula.

By contrast, the informal process of religious socialization has remained close to tradition; parents, grandparents, other elderly relatives, and neighbors teach children, by word and deed, Turco-Islamic lore, the meaning and ritual of holydays, and Islamic ethics.

Value System. As Islam developed and spread, it incorporated elements of the propagating and receiving people's cultures. Consequently, today many of the values that Muslim Turks regard as religious originated with early Turkish and Arab culture and eventuated as organic parts of Islam.

According to their religious value system, the idealized Turk is courageous, brave, and strong; moderate in all activities; respectful of the learned and elderly; loyal to kin and friends; guided by a keen sense of honor and shame; concerned with his and others' dignity; patient and enduring in the face of hardship; and generous, hospitable, and friendly.

Historically the Turk was a *ghazi* (champion of Islam), who defended the faith against the Crusaders, Byzantines, and Mongols. Today's Turks still maintain this traditional image, but now associate it with patriotism as well as Islam; to perform one's military duty is equivalent to fulfilling a religious obligation. This association is promoted in the secular schools, as the following sentences from an official religious text book used in Turkey's middle school *(orta okul)* illustrates (Hocaoğlu 1968:59-60):

> The state is the national organization that ensures security within the country and possesses the strength to oppose external danger. . . . Today we have a state named the Turkish Republic which the whole nation honors and obeys. . . . Allah commands that every Muslim and Turk love his country, work to advance it, and obey his state . . . . The soldier who dies in battle [for his country] is a martyr [*şehit,* or Islamic martyr]; the one who survives is a *ghazi.* After Muhammad, they are the most important people.

Evidently, modern Turkish nationalism is successfully capitalizing on these religious values to promote its secular cause.

The idealized Turk is neither envious of others nor contemptuous of his own situation. He works to improve his lot, but is not obsessed with the acquisition of either wealth or power. Moderation in everything — sex, consumption of food, acquisition, etc. — is his goal. Unfortunately, Western contact and modern commercialism function to devalue contentment and moderation by creating dissatisfaction with what one possesses and instilling a desire to consume what one does not yet own. The anthropologist Carleton Coon finds the entire Middle East in the same dilemma (quoted in Hamady 1960:139):

> The West has tended to widen the social gulf between rich and poor in the Middle East by dangling in the faces of the poor conveniences and luxuries of which they had never before heard and which they now cannot have, while giving the rich new and expensive tastes, and the need for more and more income.

The humble, but content Turkish villager is regarded as a fossil of Turkey's "backward" past by many Western developmental experts and modern, achievement-oriented Turks.

The importance of hospitality and generosity among Turks and other Middle Easterners is difficult to exaggerate. Any Middle Easterner who enjoys a reputation for these two virtues is respected and admired by members of his community. Guests in a Turkish home must be treated like royalty. They are offered the best places, food, and drink; everyone in the household turns his full attention to their comfort. Hosts are duty-bound to express the joy and honor that the visit brings them. In return, guests must be exceedingly polite and grateful. One of the most appreciated forms of thanks they can offer is the phrase: "May Allah accept you," denoting that generosity and hospitality are pious virtues.

A Turk should demonstrate his generosity and consideration for others on every social occasion. For instance, he should never eat, drink, or smoke in the presence of another without first offering to share or give over what he has. On occasion this means readily giving up the only water, food, or cigarette he possesses.

Although generosity and hospitality are still highly valued, many Turks complain that a sense of commercialism increasingly permeates their social relations. For example, in the past, townspeople considered it shameful to sell the produce of their family gardens; they customarily gave the fruits and vegetables away to friends and the needy. As one townsman reminisced, "I remember townspeople returning from the vineyards with their donkeys loaded down with grapes. They had so many, they would shout, 'Grapes, grapes,' along the way, and give some to everyone they met. Only the full-time farmers sold agricultural produce then. Today, people will sell anything."

Mansur (1972:65) makes a similar observation of families in the Turkish town of Bodrum who were recently encouraged to offer tourists room and board in their homes.

The idea of taking money from a guest was met with bewilderment and even horror and many of the earlier tourists stayed in some of the best homes of Bodrum without paying. In 1960, the Tourism Association devised a way to save the hosts from embarrassment: they would get the money from the tourists and give it to the hosts afterwards. This usage slowly established itself, some tourists leaving the money under the pillow before leaving and people began to earn some money in this way. 'Now', says the Association's general secretary, 'the people who were ashamed to take money five years ago hang around the bus station to grab tourists before the neighbor has a chance to do it!'

Customarily in Susurluk each member of a group seated together in a coffeehouse voluntarily pays for a round of drinks. Those who refuse to do so (and townsmen claim their number is increasing) are accused of behaving like Germans. Townspeople, correctly or not, attribute any omission of sharing or hospitality to European influence. One local "German" defended himself to me by arguing that he saves several liras a day by paying only for his own tea and not offering cigarettes to others. The listeners seated nearby countered that the "German" might be saving money, but he was certainly losing friends. "Who wants to sit with someone who prefers pennies to people!"

Associated with hospitality and generosity is the extremely important institution of friendship. True friends are loyal confidants; they share each others joys, sorrows, and material possessions. Townspeople told me that prior to

1950, it was common for close friends to establish spiritual links between themselves by becoming *ahiret* kin. The word *"ahiret"* derives from a root meaning "other world" or "afterlife." *Ahiret* designates especially close friends, who are considered inseparable in this world and the next. If only one attains heaven, he has the right to intercede with Allah for the other. The institution, which elevates friendship from the secular, worldly level to the sacred, spiritual level, was customarily established in a simple ceremony following a communal meal. After all had eaten, the two friends rose and announced that they were entering an *ahiret* relationship. They exchanged gifts, and guests congratulated the two and offered best wishes.

This spiritual bond can be established between people of the same or different ages, sexes, and socio-economic statuses, and these three variables contribute to the nature of the relationship. For example, if a rich man of forty became the *ahiret* of a poor man of twenty, their relationship would be similar to that of father-son or uncle-nephew, and the rich man would materially help the poor one. My Turkish landlady and I became *ahiret*s and our relationship was that of mother-son. She assured me that even if I remained a non-believer, she would save me on Judgement Day.

Townspeople claim that the establishment of *ahiret* relations between friends has become uncommon during the past twenty years, but they are not sure why. Friendships remain important, but they are rarely spiritualized. This secularization of friendship may be part of the general secularization process occurring in government, the economy, education, and the crafts industry — the situational contexts of many friendships.

Ideological-Ritual System. Muslim theologians generally divide the fundamentals of their religion into beliefs and duties (Hitti 1970). Five dogmas, resembling the creeds of the Judeo-Christian religions, comprise the essential beliefs of Islam. They are:

1) Belief in Allah as the only God and the eternal, preexistent and self-subsistent deity.

2) Belief in the prophets of Allah. (The *Quran* mentions 18 Old Testament and three New Testament prophets.) Belief that Muhammad is the last and the greatest prophet, the recipient of Allah's final word.

3) Belief in the *Quran* as the word of Allah conveyed to Muhammad through the Angel Gabriel.

4) Belief in the Angels of Allah, as delineated in the *Quran,* and the Devil — the fallen Angel.

5) Belief in Judgement Day, when all people will rise from the dead to be assigned places in either Heaven or Hell on the basis of their worldly deeds.

Muslims must supplement these beliefs with the fulfillment of certain duties and the performance of special ritual. The following five Islamic obligations constitute the "Pillars of Islam."

1) Profession of the faith. "There is no god but Allah, and Muhammad is His Prophet." This pronouncement constitutes an act of piety, and believers repeat it frequently throughout their lives. A non-Muslim desiring conversion to Islam need merely utter the formula with sincerity to affect his acceptance into the community of believers. He then becomes bound to fulfill the remaining obligations.

2) The second pillar is prayer said in Arabic five times daily: at dawn, noon, mid-afternoon, sunset, and in the early evening. The *müezzin* announces these times with his call to prayer from the minaret. Believers may pray in any clean place, alone or in a group, but always facing Mecca. They are enjoined to pray in congregation on Friday noons. At these times men form straight rows in the mosques and pray together, standing, kneeling, bowing, and touching their foreheads to the floor in unison. (For illustrations of these postures see Coon (1966:107).)

Susurluk's commercialization and industrialization have secularized the day for many townsmen who now work at jobs which make the frequent interruptions for prayer inconvenient, if not impossible. Those who do observe this pillar are mostly elderly men and women whose duties or lack thereof permit the intermittent prayers to provide a spiritual ordering for their comparatively leisurely days. They usually perform the prayers in their homes, but on pleasant days elderly men like to walk to the mosque to join friends in common devotions and later gather together in a coffeehouse for a chat. Women visit the mosque on special occasions only, and then pray separately from men in a curtained balcony. Children say their prayers rarely, and working men tend to do so only on special holidays in the mosque.

Prior to 1935, the year the Turkish government adopted Sunday as a legal holiday in order to conform to European standards, Friday was the customary day of rest and prayer. Now it is an ordinary business day, and Susurluk's new economic structure has reduced the proportion of the male population that can observe Friday prayers in communal fashion.

3) The *Ramazan* Fast. All adolescent and mature Muslims of good health, who are not engaged in a strenuous journey, must abstain from eating, drinking, smoking, and sexual intercourse from sunrise to sunset during *Ramazan,* the ninth lunar month in which Muhammad received his first divine revelation. Muslims may turn their attention to food and sex only during the hours of darkness, "until," as the *Quran* instructs, "a white thread can be distinguished from a black thread at dawn." Because the Islamic lunar calendar is shorter than the solar-based calendar, which Turkey adopted from Europe in 1926,

Ramazan moves up ten or eleven days each solar year and can fall in any season.

The fast promotes solidarity among community members who endure it together. It also alters the routine of modern commerce and industry. Normally two meals, instead of the usual three, are taken during the days of *Ramazan*. The first is a couple of hours before dawn, when Susurluk's Gypsy musicians go through the streets beating on drums to awaken the faithful for prayers and food. The second meal — the *iftar* — follows the end of the day's fast period, which is marked by a cannon shot and the *müezzin*'s call from the minaret to the fasters' straining ears. With this hungrily-awaited announcement, men leave their shops and places of work to rush home and eat with their families. Grocers leave their unattended stores open so that those needing last minute items may help themselves. Official offices change their work hours to permit fasting employees the opportunity of joining their families for *iftar*.

Most townspeople begin *Ramazan* intending to keep the fast, but many give up before the month is over. Out of respect and a sense of guilt, non-fasters neither eat, drink, nor smoke in public. Of the half-dozen restaurants in the town's central business district, only one did not close completely for *Ramazan,* and that one served food just at the evening meal. The small snack stands normally set up on Wednesdays for the market-day crowd, were absent during *Ramazan*. The general Islamic prohibition against alcoholic drink is strictly observed during this month; store owners remove all wine, beer, and liquor from their shelves, and barkeepers take a vacation.

During *Ramazan,* bakeries discontinue their regular bread and bake a delicious, slightly leavened flat bread called *"pide,"* that townspeople purchase hot from the ovens an hour or so before *iftar*. Although there is fasting during the day, the evening meal tends to be most elaborate; special dishes are prepared and more meat than usual is consumed. It is a time of generosity in eating and giving. Families earn *sevap* (Allah's reward for a pious deed) by inviting guests to the evening meal or by sending prepared dishes to neighbors. The municipal government, the Aid Society, and rich businessmen distribute food, flour, and cooking oil to the town's needy.

In addition, each Muslim who is able must give alms, called *"sadaka-i fitir,"* to the poor or charitable organizations at the end of *Ramazan*. As these are small — but numerous gifts — one to two and one-half liras to each of many recipients, most families hoard change during *Ramazan,* causing transactional difficulties in the market place. Merchants run out of change, and banks get so low they refuse to give out what they have. Exact change is needed for practically all purchases, or else sales must be made in amounts that can be covered by the buyer's paper money.

Certain business activities become brisk during *Ramazan*. The municipality must grant tailors and shoemakers permission to work extra long hours to ready their orders by the end of the fast month when townspeople dress in their newest for the Sweets Holiday. Candy-makers also work extra hard in preparation for the forthcoming celebration.

Long, friendly conversation is characteristic of *Ramazan*. Both women in their homes and men in the small retail and craft shops gather together and talk in the most amiable way. This helps them keep their minds off food (which is never discussed) and share the burden of the fast socially. As tempers can become unusually short during the long days without food or drink, everyone is particularly careful not to discuss delicate topics.

The elderly find the religious justification for *Ramazan* sufficient. They claim that fasting cultivates obedience to Allah, patience, and will power and contributes to an appreciation of the condition of the poor and hungry. Younger, more educated Muslims find it necessary to add scientific justifications, such as the promotion of health. They claim *Ramazan* is beneficial because people eat less, rest their stomachs, and reduce. Privately, however, many of these same persons confess that they often gain weight during the month because of the rich meals eaten at night.

4) Almsgiving. All Muslims are obliged to care for the sick and needy. The former Islamic states levied a special tax, known as the *zakat,* and distributed the proceeds to the poor. This practice has ceased; now all alms are voluntary. The people of Susurluk are instilled with the idea of giving, which usually is done on a face-to-face basis and is interwoven with holydays and life-cycle rituals: births, circumcisions, weddings, funerals, anniversaries of the deceased, etc.

The national government is attempting to capitalize on this generosity by depersonalizing it. The government encourages citizens to fulfill their religious obligations by making donations to national charitable and patriotic organizations such as the Red Crescent (Turkey's equivalent of the Red Cross), the Children's Protection Society, and the Civil Aviation Society.

5) The Pilgrimage to Mecca. The pilgrimage *(haj)* to Mecca, made during the twelfth lunar month, is a once in a lifetime obligation for healthy and financially able Muslims. Pilgrims usually make the trip at a mature age and regard it as their life's crowning achievement. Many pray years in advance for the capacity to participate in this most stirring event.

In Ottoman times the sending and welcoming of pilgrims constituted major social events in villages, towns, and cities. During the Republican era, however, the pilgrimage was officially discouraged and sharply curtailed. With the election of the Democrats in 1950, restrictions were eased and foreign currency was made available to a new surge of pilgrims.

The religious journey to Mecca and the subsequent ritual there, deepen the feeling of international Islamic brotherhood.

> Once a year . . . Mecca becomes so religiously magnetized that it attracts hordes of men and women from the four quarters of the globe. . . . The social, economic, and intellectual effects of such gatherings are not easy to exaggerate. Next to the universal canon law *(shari'ah)* and the liturgical common use of Arabic, *al-hajj* [the pilgrimage] ranks as the greatest unifying force in Islam. As believers — black and white, rich and poor, high and low, Arabs, Turks, Persians, Hindus, and Sudanese — worship together they heighten their awareness of the solidarity of Islam as a religious fraternity [Hitti 1970:39].

Both in 1968 and 1969 about 25 townspeople and 25 villagers from the sub-province of Susurluk participated in this international event.

During the week preceding departure, the potential pilgrim *(hajji)* receives well-wishers, who forgive him all material and spiritual debts incurred to them in the course of his life. Now, in the event Allah takes him while on the journey, the *hajji* may enter heaven unencumbered by worldly obligations. The well-wishers also ask to be remembered in Mecca.

On departure day the *hajji*, accompanied by relatives and friends, walks to the mosque where all pray for guidance. They then go to the charter bus which takes pilgrims from town and the nearby villages on the sacred journey. Throngs of excited people, numbering several thousand, crowd the bus station to see the travelers off. ''May your trip be holy!'' ''May your way be open!''

Upon return, the *hajji* receives a tumultuously warm reception from relatives and friends as he disembarks from the bus. The welcomers then walk their *hajji* home through the town streets exclaiming in unison that ''Allah is most great.'' In gratitude for his safe return, the *hajji's* family sacrifices an animal just before he sets foot in his home.

In Ottoman days returning *hajji*s wore either the Arab robe with full sleeves and long skirts or the white, seamless garment issued to pilgrims in Mecca. The Republican government prohibited these, and now *hajji*s wear a skull cap and pilgrim's shawl. Otherwise, their dress is Western.

For a week the *hajji* receives a steady stream of visitors; the young kiss and the older ones clasp his right palm, for it has touched holy ground. The pilgrim offers his guests Saudi Arabian dates and water from the sacred Zemzem well in the Kaaba Court at Mecca. He also distributes gifts: wraps for the women, pearls for the girls, skull caps for the men, rings and rosaries for all. The community reciprocates by granting the *hajji* special deference for the remainder of his years.

Not all townspeople share in the enthusiasm of the pilgrimage. The anti-religious regard it as an unnecessary extravagance: "All the money spent outside the country is wasted." Anyone who makes the trip more than once is suspect of ulterior motives, such as smuggling.

The most important of the several religious holidays celebrated in Susurluk are the Sweets Holiday *(Şeker Bayramı),* which ends the *Ramazan* fast, and the Feast of Sacrifice *(Kurban Bayramı),* which falls about ten weeks later. Known respectively as the "Minor Feast" and the "Major Feast" in Arab countries, they are official holidays in Turkey. Both are times of spiritual and social renewal.

Townspeople thoroughly clean and often repaint their homes in preparation. Those who can, order suits and shoes. Formerly the townswomen, like the village women today, sewed new peasant dresses and dyed their hands, feet, and hair with henna. Now they favor Western clothing and some use light make-up.

The holidays last three and four days and begin with men praying together in the mosque. Later, families visit the cemetery to lay wreaths (a Republican custom copied from Europe) on the graves of deceased relatives and distribute food to the few poor congregated there. Younger relatives bring holiday greetings to older ones and kiss their hands. Everyone exchanges salutations in the street, and those whose relations may have become strained during the past year earn Allah's blessing by coming together in renewed friendship.

In addition to informal visits with relatives and friends, members of various town associations (e.g., the wagoners, the police force, local party branches) visit the mayor and sub-provincial governor as units. The two dignitaries sit together in the town's wedding hall and accept holiday wishes from groups and individuals on behalf of the town and sub-province.

Special candy and pastries characterize the Sweets Holiday, while meat dishes distinguish the Feast of Sacrifice. On the first morning of the sacrificial feast each adult male, who is financially able, should sacrifice a healthy sheep or goat with its head turned toward Mecca. The ritual may be either votive or freewill. Often, a Muslim vows to sacrifice an animal for a divine favor, such as a dear one's recovery from illness or a child's educational success. In such instances, the sacrificer gives all of the animal's meat away, consuming none himself. By contrast, a family making a freewill sacrifice generally keeps one-third of the meat and distributes the rest to friends, relatives, and the poor. Some Muslim theologians believe this ritual commemorates Abraham's willingness to sacrifice his own son to God.

The sacrificed animal has a spiritual connection with the sacrificer, and those who share in the consumption of its meat enter or reaffirm a spiritual bond with the donor. The meals prepared from these holyday animals are communal in a socio-spiritual sense.

The vast majority of townspeople enthusiastically participate in all or parts of the ritual comprising these two religious holidays. As in the case of *Ramazan,* however, some of the more educated Muslims seek non-religious justification for their involvement. One local primary school teacher, for example, thinks the main contribution of the holydays is sociological. Although he strongly opposes institutionalized religion with its clergy, he wrote a positive editorial on the social functions of Islam:

Muslims from all over the world celebrate the same two occasions: the Sweets Holiday and the Feast of Sacrifice. On these days antagonists make peace, grudges are forgotten, and the atmosphere is filled with brotherly love. These holidays have social importance: the poor are clothed, and meat enters the homes of those who seldom see it. Citizens with means sacrifice animals, distribute meat to those who have none, donate the pelts to the Civil Aviation Society, and give money to the poor. Ours is the most perfect religion, because it wants people to love and help each other. These are the basic reasons for our holidays.

The Islamic pillars, the religious holidays, sacred remedies, votive offerings to the deity, and the Muslim life-cycle rituals occurring at birth, male circumcision, marriage, and death pervade the individual, family, and community with ubiquitous reminders interspaced on several temporal dimensions (lunar, biological, social, etc.) that they are active participants in a fellowship of spiritual dynamics. The Turkish author Selahattin Şenelt describes the complex image of involvement that the word "religion" generates in the minds of Turkish Muslims (quoted in G. L. Lewis 1965:81):

The Friday prayers, the evening prayers, the Prophet's Birthday and the sweets we had on it, pilgrimages to holy places, kissing our elders' hands, the meat of sacrifice, private devotions, rosaries, alms-giving, presents, donations, clothing the orphan and comforting the fatherless, feeding the poor, the drinking-fountains built by the pious, and good works, the Koran and its recitation, circumcision, duties, prayers on special occasions, congregations, the Beard and the Cloak of the Prophet, Ramadan and its night-prayers, its meals before dawn and after sunset and the gifts we were given at them, and the holiday that ends the Month of Fasting; the Night of Power, the candles, the votive offerings, the cry of the muezzin, the mosques, the fountains, the tombs, the prostrations, the hymns, the sermons and homilies, the Amens, the invocation of the Name of God, the tears, the sobs, the seed-cakes and the lighted minarets of festal days, the sweets and the roundabouts.

Conclusion

Islam prescribes specific rules and guide-lines for practically every human thought and activity. In the Ottoman period Islam was so thoroughly integrated with all areas of social action: kinship, economics, politics, education, that any socio-cultural change had religious implications. Given this conservative structure, religion limited the flexibility and reduced the range of human behavior.

The Turkish reformers appreciated the strength of Islam's conservative role and concluded that their envisioned revolution could be successful only if Islam's prominent position as the central symbol and cohesive force of Turkish society was significantly weakened or eliminated. The reformers disestablished Islam in politics, government, and education, replacing it with a secular, nationalistic ideology that stresses allegiance and loyalty to the state. With Islam attenuated in these areas, the potential was created for new, broad initiatives in westernization. Attempts were made to extend westernization into the core of Islam itself. Some reformers advocated a protestantized form of Islamic service with the congregation wearing shoes, sitting in pews rather than prostrating in a "demeaning manner," listening to sacred music, and the like. Except for a few nationalistic measures such as changing the call to prayer from Arabic to vernacular Turkish, these suggested imitations were rejected by Ataturk, who preferred to reduce Islam to the realm of the individual conscience.

However, the initiation of multi-party politics and the popular support for parties with liberal attitudes toward religious expression proved Islamic sentiment too strong for such narrow relegation. The government now takes a utilitarian approach to religion; it regards Islam as a vital force which can be harnessed for the good of the state. Thus the government has sponsored (and controlled) more and more religious activity: religious instruction in the schools, Quranic readings on official radio, governmental proclamations on Islamic holidays, financial support and training of Muslim clergy.

Simultaneously the government competes with religion in the area of communal ritual by instituting and encouraging patriotic ceremonies: military parades, the celebration of patriotic holidays, the flag ceremony, the national anthem, the portraits and statues of Ataturk, etc. Upon mention of the words "Turkish State," a modern Turk could conjure up a list of patriotic ritual and symbol as impressive as the one generated above by the word "religion."

Turkey has experienced a general process of secularization, similar to that witnessed in other modernizing countries. During the Republican party era the process appeared revolutionary, and with the election of the Democrats observers began describing an Islamic revival. Now it is obvious that Islamic sentiment held strong throughout the entire period, first seeking concealment from official disapproval, then emerging florescent in the spring of a more liberal political atmosphere. But pervading this oscillation is a secularization process which increasingly removes, or at least attenuates, the role of religion from many spheres of human life and provides people with a greater array of potential alternatives for living.

Hafïz duasĭ; *reciting the Quran*

Funeral Procession

Last Rites

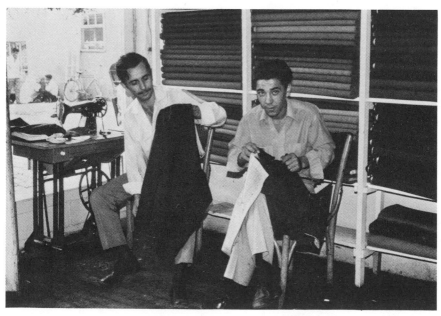

"Mustafa, the tailor," and apprentice

CHAPTER X

Conclusion

Susurluk's experience fits a general pattern of change shared by many small urban communities throughout Turkey, the Middle East, and the Third World. The town's interrelated processes of socio-cultural, economic, political, and educational change correspond closely to Smelser's model of modernization outlined in the first chapter.

Formerly characterized by subsistence agriculture and a limited market economy, this small town has been transformed, with the consent of its residents, into an industrial, commercial, and governmental center having a much greater degree of regional, national, and international involvement. The town's new economic structure, marked by increased industrialization and a more highly differentiated occupational configuration, has largely resulted from the construction and operation of the sugar refinery, improved agricultural technology, expanded markets for agricultural produce, and the development of local craft and commercial industries. The new occupational opportunities attracted people from cities and the surrounding villages, and the resultant mingling of urbanites, townspeople, and former peasants created a new atmosphere of socio-cultural heterogeneity.

Susurluk's greater regional, national, and international integration has been promoted by expanded educational opportunities, popular mass media participation, improved travel facilities, active participation in a multi-party political system, labor emigration to Turkey's major cities and Europe, and its newly created and externally directed industries and financial institutions. One result of tightened integration with national systems has been a diminution of the town's responsibility for and authority over many economic, educational, and governmental decisions of local consequence.

Change has included a general process of secularization. Religion's influence in legal, political, educational, and economic spheres has declined, so that social behavior in these areas is guided increasingly by non-religious norms. For instance, judges administer Western legal codes; teachers may employ the educational philosophies of Dewey, Rousseau, or Pestalozzi; and businessmen may manage their affairs with primacy given to the profit motive. Norms guiding social relations have been differentiated into a series of secular codes and the religious code which now dominates in a diminishing range of human affairs. As a consequence, modern Turks may choose from a comparatively wide array of alternatives for expressing their thoughts, motives, and emotions.

Concomitant to these developments has been the genesis of a mass culture of material aspirations nurtured by the mass media and greater exposure to life-styles in Turkey's modern cities and the industrially advanced West. A tide of aspirations, swelling beyond the consumption limits imposed by the local economy, has created, what I call, a "Culture of Discontent," characterized by manifest dissatisfaction with locally available income and consumption opportunities and a pressing desire to abandon Susurluk and even Turkey in pursuit of a "better life."

In the 1950s Susurluk experienced the industrial revolution already ancient history in Europe. But, in many respects the townspeople have caught up to the Western world; what they lack in living standards, they compensate for in aspiration. Now, shoulder to shoulder, they march in step with all of mankind into a future of dramatic changes more consequential than the transition from agriculture to industry.

Successful adjustment to this changing situation has necessarily required people to alter their perceptions of the world and innovate strategies designed to achieve new goals through the utilization of available personal skills, social ties, and material resources. Consequently, traditional kinship relations, sex roles, friendship bonds, employment and investment options, educational preferences, and criteria for individual evaluation have all been altered to varying degrees by people seeking to accomplish the diverse objectives comprising their modernized lives.

The complex processes of change occurring in Susurluk derive their essence, meaning, and dynamics from the aspirations and actions of individual persons. The life movements of thousands of people taken together in their kaleidoscopic variety form the images depicting Susurluk's story. Although each person is unique, the ambitions of one young man, whom I will never forget, are shared by many townsmen.

Shortly after my initial arrival in Susurluk in August of 1969, I met Mustafa — a slightly built, light complexioned bachelor of twenty-nine years, who worked as a journeyman tailor in the shop of a friend. Mustafa emitted an aura of security, confidence, and peace of mind. He belonged in Susurluk; the town constituted a natural habitat to which he had attained a kind of optimum social adaptation.

He was born and raised here, and during his developing years he earned a fine reputation for his friendliness, good nature, and honesty. After both his parents died, he, his younger brother, and grandmother continued to live together in the family home located in Burhaniye Quarter, one of the town's ethnically mixed sections. He grew up enjoying a wide circle of friends and the support of his many relatives, who ranged from store and restaurant owners to the head of the municipal police force. Shortly after finishing primary school, he entered his apprenticeship and eventually developed the skill and dexterity that separate accomplished tailors from mere needleworkers. He could convert a measure of cloth into a finely styled men's suit in about a day and a half of concentrated effort. His employer knew that Mustafa's reputation as one of the town's top young tailors and his wide ranging social ties contributed to the steady stream of customers to the shop. Having inherited a civic spirit from his father, Mustafa engaged himself in numerous town activities, often serving as co-chairman or member of the committees involved. He developed into one of those informal town leaders whose active participation in a variety of town-wide organizations contributed to the community's direction, cohesion, and spirit.

His daily routine pleasantly mingled work with social involvement. Dressed smartly in one of his own suits, he strolled to work at a leisurely morning hour, always sure to walk three blocks out of his way to pass the home of a special girl. Once in the shop, he chose his own work pace — now stitching intensely, now stopping to joke and sip tea with visitors. At noontime he strolled home by his usual circuitous route to lunch on a fine Turkish meal either prepared by his grandmother from their own garden or brought over by one of his many married sisters, aunts, or cousins. In the afternoon he continued working and socializing in his shop until dinner time, when he either went home or crossed the street to his brother-in-law's restaurant to dine with a group of friends. He also shared his evenings with friends, either watching a movie, attending a civic meeting, or drinking and dancing farewell to a fellow bachelor about to be married.

During the late 1960s Mustafa's horizons were broadened by reports of friends who had emigrated to Europe for work. Initially Mustafa had discounted any ideas about leaving town or the country, but now presented with the evidence of his friends' success and the town's favorable reaction to it, he began to question his earlier decision. The constant encouragement to emigrate given him by his restaurateur brother-in-law, who had himself worked in the Cologne Ford Factory, also made its impression. In the fall of 1969, one of his friends returned from Switzerland raving about the high wages and good living in that "most civilized of all countries." He claimed to have special connections and to be able to secure fine jobs for close friends willing to invest TL 2000 in their cause. In true Turkish fashion Mustafa bargained him down to TL 1000 — his entire savings. The "friend" took the money from Mustafa and several other young men and returned to Switzerland, promising to send word in a month or two.

The more Mustafa discussed Switzerland with townspeople, the more encouragement he received, and the more enthused he became about trying life in a European country. But his newly engendered hopes were met with silence. After several months passed without word, Mustafa and his friends became despondent and a little ashamed for having been taken.

During the early part of 1970, a major Turkish newspaper carried a series about a small group of Turkish tailors who had secured jobs in a Rochester, New York clothing factory. Mustafa excitedly asked me to help him apply for work there. Reluctantly I did so. I compared industrial, gray Rochester with this small, peaceful town nestled between green rolling hills and crowned with clear blue skies and warm sunshine throughout much of the year. I was convinced that even at ten times his current income, Mustafa would not achieve the kind of social fulfillment he enjoyed in Susurluk. But no amount of comparative reasoning could dissuade him from his new ambition. Again, friends and relatives offered encouragement, some even expressed envy.

Mustafa enrolled in the free English language course given in the evenings to adults by the local Peace Corps volunteer and myself. Owing to his persistent desire to learn and his natural facility for language, Mustafa made steady progress. Now when friends dropped by the shop to ask about his American plans, he would claim they were 100% sure and then would good-naturedly spout out a few English sentences to demonstrate that he was more prepared than ever to go. Any lower assessment of his chances by me had no impact on his dreams.

The application process stretched out over several months, and only by spring of 1970 did a card finally arrive from Rochester informing us that Mustafa's application was on file. Summer passed without further word, so in August, shortly before I left Susurluk, I wrote Rochester again, asking about Mustafa's chances.

During those final weeks in Susurluk, Mustafa and I spent many evenings together conversing and drinking raki in the town park. He never tired of imagining how we would be together in America, sharing our leisure time and doing many of the things we enjoyed in Susurluk, but, of course, on a much grander scale. He would work hard, save money, and then buy a car, a television, a modern home — "the complete set." He would marry an American girl and their children would grow up amidst prosperity.

By September of 1970 I was back at Harvard beginning to reassess the Susurluk experience, when a letter arrived from Mustafa. Enclosed was his original application, returned by the Rochester plant, with a note explaining there was no work. But only part of a dream had been shattered; Mustafa assured me he would get to America one way or another.

We corresponded for a year; then my letters went unanswered. When I returned to Susurluk in the summer of 1972, Mustafa was not there. Friends related how he had become depressed and dispirited in Susurluk and decided to seek his fortune in Istanbul. A relative gave me Mustafa's business address, and I found him at summer's end working in a back alley tailor shop in Istanbul's heavily congested Beyoğlu district. He gave me a warm welcome; we embraced and he pulled up a chair for me by his sewing machine so that we could catch up on each other's recent history. As we talked Mustafa continued to sew in a rapid, compulsive manner. The poorly lit, drab complex of three cubicles constituting the shop contained five other tailors who worked in a steady silence. The scene contrasted sharply with that of the cheerfully bright and airy Susurluk shop, which opened fully to the sunshine and people of the street through its two large store-front windows.

Mustafa explained that Susurluk had become too confining, so he had a friend find him a job with an Istanbul tailor. He soon married a young lady working in the same shop, and later switched to his present location hoping to earn more money. He was struggling to survive in this metropolis. With two incomes he and his wife could cover the rent for a small walk-up apartment on the fifth floor of an old tenement house, food at the highest prices in Turkey, and incidental expenses. But they could save very little, as he was repaying the loan that permitted him to marry. And now that his wife was pregnant, a baby and one less income loomed in his future. Alone in Istanbul, without relatives and close friends, his life had taken a serious turn.

He invited me home for dinner, but I insisted that as his brother I had the right and obligation to offer him and his bride a wedding meal, however belated. So we dined out together on fine Russian food and tasty Turkish wine at the restaurant of the famous Russian sisters who had found refuge from the Bolsheviks in Istanbul. However pleasant our reunion, Mustafa displayed no pleasure in reminiscences. As he explained at my final departure, Susurluk was a place of the past. He had rejected it and could never return. He had left home for a better future, and although he was just getting by in Istanbul, he still felt, or at least said, he had come somewhere. He often thought of America and Europe, but could no longer indulge in the fantasies of his youth.

Mustafa is but one of millions participating in a new "Culture of Discontent," created largely, but inadvertently by the world's more modern countries. Like the "grocer of Balgat" (Lerner 1958) and the "peasant of Las Bocas" (Erasmus 1961), the "tailor of Susurluk" engendered a level of aspirations far exceeding the bounds of his local opportunities. Made to want what only a few privileged can afford, he rejected a past, even an evolving present, in impatient pursuit of a distant, probably unattainable future.

Over the past several decades rich countries have been convincing poor ones that they too could attain high levels of economic development if only they would follow this developmental plan or embrace that socio-political ideology.

Are these convictions warranted? The American people, who represent only six per cent of the world's population consume an enormously greater proportion of the world's yearly output of non-renewable resources. During the early 1970s, for example, the United States consumed about two-thirds of the world's annual output of copper, coal, and oil. Is it possible for all peoples of the world to consume at the American rate?

Meadows and his associates (1972) have argued persuasively that given the finite nature of the earth's ability to supply the resources necessary for human survival, "if the present growth trends in world population, industrialization, pollution, food production, and resource depletion continue unchanged, the limits to growth on this planet will be reached sometime within the next one hundred years." If it is true, as evidence indicates, that current growth rates in population and material output "cannot be sustained even for the lifetimes of children being born today," how realistic is it to expect a major proportion of Third World countries to reach Western standards of living even within the next century?

L. R. Brown (1972a; 1972b) has presented some provocative facts about current world trends. The gap between rich and poor countries, which originated in relatively recent history, is widening at an alarming pace. In 1850, the ratio between per capita incomes of industrialized societies and the rest of the world was about two to one. It jumped to about ten to one in 1950, to about fifteen to one in 1960, and may reach thirty to one by the end of our century. The world community has been divided economically into rich, industrial, well-fed, consumption-oriented people living in the United States, Canada, Europe, the USSR, and Japan and poor, hungry, aspiring people struggling to survive in Latin America, Africa, and Asia. That the majority of mankind falls into the second group is no credit to human history.

Other world trends also offer those sharing the "Culture of Discontent" little encouragement. At its current annual growth rate of 2%, today's world population of about 3.6 billion people can easily double in only thirty-five years. Ironically, population is growing fastest in those countries where hunger, malnutrition, and unemployment are most prevalent. As a result of these increasing numbers, unemployment rates in countries like India, Pakistan, Ceylon, Malaysia, and the Philippines, and in much of Latin America exceed 15% and continue to rise. Underemployment rates may even be higher. For these millions without viable sources of income, our twentieth century offers despair and misery.

Urbanization in the Third World is also increasing at a dangerous rate. Cities which now cannot provide jobs and basic services such as housing, sanitation, water, sewers, police and fire protection, and education for their estimated 600 million inhabitants may grow 500% in the next thirty years. The hopes of peasants fleeing to these swarming metropolises in search of a better life will be shattered by the poor, congested, and diseased slums which will become their homes.

Ultimately, the most adverse consequence of the world's growing industry, population, and avid consumptive demands is the steady deterioration of the natural environment. Air, land, and water pollution; chemical poisoning; deforestation; and the depletion of mineral resources are creating an unattractive, unhealthy, and increasingly uninhabitable world.

Mankind's salvation requires momentous changes in values, motivations, and social institutions. The cultural equipment that has served man in the past is now causing his destruction. Such "axioms" as "Growth is good," "What's good for the economy is good for the country," "Be fruitful and multiply," "My country right or wrong," are proving increasingly inconsistent with survival. As soon as possible man must sharply curtail his population and economic growth. Conspicuous production and consumption — both civilian and military — must be stopped and the resources saved must be transferred to the poor so that they may at least enjoy the basic necessities of life. The nations of the world must plan and act together to achieve a design for living which ensures each a relatively equal minimum living standard consonant with the finite constraints of our earth.

To accomplish this, the societies of the world must actively reject certain aspects of the predominantly Western concept of man and embrace a different self-image and mission. The idealized concept of man which dominates in much of modern Western civilization stresses human centrality and omnipotence — man's right and ability to subjugate nature to serve his selfish ends; individualism — the precedence of the individual's interests over those of society; and materialism — emphasis on the "virtues" of conspicuous production, acquisition, and consumption.

A much more human self-image and social ethic can be created from values prevalent today, however grossly overshadowed, in many of the world's cultures. Man must consider himself part of, rather than apart from nature. He is a humble component of an intricate biospheric complex which he must cease exploiting mindlessly and endeavor to understand. Mankind must cultivate a better appreciation for nature as well as itself and must learn to live together in harmony.

Individualism must be balanced by social responsibility. Our individual actions — both personal and national — have had grave consequences for others. No individuals or nations have the moral right to monopolize large, inordinate portions of the world's resources to the detriment of others.

Mankind must cultivate an ideology of anti-materialism which repudiates conspicuous production, acquisition, and consumption and all values promoting them. Human success, fulfillment, and happiness must cease being defined in terms of quantity of material goods possessed and destroyed.

The Turks and many other peoples of the world — prosperous and poor, ''arrived'' and aspiring — can rediscover the values necessary for this image and social ethic in their traditional mores and religious systems. By assigning these values new primacy, we will have progressed towards a solution to the predicament of mankind.

APPENDIX A
Socio-Cultural Characteristics of Adult Sample

The following tables show the ethnic, occupational, age, educational, and residential characteristics of the adult male sample.

Ethnicity of Respondent's Father

	Married	Bachelor	Total	
	Number	Number	Percent	Number
Manav	34	21	30.4%	55
Balkan Turk	51	22	40.3%	73
Yürük-Turkmen	3	—	1.7%	3
Other Province Turk	4	1	2.8%	5
Crimean Tatar	2	—	1.1%	2
Azeri Turk	1	—	.6%	1
Albanian (Arnavut)	2	2	2.2%	4
Bosnian (Boshnak)	1	—	.6%	1
Gypsy	5	1	3.3%	6
Circassian	18	6	13.3%	24
Georgian	2	2	2.2%	4
Dagistani	1	—	.6%	1
Kurd	2	—	1.1%	2
Totals	126	55	100.1%	181

(blanks = 1)

Respondent's Occupation

	Married	Bachelor	Total	
	Number	Number	Percent	Number
Teacher, government or institutional official	19	5	13.2%	24
Skilled or semi-skilled craftsman or worker	46	18	35.2%	64
Merchant, commerce	15	6	11.5%	21
Policeman, watchman	10	—	5.5%	10
Transportation	12	3	8.2%	15
Agriculture	6	—	3.3%	6
Unskilled	18	6	13.2%	24
Student	1	17	9.9%	18
Totals	127	55	100.0%	182

Age of Respondent

Ages	Married Number	Bachelor Number	Total Percent	Total Number
18 - 26	10	52	34.0%	62
27 - 35	57	3	33.0%	60
36 - 44	43	—	23.6%	43
45 - 53	11	—	6.0%	11
54 - 68	6	—	3.3%	6
Totals	127	55	99.9%	182

Respondent's Education

Educational Level:	Married Number	Bachelor Number	Total Percent	Total Number
None	9	—	5.0%	9
Attended primary school	11	2	7.1%	13
Finished primary school	70	20	49.5%	90
Attended middle school	13	7	11.0%	20
Finished middle school	10	3	7.1%	13
Attended high school	1	9	5.5%	10
Finished high school	8	5	7.1%	13
Attended university	4	9	7.1%	13
Finished university	1	—	.6%	1
Totals	127	55	100.0%	182

Respondent's Quarter of Residence

Quarters:	Married Number	Bachelor Number	Total Percent	Total Number
Han	27	12	21.4%	39
Orta	21	7	15.4%	28
Kışla	15	9	13.2%	24
Burhaniye	17	7	13.2%	24
Sultaniye	17	6	12.6%	23
Yeni	30	14	24.2%	44
Totals	127	55	100.0%	182

APPENDIX B
Villages in Susurluk Sub-province

Village Name	Km. Distance from Town	Terrain	1965[1] Population	Major[2] Ethnic Groups
Aziziye	9	valley	131	Circassian
Babaköy	16	plain	1,123	Balkan Turk, Yürük
Balıklıdere	5	plain	801	Circassian, Balkan Turk
Bozen	23	hill	568	Balkan Turk, Yürük-Turkmen
Buzağlık	3	plain	277	Balkan Turk
Dere	14	valley	1,079	Manav
Duman	6	hill	274	Yürük-Turkmen
Ekinlik	7	hill	146	Balkan Turk
Gürece	17	hill	426	Balkan Turk
Kadıkırı	8	hill	111	Circassian
Kalfa	13	hill	190	Balkan Turk
Karaköy	5	hill	323	Yürük
Karapürçek	16	plain	2,247	Balkan Turk, Manav
Kayıkçı	4	plain	455	Balkan Turk, Manav
Kizildere	12	hill	610	Georgian, Yürük
Kocapinar	5	hill	260	Balkan Turk
Kulat	17	hill	289	Balkan Turk
Kurucaoluk	12	hill	398	Balkan Turk
Paşaköy	14	hill	248	Yürük-Turkmen
Söğütçayır	8	hill	686	Yürük, Balkan Turk
Sultançayır	7	valley	567	Circassian, Balkan Turk, Nogay, Crimean Tatar
Sülücek	10	hill	149	Yürük
Tütünlük	11	hill	132	Balkan Turk
Yağcı	9	plain	766	Balkan Turk
Yahyaköy	10	plain	736	Balkan Turk, Circassian
Yaylaçayır	18	hill	435	Balkan Turk
Yıldız	18	plain	1,588	Manav, Circassian, Balkan Turk

Villages in the Göbel District of Susurluk

Village Name	Km. Distance from Town	Terrain	Population	Major Ethnic Groups
Göbel	15	plain	2,677	Balkan Turk
Beyköy	19	plain	678	Manav
Ilıcaboğaz	24	plain	380	Balkan Turk, Circassian
Iclaliye	24	plain	206	Balkan Turk
Kepekler	21	plain	275	Manav
Muradiye	24	plain	1,278	Balkan Turk, Circassian
Okçugöl	17	plain	274	Balkan Turk
Söve	21	plain	940	Balkan Turk, Yürük
Ümiteli	16	plain	884	Balkan Turk, Manav

Villages in the Omerköy District of Susurluk

Village Name	Km. Distance from Town	Terrain	1965 [1] Population	Major [2] Ethnic Groups
Omerköy	21	plain	1,130	Balkan Turk, Manav
Alibey	26	hill	445	Yürük, Bosnian
Asmalıdere	27	hill	400	Balkan Turk
Danaveli	19	hill	311	Chepni
Demirkapı	16	plain	966	Circassian, Balkan Turk
Eminpınar	31	hill	375	Muhacir
Gökçedere	24	hill	552	Yürük, Balkan Turk
Kayalıdere	25	hill	227	Yürük-Turkmen
Kiraz	20	hill	154	Yürük
Odalıdam	27	hill	151	Yürük-Turkmen
Reşadiye	29	plain	877	Balkan Turk

[1] 1965 population figures wire taken from *Balikesir Il 1967 Yilliği* (1969: 9-96).

[2] Ethnicity information was adapted from Ozer (1963:35-36) with many major corrections based on field notes.

References

Abadan, Nermin
    1967   "Turkey." in Raphael Patai, ed. *Women in the Moslem World.* (New York: The Free Press).

Altunbaş, Abdullah
    1969   *Susurluk Ilçesi.* (Susurluk, Turkey: (mimeo)).

Babinger, Franz
    1927   "Karami Mehmed Pasha." *The Encyclopedia of Islam.* vol. 2, (Leiden: E. J. Brill).

Balıkesir 1967 Il Yıllığı
    1969   (Istanbul: Çelikcilt Matbaası).

Başgöz, Ilhan and Howard E. Wilson
    1968   *Educational Problems in Turkey 1920-1940.* (The Hague: Mouton and Co.).

Bayatlı, Osman
    1942   *Bergamanda Efsaneler Adetler.* (Bergaman, Turkey: Vakit Matbaası).

Belgesay, M. R.
    1957   "Social, Economic, and Technical Difficulties Experienced as a Result of the Reception of Foreign Law." *International Social Science Bulletin,* vol. 9, no. 1, pp. 49-51.

Bradburn, N.M.
    1960   "The Managerial Role in Turkey: A Psychological Study." Unpublished Ph.D. dissertation, Harvard University.
    1963   "N Achievement and Father Dominance in Turkey." *Journal of Abnormal and Social Psychology,* vol. 67, no. 5, pp. 464-468.

Brown, Lester R.
    1972a   *World Without Borders.* (New York: Random House).
    1972b   "An Overview of World Trends." *The Futurist,* vol. 6, no. 6, pp. 225-232.

Coon, Carleton S.
    1966   *Caravan: the Story of the Middle East.* (New York: Holt, Rinehart, and Winston).

Daily News
    (Ankara, Turkey).

Deny, J.
    1960   "Ahmed Wafik Pasha." *The Encyclopedia of Islam.* (New edition), vol. 1, (Leiden: E. J. Brill).

Dereli, Toker
    1968   *The Development of Turkish Trade Unionism.* (Istanbul: Sermet Matbaası).

Dundar, Nuri
  1933   *Derleme, Susığırlık.* (Balıkesir, Turkey: Vilayet Matbaası).
Erasmus, Charles J.
  1961   *Man Takes Control.* (Minneapolis: University of Minnesota Press).
Erdentuğ, Nermin
  1959   *A Study of Social Structure of a Turkish Village.* (Ankara: Ayyıldız Matbaası).
Forget, Nelly
  1962   "Attitudes towards Work by Women in Morocco." *International Social Science Journal,* vol. 14, no. 1, pp. 92-124.
Foster, George M.
  1973   *Traditional Societies and Technological Change.* 2nd ed. (New York: Harper & Row, Publishers).
Frey, Frederick W.
  1964   "Education: Turkey." in R. E. Ward and D. A. Rustow, eds., *Political Modernization in Japan and Turkey.* (Princeton: Princeton University Press).
The Glorious Kuran
  1953   Mohammed M. Pickthall, trans. (New York: The New American Library).
Goode, William J.
  1963   *World Revolution and Family Patterns.* (New York: The Free Press).
  1968   "The Theory and Measurement of Family Change." in E. B. Sheldon and W. E. Moore, eds., *Indications of Social Change.* (New York: Russell Sage Foundation).
Goodenough, W. H.
  1956   "Residence Rules." *Southwestern Journal of Anthropology,* vol. 12, no. 1, pp. 22-37.
Hamady, Sania
  1960   *Temperament and Character of the Arabs.* (New York: Twayne Publishers).
24 Haziran
         (Susurluk, Turkey).
Hess, Robert D. and Judith V. Torney
  1967   *The Development of Political Attitudes in Children.*
         (Chicago: Aldine Publishing Co.).
Hitti, Philip K.
  1970   *Islam, A Way of Life.* (Minneapolis: University of Minnesota Press).
Hocaoğlu, Mehmet
  1968   *Din Bilgisi, Orta I.* (Istanbul: Bahar Matbaası).
Ibn Battuta
  1929   *Travels in Asia and Africa.* H. A. R. Gibb, trans. (London: Routledge and Kegan Paul).
Iller Bankasi Belediye Yıllığı
  1950   "Susurluk." Vol. 3. (Ankara: Güney Matbaacılık).

International Social Science Bulletin
1957   "The Reception of Foreign Law in Turkey." vol. 9, no. 1.
Ismael, Tareq Y.
1970   "The Heritage of Islam." in T. Y. Ismael, ed., *Governments and Politics of the Contemporary Middle East.* (Homewood, Ill.: Dorsey Press).
Karpat, Kemal H.
1959   *Turkey's Politics.* (Princeton: Princeton University Press).
Kazamias, Andreas M.
1966   *Education and the Quest for Modernity in Turkey.* (Chicago: University of Chicago Press).
Kiray, Mubeccel
1964   *Ereğli – Ağır Sanayiden Önce bir Sahil Kasabası.* (Ankara: Devlet Karayolları Matbaası).
Lerner, Daniel
1958   *The Passing of Traditional Society.* (New York: The Free Press).
Levy, Marion J.
1966   *Modernization and the Structure of Societies.* (Princeton: Princeton University Press).
Lewis, G. L.
1955   "The Secret Language of the Geygelli Yürüks." *Zeki Velidi Togana Armağan.* (Istanbul: Maarif Basımevi).
1965   *Turkey.* 3rd ed. (New York: Frederick A. Praeger).
Lewis, W Arthur
1965   "Beyond African Dictatorship." *Encounter,* vol. 25, no. 2, pp. 3-18.
Luzbetak, Louis J.
1951   *Marriage and the Family in Caucasia.* (Vienna: St. Gabriel's Press).
Magnarella, Paul J.
1970   "From Villager to Townsman in Turkey." *The Middle East Journal,* vol. 24, no. 2, pp. 229-40.
1972   "Turkish Townsmen View Apollo." *The Middle East Journal,* vol. 26, no. 2, pp. 181-183.
1973   "The Reception of Swiss Family Law in Turkey." *Anthropological Quarterly,* vol. 46, no. 2, pp. 100-116.
Makal, Mahmut
1954   *A Village in Anatolia.* Wyndham Deedes, Trans. (London: Vallentine, Mitchell and Co.).
Mansur, Fatma
1972   *Bodrum, a Town in the Aegean.* (Leiden: E. J. Brill).
McClelland, David C.
1961   *The Achieving Society.* (Princeton: Van Nostrand).
1963   "National Character and Economic Growth in Turkey and Iran." in Lucian W. Pye, ed., *Communications and Political Development.* (Princeton: Princeton University Press).

Meadows, Donella H. *et al.*
    1972   *The Limits to Growth.* (New York: Universe Books).
Mutluçağ, Hayri
    1967   "Borasit ve Anadolu'da Yabancı Çıkarları." *Belgelerle Türk Tarihi Dergisi,* vol. 1, pp. 24-35.
Nash, Manning
    1967   *Machine Age Maya.* (Chicago: University of Chicago Press).
Ostrogorsky, George
    1957   *History of the Byzantine State.* Joan Hussey, trans. (New Brunswick: Rutgers University Press).
Ozer, Kemal
    1963   *Susurluk Ilçesi.* (Balıkesir, Turkey: Türk Dili Matbaası).
Redfield, Robert and Milton B. Singer
    1954   "The Cultural Role of Cities." *Economic Development and Cultural Change,* vol. 3, pp. 53-73.
Robinson, Richard D.
    1949a   "Attitudes in Gaziantep." in *Letters from Turkey, RDR-37.* (New York: Institute of Current World Affairs).
    1949b   "Communism in the Villages." in *Letters from Turkey, RDR-38.* (New York: Institute of Current World Affairs).
    1963   *The First Turkish Republic.* (Cambridge: Harvard University Press).
    1967   *High-level Manpower in Economic Development: The Turkish Case.* (Cambridge: Harvard University Press).
Rustow, Dankwart A.
    1957   "Politics and Islam in Turkey 1920-1955." in Richard N. Frye, ed., *Islam and the West.* ('S-Gravenhage: Mouton and Co.).
Şahinkaya, Rezan
    1970   *Hatay Bölgesinde Köy ve Şehirde Aile Mutluluğu ve Çocuk Ölümü.* (Ankara: Ankara Universitesi Basımevi).
Schul, Bill
    1972   "What Happened in Kansas." *Intellectual Digest,* vol. 2, pp. 80-81.
Sherwood, W. B.
    1967   "The Rise of the Justice Party in Turkey." *World Politics,* vol. 20, no. 1, pp. 54-65.
Smelser, Neil J.
    1968   *Essay in Sociological Explanation.* (Englewood Cliffs, N.J.: Prentice-Hall, Inc.).
    1971   "Mechanisms of Change and Adjustment to Change." in George Dalton, ed., *Economic Development and Social Change.* (Garden City, N.Y.: The Natural History Press).
Stirling, Paul
    1965   *Turkish Village.* (New York: John Wiley and Sons, Inc.).

Su, Kamil
   1938   *Balıkesir ve Cıvarında Yürük ve Türkmenler.* (Istanbul: Resimli Ay Matbaası).
Susurluk Beş Eylul Ekspres
   (Susurluk, Turkey).
Tachau, Frank
   1972   "The Republic of Turkey." in A. A. Al-Marayati, ed., *The Middle East: Its Government and Politics.* (Belmont, Calif.: Duxbury Press).
Tercüman
   (Istanbul, Turkey).
Timur, H.
   1957   "Civil Marriages in Turkey: Difficulties, Causes, and Remedies." *International Social Science Bulletin,* vol. 9, no. 1, pp. 34-36.
Trimingham, J. Spencer
   1971   *The Sufi Orders in Islam.* (Oxford: Clarendon Press).
Tuna, Orhan
   1963   "Growth and Functions of Turkish Trade Unions." in *Social Aspects of Economic Development.* (Istanbul: Economic and Social Studies Conference Board).
Tuncer, Baran
   1968   *The Impact of Population on the Turkish Economy.* (Ankara, Hacettepe University Publications) No.3.
Turkish Digest
   1972   "President Sunay's Message." vol. 1, no. 1.
Warren, Roland L.
   1972   *The Community in America.* 2nd ed. (Chicago: Rand McNally and Company).
Yasa, Ibrahim
   1957   *Hasanoğlan: Socio-Economic Structure of a Turkish Village.* (Ankara: Yeni Matbassı).

Index